Thomas Cole

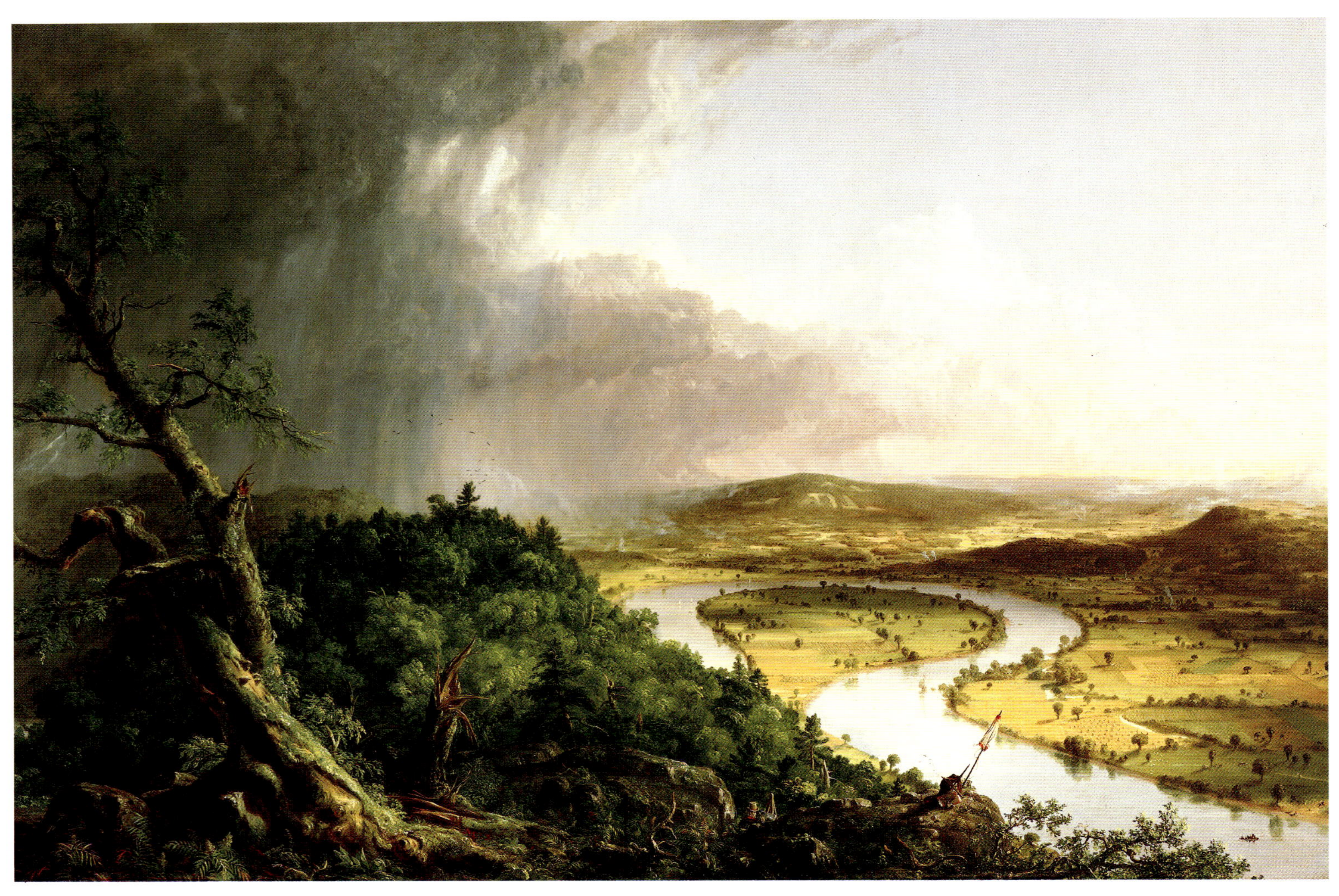

Papa,

to encourage and inspire.

deine Maxi

Thomas Cole

Earl A. Powell

HARRY N. ABRAMS, INC., PUBLISHERS

Editor: Mark Greenberg
Designer: Ellen Nygaard Ford
Photo Research: Lauren Boucher

FRONT COVER:
The Notch of the White Mountains (Crawford Notch) [detail]
1839. Oil on canvas, 40 x 61½"
National Gallery of Art, Washington, D.C., Andrew W. Mellon Fund

BACK COVER:
Self-Portrait
c. 1836. Oil on canvas, 22 x 18"
Courtesy of the New-York Historical Society, New York City

ON THE TITLE PAGE:
The Oxbow (The Connecticut River near Northampton)
1836. Oil on canvas, 51½ x 76"
The Metropolitan Museum of Art, New York,
Gift of Mrs. Russell Sage, 1908

Library of Congress Cataloging-in-Publication Data

Powell, Earl A.
Thomas Cole / Earl A. Powell.
p. cm.
Includes bibliographical references.
ISBN 0-8109-3158-3
1. Cole, Thomas, 1801–1848—Criticism and interpretation.
2. Hudson River school of landscape painting. I. Title.
ND237.C6A4 1990 90-121
759.13—dc20 CIP

Paperback edition published in 2000 by
Harry N. Abrams, Incorporated, New York

Clothbound edition published in 1990 by
Harry N. Abrams, Inc.,
New York

Printed and bound in Japan

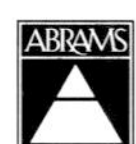

Harry N. Abrams, Inc.
100 Fifth Avenue
New York, N. Y. 10011
www.abramsbooks.com

Contents

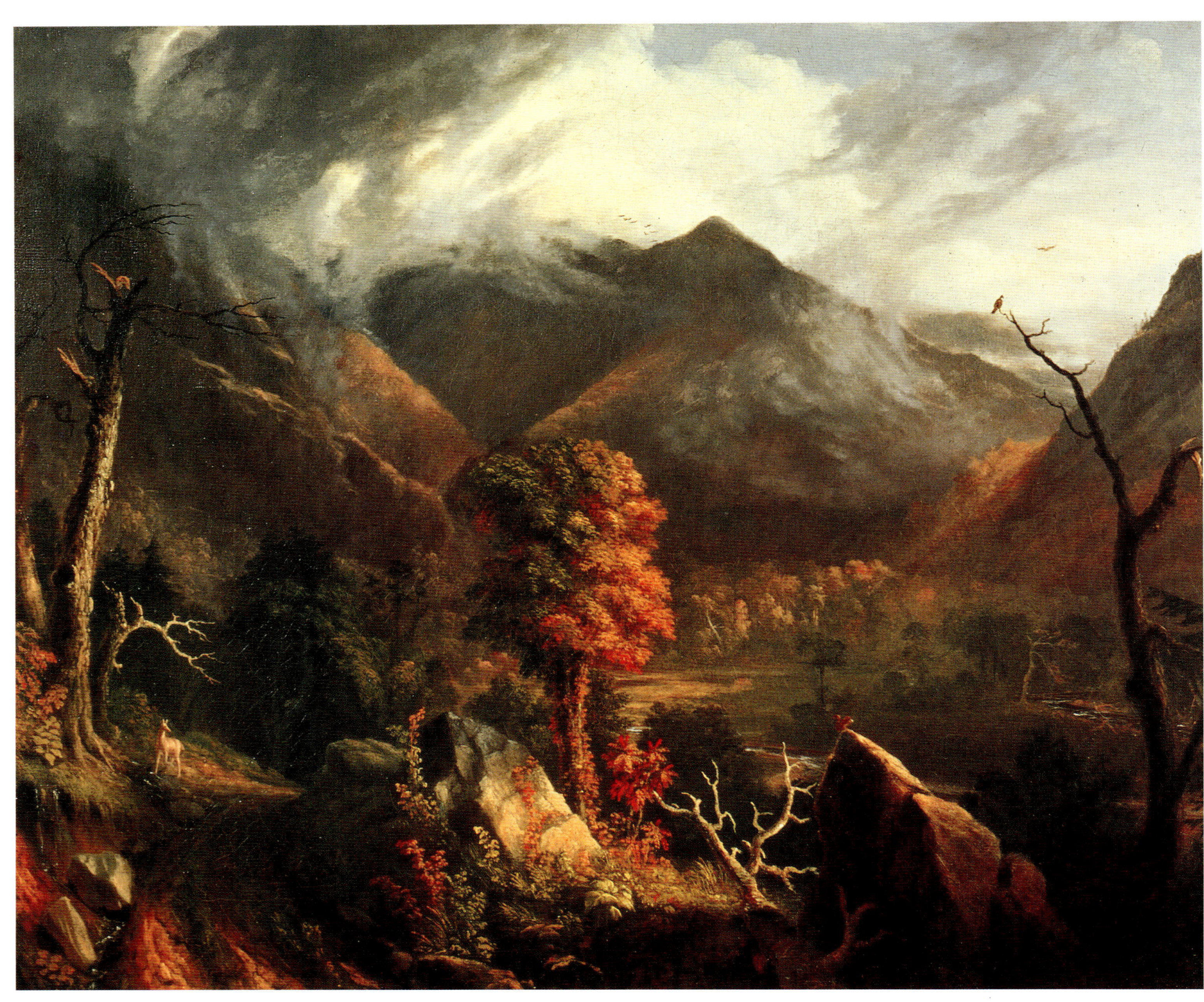

View in the White Mountains

c. 1827. Oil on canvas,
27⅛ x 32¼″
The Fine Arts Museums
of San Francisco,
Museum Purchase,
M.H. de Young Art Trust Fund

Acknowledgments

It has been a pleasure to prepare this study of Thomas Cole, America's first great landscape painter, and its realization has been made possible through the commitment and support of several individuals whose contributions I would like to acknowledge with gratitude. Mark Greenberg, the editor for this project, has been a pleasure to work with, and his informed and constructive criticism of the manuscript was extremely helpful. I would also like to thank Professor John Wilmerding of Princeton University, Ms. Frances Smythe, Editor, National Gallery of Art, and Mr. Mitch Tuchman, Editor, Los Angeles County Museum of Art, for reading the manuscript and providing me with their thoughts and helpful insights. I am grateful to the Baltimore Museum of Art and Professor Howard Merritt for permitting the inclusion of the annotated list of Cole's paintings, which first appeared in 1967 in the Baltimore Museum's *Annual II: Studies on Thomas Cole, An American Romanticist.*

I would also like to thank my wife, Nancy, who has been more than generously supportive of the personal time required to work on this important project.

Earl A. Powell

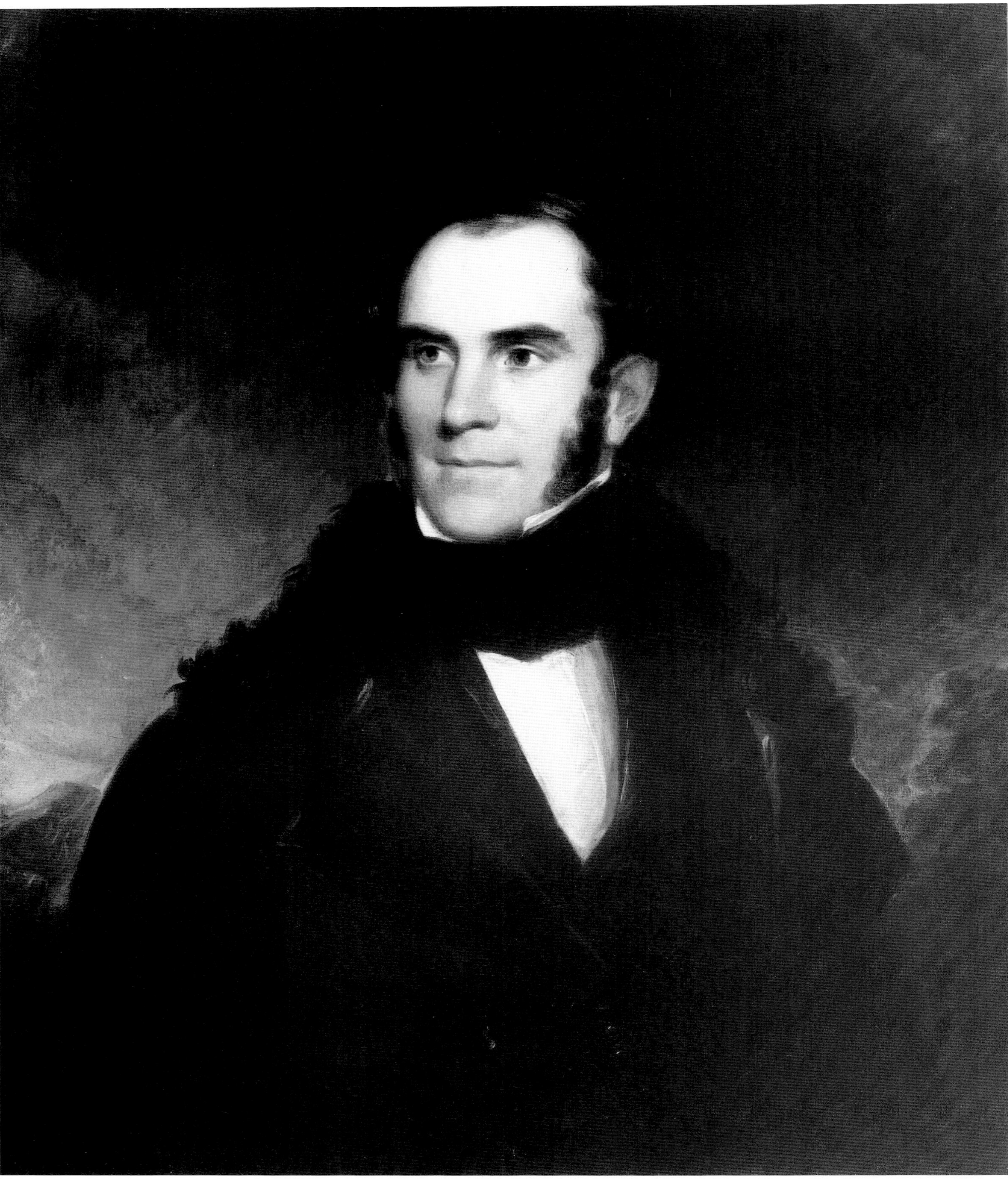

Introduction

For the generation of artists who rose to prominence in the years following the establishment of the Republic, the creation of an American cultural and artistic identity was a challenge of national importance. This goal was central to the development of American art of the Romantic era. To achieve it, painters and sculptors of this period looked deep into the historical roots of Western culture to Greece and Rome and to the literature of the day for inspiration. They faced the difficult challenge, however, of assimilating European aesthetics and styles while simultaneously attempting to transcend them in their effort to create a uniquely American art.

These artists inherited from the Colonial period a distinguished portrait tradition characterized by the brittle realism of John Singleton Copley and the more elegant rococo brushwork of Gilbert Stuart. But the American Revolution did not engender the wider appreciation of imaginative literary themes or historical subject matter that prevailed in Europe. Benjamin West had achieved great success as president of the Royal Academy in London, but his Neoclassical historical and mythological works did not suit the popular taste of America. A new nation, however, required a distinctive artistic tradition, and the arts of the young republic slowly began to expand and move appreciably beyond the limited restrictions of the portrait tradition. Nationalism and Romanticism came together in the first quarter of the nineteenth century to inspire important new developments in literature and painting, which resulted in the emergence of landscape as a metaphor for the new country.

The aesthetic ideas that swept Europe during the Age of Revolution deeply affected American creative initiative. Milton and Byron were widely read and deeply influential on both sides of the Atlantic. In literature, Washington Irving and James Fenimore Cooper emerged as the American counterparts to William Wordsworth and Samuel Taylor Coleridge. Washington Allston, trained in Europe under Benjamin West, was the first American painter who was able to enlarge upon the portrait tradition and introduce biblical as well as mythological and landscape subjects into his vocabulary. His interest in Romantic literary themes and the moods of nature opened up new creative possibilities for Ameri-

Asher B. Durand
Portrait of Thomas Cole

1838. Oil on canvas,
30½ x 25″
The Berkshire Museum,
Pittsfield, Massachusetts,
Gift of Zenas Crane

can artists, but even Allston was not to experience success in his native country. The reason was that his work was not considered "American." James Jackson Jarvis, in his important book *The Art Idea,* commented on the reason for this failure: "It is somewhat strange that Allston, who gave up wealth and distinction abroad to love of country, should have been in his arts so completely foreign in feeling and motives. There is not a trace of American influence in either. His subjects, including his landscapes, were almost exclusively taken from Europe and literature of the past, or else composed under the overshadowing influences, generally mixed, of the great masters he had copied and studied." (Jarvis, 173)

By 1825, when the landscape paintings of Thomas Cole were praised by New York's artistic establishment, a new appreciation for nature had developed, and Cole's art seemed to catalyze interest in what was then perceived as America's greatest natural and moral resource, wild nature. Cole was recognized for having developed a native landscape vision that united American nature with the inherited tradition of the picturesque, the sublime, and the beautiful, to create a compelling body of landscape paintings, which emphasized America's unique natural heritage. His art fused European aesthetics with an imaginative landscape vision to celebrate the one aspect of America that Europe could not rival, a vast wilderness landscape so expansive as to be virtually incomprehensible in its scale and majesty, a literal manifestation of the sublime.

Cole's art united God and nature and, particularly in his early picturesque work, provided American audiences with the visual equivalent of Cooper's famous *Leatherstocking* novels, whose themes, in fact, inspired a group of paintings. His art introduced a new chapter into American artistic history, one in which nature, specifically the wilderness, captured the American imagination and became a new national symbol. In this body of work the American Romantic imagination achieved maturity.

The American landscape had always exerted a strong hold on the imagination and still does today. Its vast expanse, extending in a virtually limitless plane to the west, had originally been viewed by the first settlers as the ruins of paradise. But in the seventeenth century nature was a threatening and hostile force, filled with mystery and even death. It was not until the coastal colonies became well established and the frontier had been pushed well inland that a nostalgia for the wilderness developed. This longing for a natural condition coupled with the knowledge that at the same time it still existed, gave the landscape art of Thomas Cole its unique stature as a nationalist symbol embodying the myth of America.

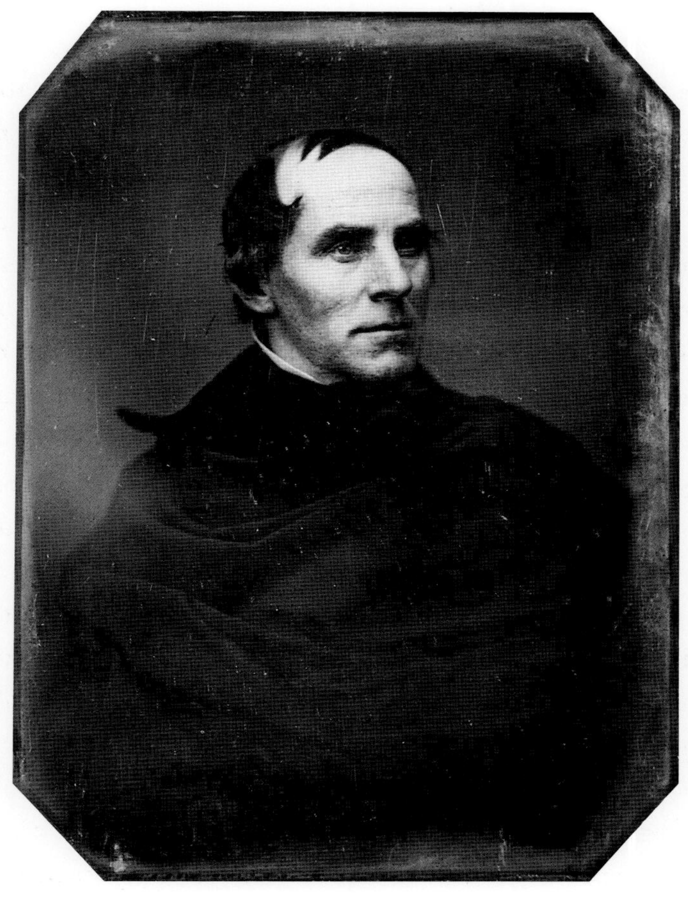

Attributed to Mathew Brady
Thomas Cole

c. 1845. Daguerreotype,
5⅜ x 4″
National Portrait Gallery,
Smithsonian Institution.
Washington, D.C.,
Gift of Edith Cole Silberstein

Cole was not the first American landscape painter, but he became America's most important painter of landscape by enlisting his art in the service of American nature and elevating landscape to a plane of historical importance. His ambition was to raise the landscape to the level and stature of history painting by emphasizing America's wilderness and its association with God. Cole's philosophy of naturalism was strongly influenced by the English Romantic poets, by the picturesque, and by Archibald Alison and his theory of association. But his art was uniquely American, inspired by the sublime imagery of the eastern mountains and the uncultivated wilderness of the New World.

Cole is generally recognized as the father of the so-called Hudson River School, a critical term that became associated with his art following his death and that also encompassed the work of his fellow landscape painters and friends Asher B. Durand, Frederic E. Church, Jasper Francis Cropsey, and others. He was the first, however, to exalt the landscape in his art, and his celebration of the American wilderness was unique in its time. His work elevated him to the highest level of America's artistic establishment.

1. Early Years

Little is known of Thomas Cole's childhood and education in England. His early years, prior to his family immigrating to America, are obscured beneath a changing economic situation. What is known is that he grew up during the height of the Romantic era in Great Britain and his early education included reading Milton, Spencer, Thomson, and Wordsworth and the Lake Poets, from whom he certainly gained an innate appreciation of biblical literature, poetry, and nature and the landscape. In England the face of nature was undergoing enormous change as agrarian lands and the natural landscape gave way to a nascent industrialized economy.

Thomas Cole was born on 1 February 1801 at Bolton-le-Moor, Lancashire, the seventh of eight children and the only son of James and Mary Cole. His father was a woolen manufacturer who experienced business difficulties in Bolton—a textile center in the heart of Britain's industrial landscape—and relocated to Chorely where Thomas was apprenticed to a calico designer and learned the art of engraving. Thomas was an imaginative and thoughtful young man, given to reading the poetry and literature of the Romantic era, and even in his early youth he was attracted to the landscape. His biographer, Louis Legrand Noble, recounted that it was Cole's "delight to wander off into the shady solitudes, and mingle music and lonely feelings with dreams of beauty," on long walks with his youngest sister, Sarah, in search of the picturesque. Noble is the primary source of biographical information on Cole, and his life of the artist, published in 1853, contains excerpts from Cole's journals, prose writings, and poetry. It is a fascinating compendium, important not only for the information Noble provides about Cole but also as a literary recollection of the American Romantic era.

According to early accounts Cole was a voracious reader and was infatuated with literature about the North American states. He would undoubtedly have come into early contact with the theories of the picturesque, which were central to the development of English Romantic art and literature. Indeed, the writings of William Gilpin, which were printed beginning in 1782, became a virtual manifesto for the first generation of Romantic landscape painters and poets in England and America. His *Three Essays: On Picturesque Beauty; On Picturesque*

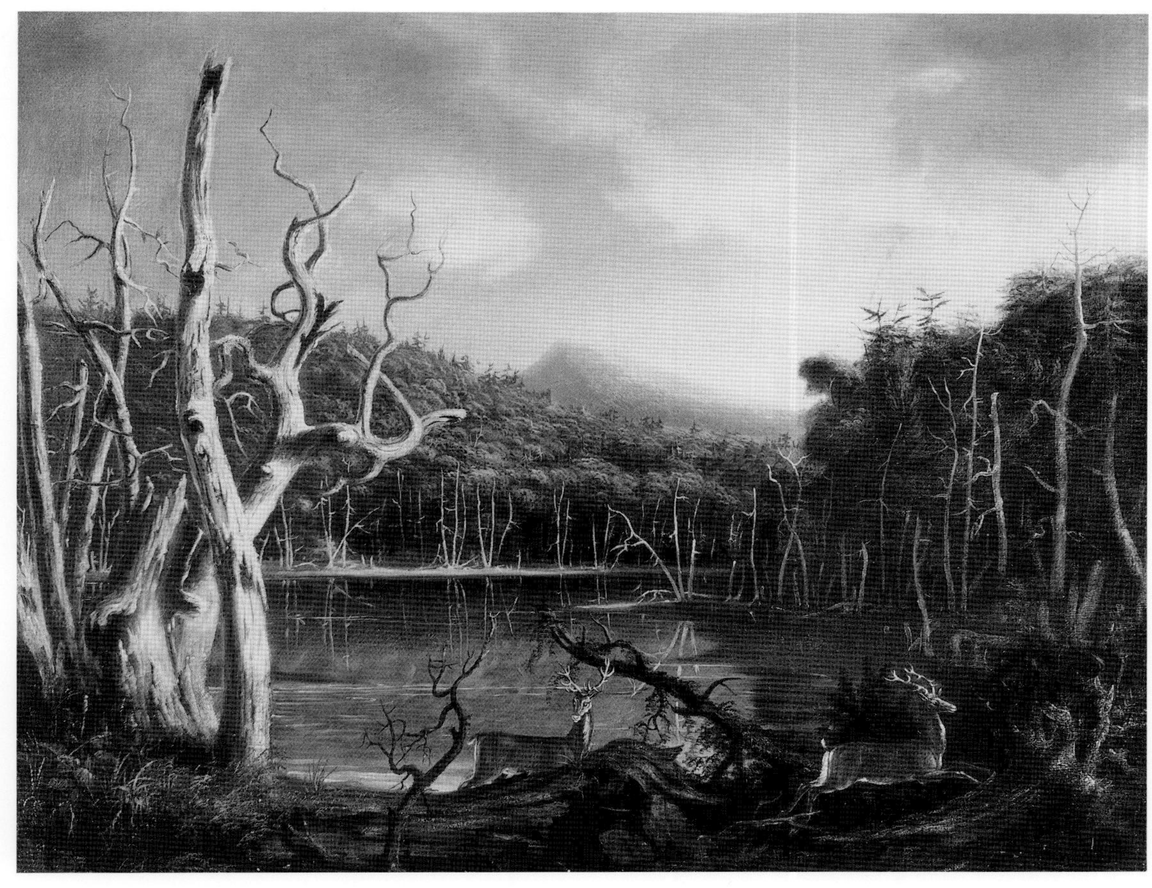

Lake with Dead Trees (Catskill)

1825. Oil on canvas,
27 x 34″
Allen Memorial Art Museum,
Oberlin College, Oberlin, Ohio,
Gift of Charles F. Olney

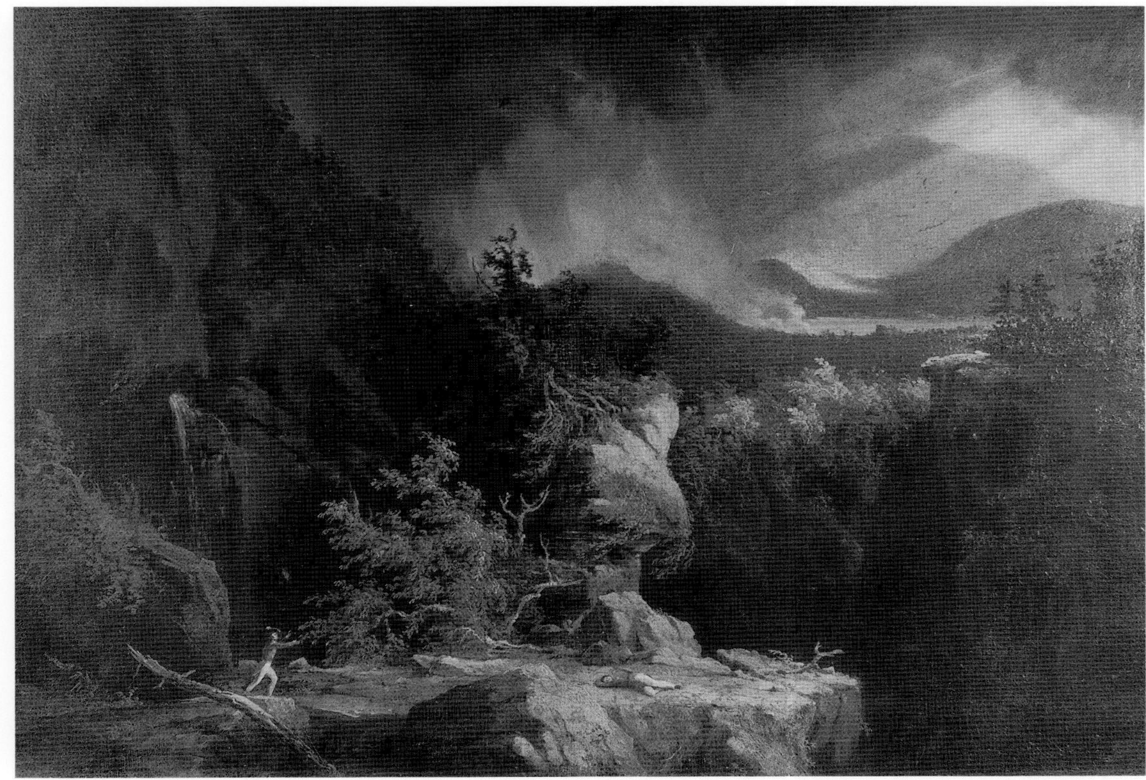

Gelyna

1826. Oil on board,
24 x 34½″
Courtesy Fort Ticonderoga Museum,
Ticonderoga, New York

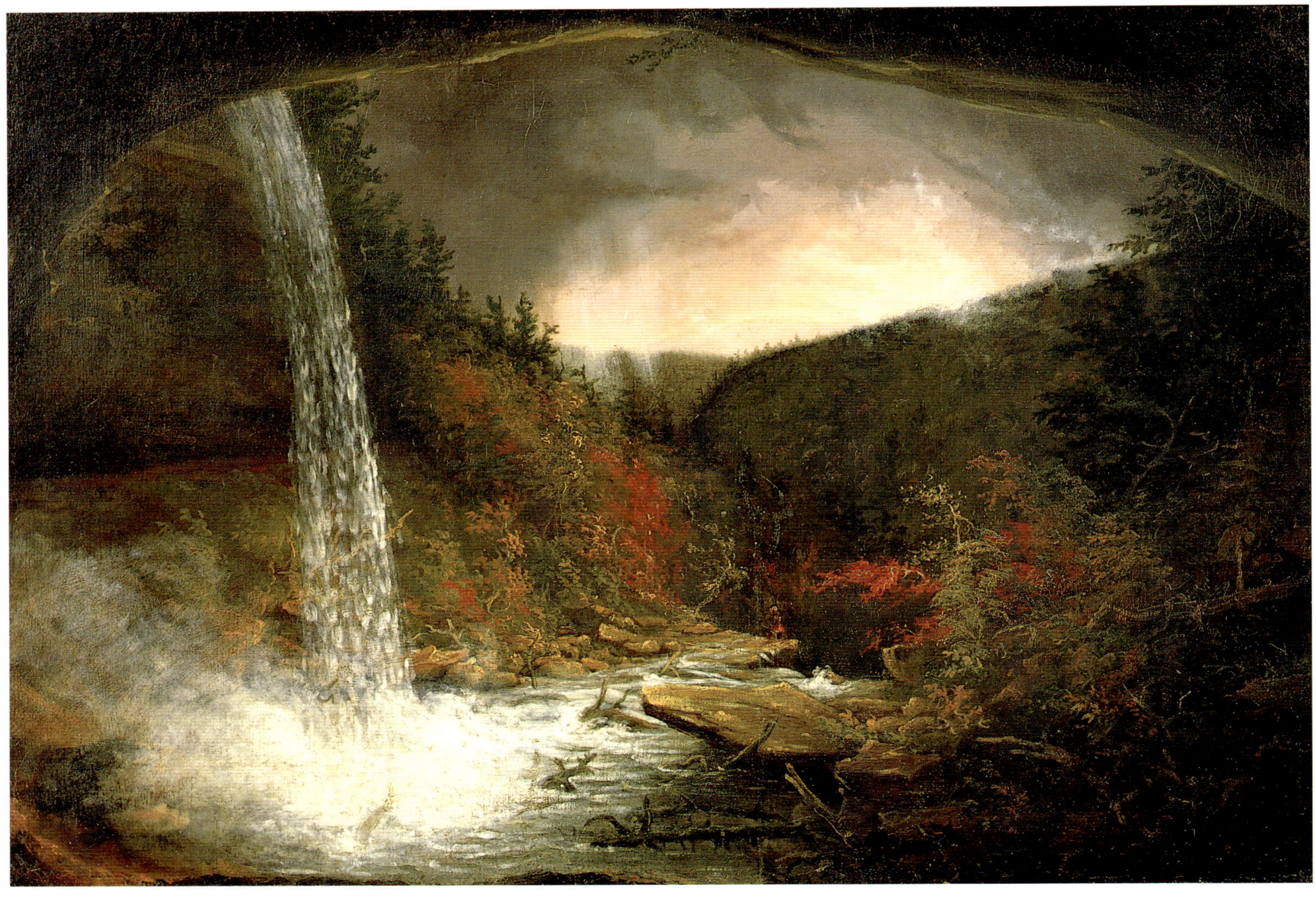

Kaaterskill Falls

1826. Oil on canvas,
25¼ x 36 3/16"
Wadsworth Atheneum,
Hartford, Connecticut,
Bequest of Daniel Wadsworth

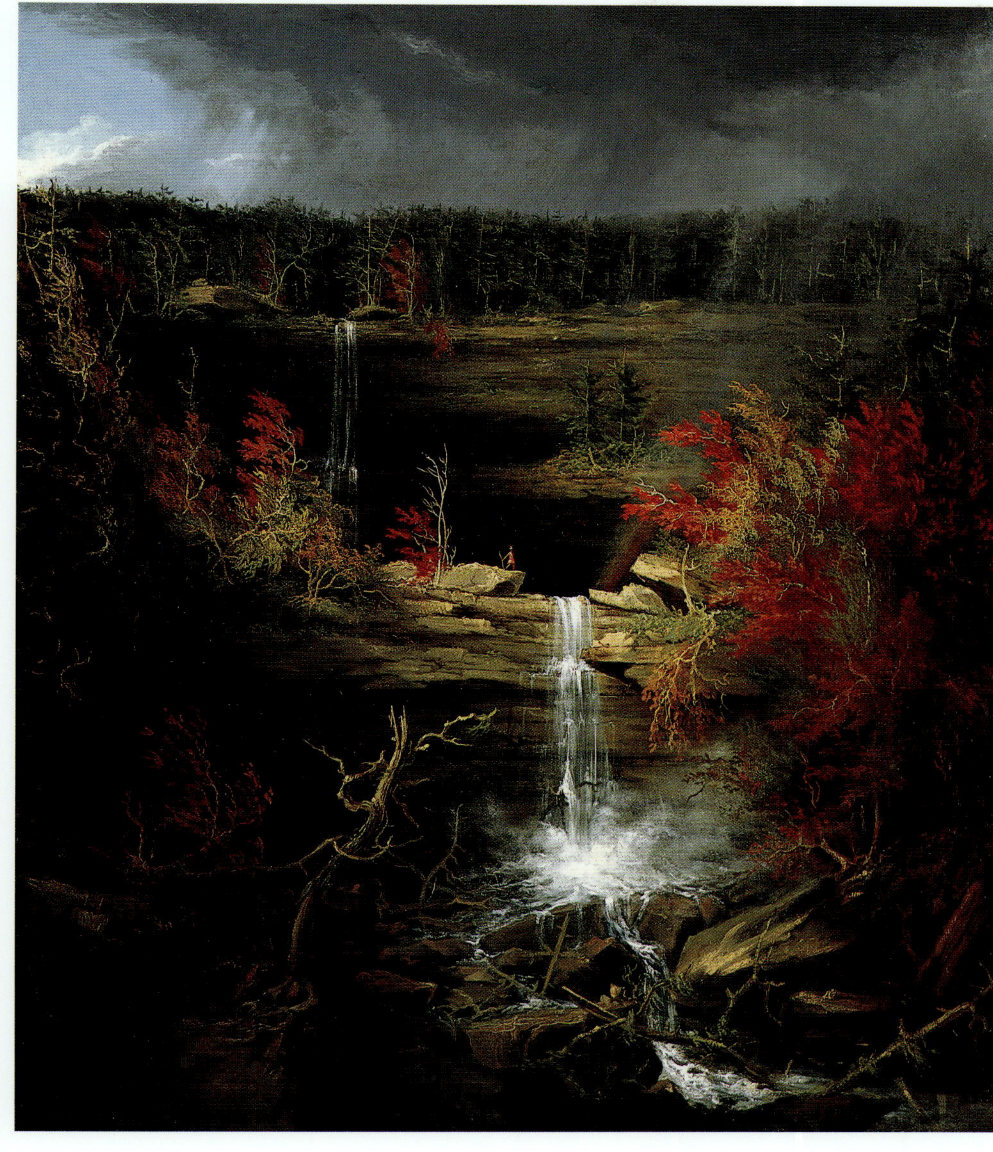

Falls of Kaaterskill

1826. Oil on canvas,
43 x 36″
The Warner Collection of
Gulf States Paper Corporation,
Tuscaloosa, Alabama

Travel; and On Sketching Landscape; To Which is added a Poem, provided its readers with a basic instructional course in the principles of the picturesque. It taught a generation more and more interested in the beauties of nature how to appreciate picturesque landscape, how to recognize the qualities of the picturesque, and how to compose artistic interpretations of its features in the landscape. Gilpin's descriptive compositions of picturesque scenery were illustrated by small aquatint landscape prints, which supported the principles of his theory and had great instructional value for emerging artistic sensibilities. He was widely read in England and America. It is not known precisely when Cole was introduced to Gilpin's theories of the picturesque, but in his first landscapes of the Hudson River and the Adirondacks it is evident that he had assimilated the theories of Gilpin and understood them well. In his later writings, in particular his fascinating correspondence with Robert Gilmor, his most important early patron, Gilpin is specifically mentioned with regard to the organization of landscape compositions.

Briefly, the picturesque involved a selective appreciation of various aspects of the landscape, usually rough and tactile features such as rock outcrops, cliffs, and clumps of trees, which a sensitized person could recognize and an artist could combine to form a landscape composition. The concept had an interesting history and will be discussed at length in a subsequent chapter.

Cole's father's economic situation soon compelled the family to seek relocation yet again, and they began to prepare for the trip to America in the hope of restoring their fortunes. Cole's early years in America would be governed by his family's constant moves in search of profitable enterprise. Prior to embarkation at Liverpool, the young Cole was apprenticed to an engraver, although no record of any work by his hand from this period is known.

The family landed in the United States in the spring of 1818 and by July had arrived in Philadelphia, where Cole's father opened a dry-goods shop. Thomas himself worked on wood engraving and produced woodcuts for printers; in the fall his family moved again, this time farther west to Steubenville, Ohio, by way of Pittsburgh. Thomas remained in Philadelphia and in January 1819 made a trip with a friend to St. Eustatius in the West Indies, where he sketched and recorded the beauty of nature in a tropical environment that must have greatly impressed him. Noble recorded that Cole was entranced by the sublimity of nature in her grander forms, commenting in his typically flowery prose, "Out of the bright ocean sprung the rifted rocks into the blue heaven; cliffs bathed their feet in the surf, and their brows in the clouds of the Atlantic; fields of flowery luxuriance, groves of dark and glistening green made the spaces between the sea-shore and the distant slopes look to his enamored eyes like Paradise: a glory sat on the rugged peaks." (Noble, 8)

Cole sketched often in the time he was there and embarked on picturesque tours of the landscape of the island that were precursors to his later tours in the upper Hudson River Valley. In May he returned and joined his family in Ohio, where he remained for much of the next two years in isolation and loneliness. It

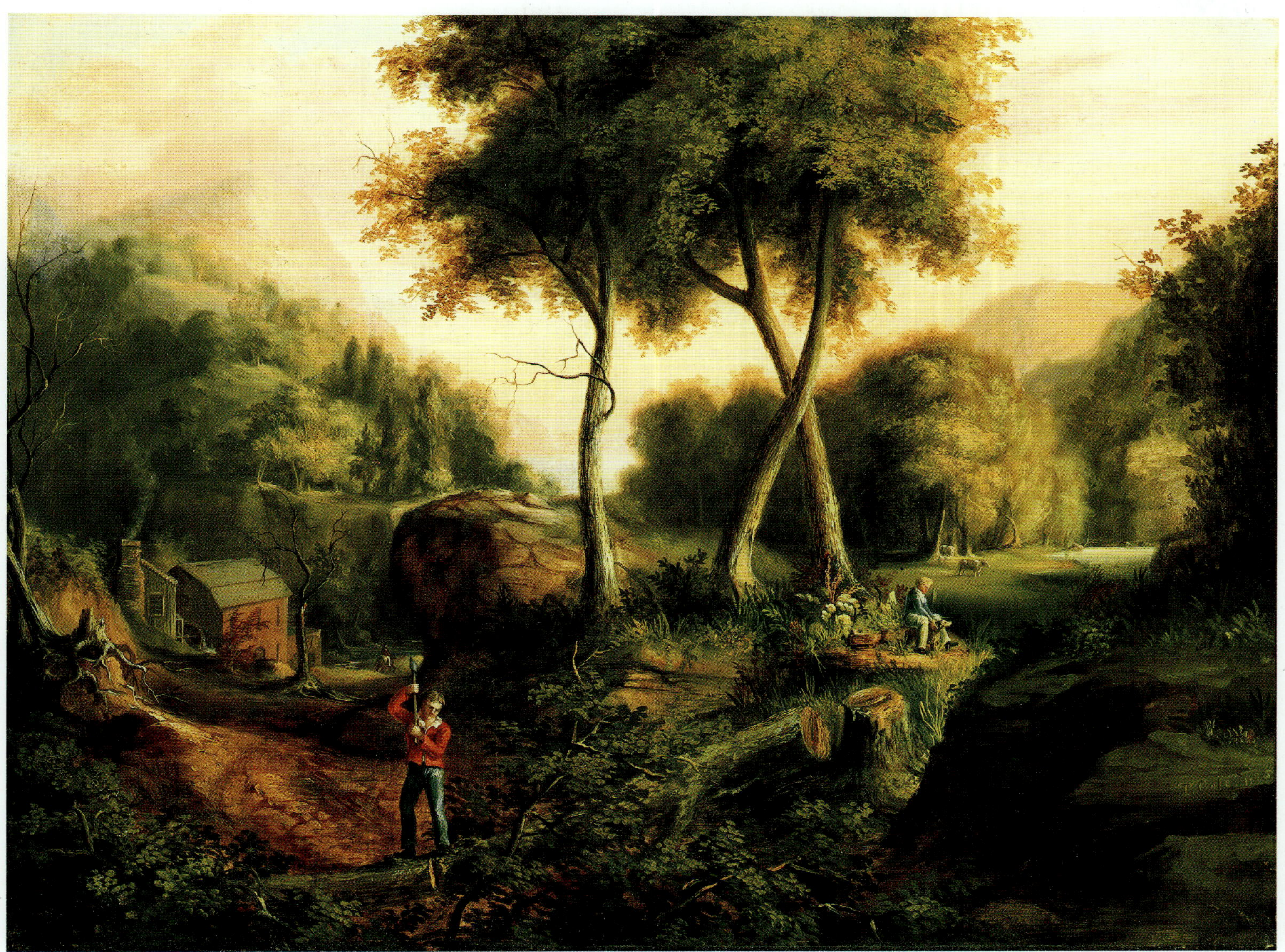

Landscape

1825. Oil on canvas,
$23\frac{3}{4}$ x $31\frac{1}{2}''$
The Minneapolis Institute of Arts,
Bequest of Mrs. Kate Dunwoody

was here, however, that he determined to be a landscape painter and consolidated his ideas and feelings with respect to nature. It was at this time that he made the acquaintance of an itinerant portrait painter by the name of Stein who arrived in the village to solicit sitters. It is difficult to know whether the paintings of this man were more inspirational than an English book of engravings that he loaned to Cole. The book apparently contained copies of the great European masters and was an inspiration to the young artist. In any event, Noble reports that this book had a catalytic effect on Cole and he resolved with conviction to become an artist.

Cole had developed the rudimentary beginnings of technique by copying engravings and sketching from nature, and he began to do portraits of friends and family. In February 1822 he finally resolved to expand his horizons and, like virtually all his contemporaries who embarked on an artistic career, he began a tour of surrounding villages to make portraits. Cole soon discovered that he was following in the tracks of the same German painter who had earlier befriended him. After several exasperating days he returned home to Steubenville, where he remained to do some scene painting for an amateur theatrical organization to pay off debts he had accumulated, and he prepared to join his parents, who had moved on to Pittsburgh. During the next year he worked for his father and gradually determined that if he were serious about becoming a painter, it would be necessary to go to Philadelphia to study. In November 1823 Cole departed for Philadelphia and what he later described as "the winter of my discontent."

Cole's winter in Philadelphia must have been shared by many a poor student. Without money and friends, he boarded with a family and lived in an upstairs room without sufficient heat and fell ill. Gradually, however, he recovered and began to paint some landscapes, which he sold, and he augmented his meager income by doing ornamental painting of birds and flowers on Japan ware. He also continued to write poetry inspired by Wordsworth and the other English Romantic poets. His time in Philadelphia was soon to end, however, and in 1825 he decided to move to New York, following his parents yet again. It was here he hoped to establish his reputation as a landscape painter.

For the first two years he maintained a studio in Greenwich Street in his father's house. His first paintings, landscape compositions, were acquired by George Bruen, who purchased three of them for the sum of twenty-one dollars. He sold others as well and was pleased with his modest success. During this time he became enamored of the landscape of the Hudson and began to explore the

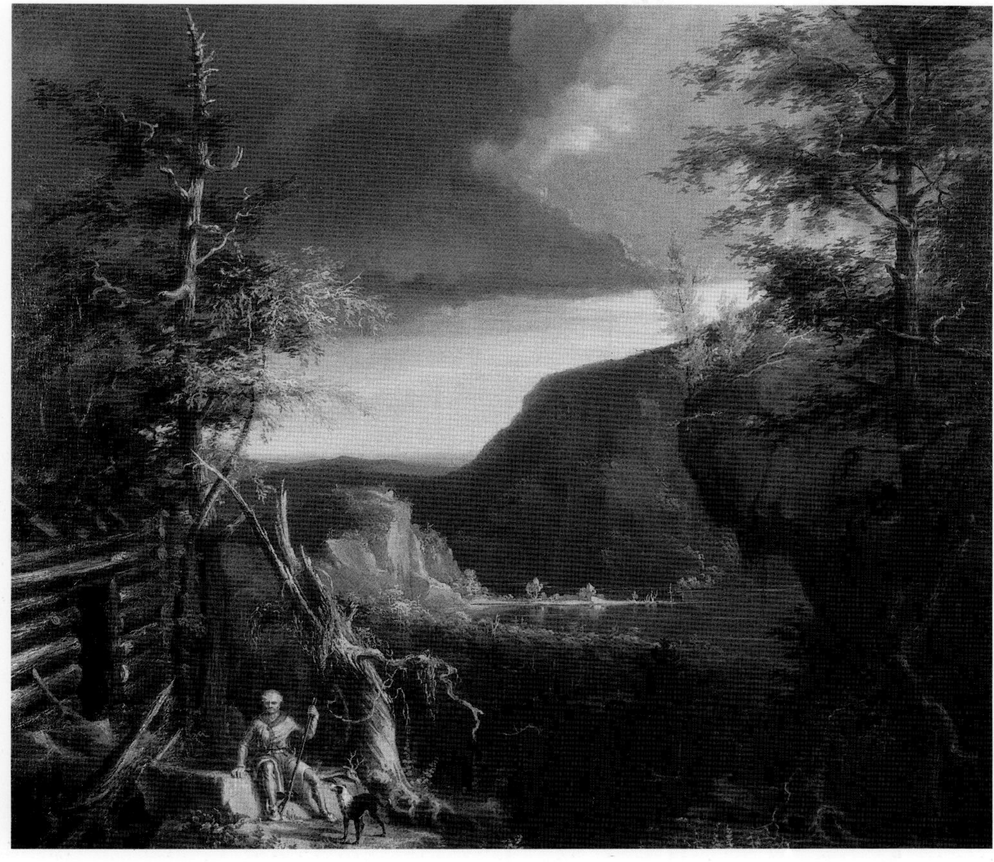

Daniel Boone and His Cabin at Great Osage Lake

1826. Oil on canvas, 38 x 42½"
Mead Art Museum, Amherst College, Amherst, Massachusetts

great river and the Catskill Mountains, which captured his imagination. When he returned to New York in 1825, he completed and exhibited three paintings entitled *A View of Fort Putnam* (now lost), *Lake with Dead Trees,* and *The Falls of the Kaaterskill;* they were offered for sale at twenty-five dollars apiece and were acquired by John Trumbull, William Dunlap, and Asher B. Durand, three of the most important and influential figures in the New York art world. According to William Dunlap, author of the monumental *History of the Rise and Progress of the Arts of Design in the United States,* which was published in 1834, John Trumbull was the first to see these youthful pictures and made the first selection, followed by Dunlap and Asher B. Durand, a fellow painter and soon to become Cole's close personal friend. Together these purchases secured the reputation and career of Thomas Cole. Soon thereafter he was solicited for landscape compositions and became one of the most celebrated painters in New York.

2. *Thomas Cole and the Picturesque*

In 1826 the National Academy of Design was established with Samuel F. B. Morse as president and a governing board of artists. Thomas Cole, through the notoriety he achieved with his first picturesque landscapes and with the support of Dunlap and other influential artists, was elected a founding member of the new academy. In the next few years Cole would build on his early reputation and produce many picturesque landscapes taken from his tours of the Hudson River Valley and the Adirondacks. His interest in the picturesque resulted in several important paintings devoted to this kind of landscape composition, which focused on the wilderness scenery of the area. He also was inspired by the mythic history of the region and, consistent with his abiding interest in history painting, developed several themes from James Fenimore Cooper's *Leatherstocking* novels. His union of the aesthetics of the picturesque with the wild scenery of America, which so entranced Trumbull, Dunlap, and Durand, also continued to provide inspiration and assured his popular success.

The picturesque, the sublime, and the beautiful were categories of emotion as well as of formal expression, and they were central to the development of Romantic landscape. In Cole's generation attitudes toward nature reflected the poetical raptures of Wordsworth and Byron. The picturesque was of most importance to Cole in his early development, and his Hudson River paintings, constructed on the basis of the theory of the picturesque, were directly inspired by the writings of Gilpin.

The body of landscape theory that developed in England and that reached its highest level in the literature and landscape painting of the early nineteenth century was characterized by a nostalgic longing for landscapes that no longer existed in Europe. The picturesque was central to this form of nostalgia; it was particularly influential in America because it was here that the ideal landscape features described by Gilpin—unexplored wilderness, primitive forests, rugged mountains, impetuous rivers—were reality. Cole was the first artist to realize fully the implications of the picturesque for the development of landscape painting in America, and his awareness of Gilpin, along with the later theorists Uve-

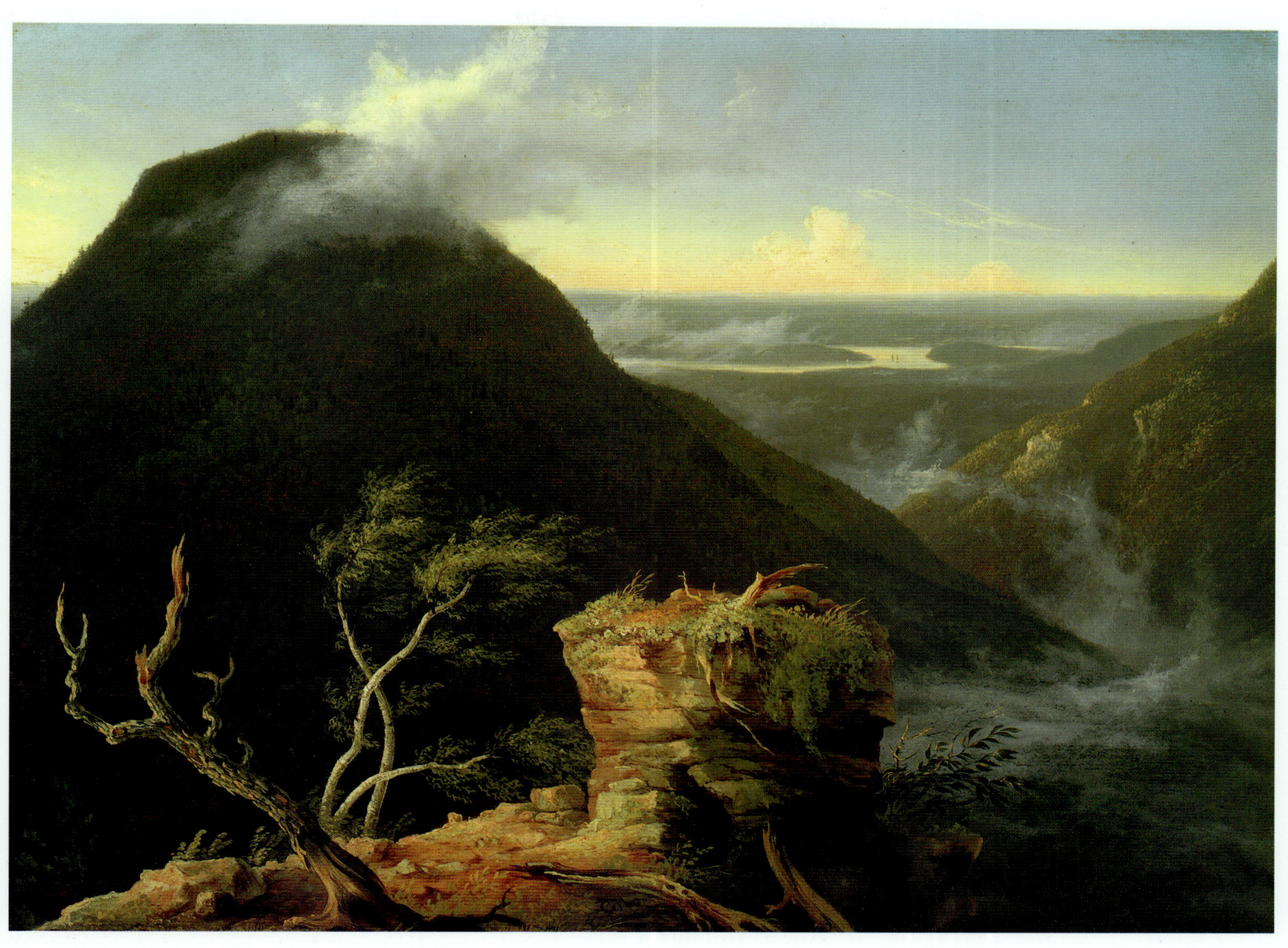

Sunny Morning on the Hudson River

c. 1827. Oil on panel,
18¾ x 25¼″
Courtesy, Museum of
Fine Arts, Boston,
Gift of Mrs. Maxim Karolik
for the Karolik Collection
of American Paintings, 1815–1865

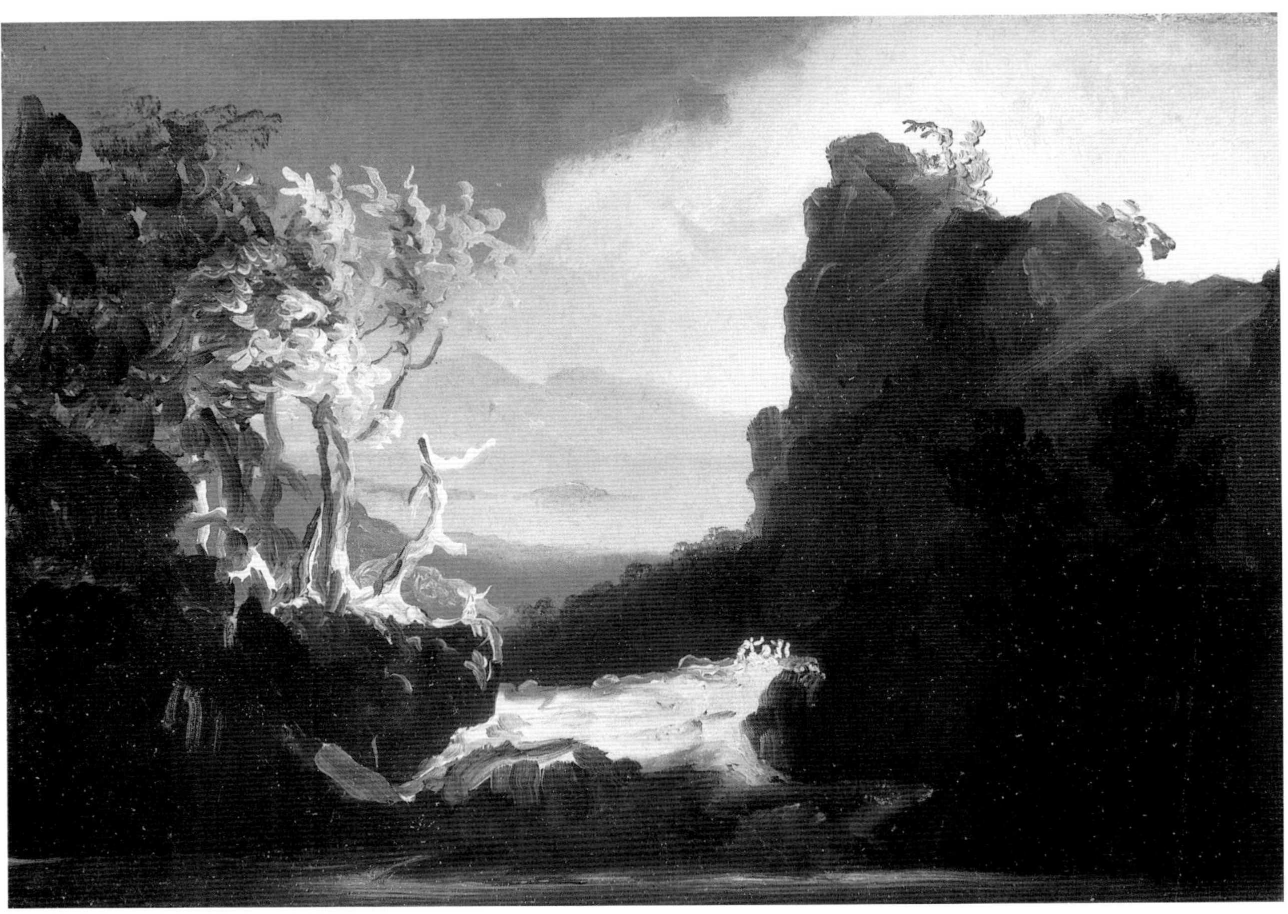

Romantic Landscape
c. 1827. Oil on academy board, 8 x 11″
Courtesy The New-York Historical Society, New York City

dale Price and Payne Knight, and his application of picturesque theory to the American landscape inaugurated a new chapter of landscape painting in this country.

As a body of landscape theory, the picturesque was one of the most important and influential English contributions to the education of American vision. It was developed by Gilpin in an attempt to adapt Edmund Burke's theories of the sublime to real world experience. As such it came to exist as an alternative to the beautiful and the sublime as an objective system by which both to experience and view nature. The beautiful was based on the idyllic, imaginative landscapes of Claude Lorrain, while the sublime, as envisioned by Burke, was a world of darkness and storm, of nature enraged in a bleak wilderness barren of vegetation, a landscape of the imagination as it contemplated the apocalypse. The picturesque represented an attitude toward landscape that was essentially transitional: it appeared simultaneously with the general shift of aesthetics that accompanied the movement away from Neoclassical imagery to Romantic subjects in the last quarter of the eighteenth century. The picturesque represented an interregnum, as Christopher Hussey noted, between classical and Romantic art that was necessary in order to allow the imagination to form the ability to feel through the eyes. (Hussey, 4)

The picturesque was a mode of viewing the world that depended on qualities, discernible in nature, that stimulated the mind and imagination. Hussey noted that "Classic art makes you think . . . imaginative art makes you feel. But picturesque art merely makes you see." (Hussey, 245) As an approach to nature, the picturesque was empirical and purely objective. It was a mode of vision that was associated with certain definable and clearly recognizable features in nature.

Gilpin was central to the dissemination and appreciation of the picturesque. His reputation in the United States rose significantly during the first decades of the nineteenth century, and his concept of the picturesque inspired the publication here of William Combe's satire "The Tour of Dr. Syntax in Search of the Picturesque." The satire was first published in *Ackerman's Political Magazine* (from 1809 to 1811). Three editions were published in Philadelphia soon after it appeared in book form in London in 1812.

Gilpin characterized the qualities of the picturesque as those that would look well in a picture and that emphasized nature in an uncivilized or uncultivated state. He believed rough, tactile surfaces were picturesque and that these aspects of the natural world could be enhanced through vibrant chiaroscuro effects. In other words, he isolated the visual qualities of nature and taught that those qualities, although they might never be found all together in a natural vista, could be located in several different aspects and united in a single composition by a gifted artist.

Gilpin believed that the most worthwhile place to search for picturesque scenery was along the banks of rivers. For Thomas Cole, the Hudson offered rich opportunities, and his 1825 sketching trip provided him with the quintessential picturesque experience. Cole's work progressed rapidly after 1825, and during these years he produced some of his most important landscapes.

Sunny Morning on the Hudson River of 1827 is a wonderful example of Cole's best picturesque work from this period; it is characterized by rich color and chiar-

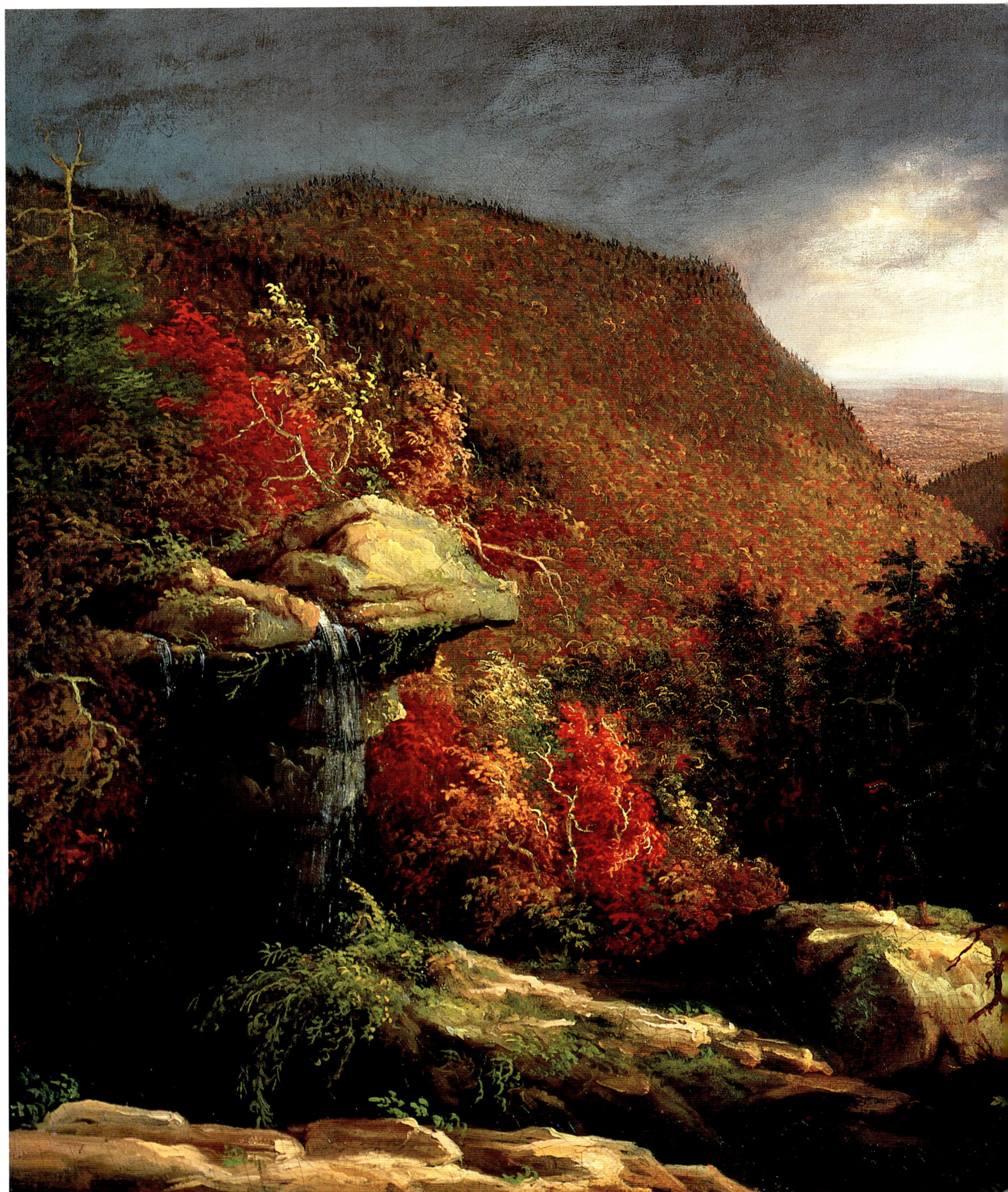

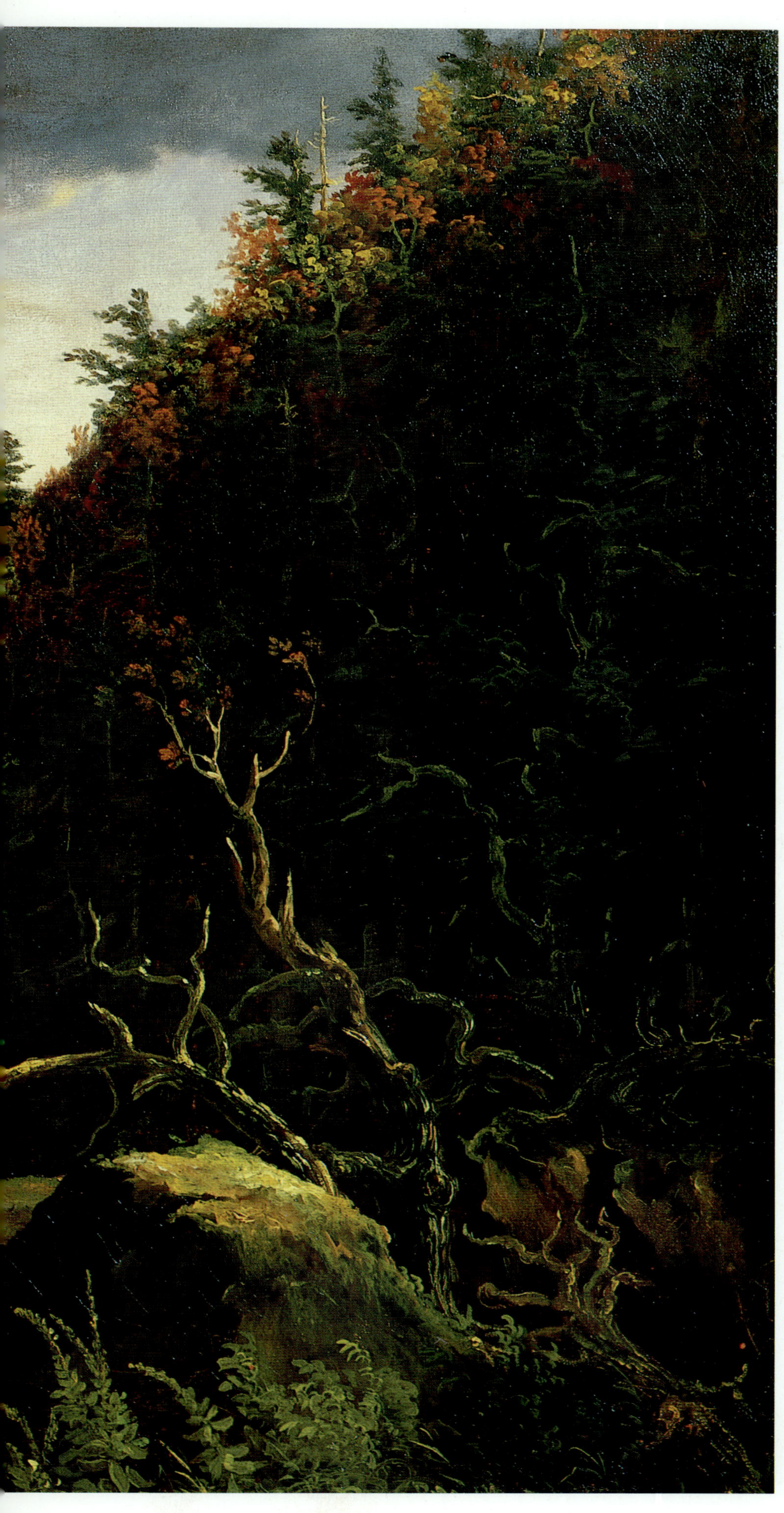

The Clove, Catskills

1827. Oil on canvas,
25 x 36″
Collection New Britain Museum
of American Art,
New Britain, Connecticut,
Charles F. Smith Fund

oscuro effects. This picture might well have been the one Cole described in his writings:

> The mists were resting on the vale of the Hudson like drifted snow; tops of distant mountains in the east were visible—things of another world. The sun rose from bars of pearly hue: above there were clouds light and warm, and the clear sky was of a cool grayish tint. The mist below the mountain began first to be lighted up, and the trees on the tops of the lower hills cast their shadows over the misty surface—innumerable streaks. A line of light on the extreme horizon was very beautiful. Seen through the breaking mists, the fields were exquisitely fresh and green. Though dark, the mountain side was sparkling; and the Hudson, where it was uncovered to the sight, slept in deep shadow. (Noble, 39)

Cole also wrote substantial verse describing his feelings before the natural spectacle of this untouched wilderness, but his description of the scene and its visualization in this canvas are a paradigm of the picturesque in American painting. The richly textured paint surfaces and theatrical use of light and shadow, which contrast the foreground trees and the excessively imaginative rock outcrop against the dark mass of the mountain in the background, are a masterful employment of the rules of picturesque composition. Cole's landscape compositions are clearly indebted to Gilpin's theories, which permitted the artist license to alter foreground effects to enhance the overall view.

There are other early works of significance in Cole's development that emphasize his commitment to the idea of the picturesque composition. *Landscape with Dead Tree* of 1827–28 shows his continuing adherence to the massing of light and dark forms with somewhat exaggerated foreground effects. According to Gilpin, the picturesque could mitigate the "terror" of the sublime and form a natural visual bridge to the aesthetics of the beautiful. Perhaps more than any other early work, *Landscape with Dead Tree* specifically visualizes that transition. The storm passing into the distance leaves nature cleansed and bright in an autumnal glory that would have a continuing fascination for Cole and other artists of his generation.

These compositional principles are likewise manifested in Cole's *The Clove, Catskills,* of 1827, where the rising diagonals of the mountains are made more emphatic by the use of chiaroscuro effects, which divide the canvas into roughly equivalent light and dark areas behind the carefully articulated organization of the rocks and trees in the foreground.

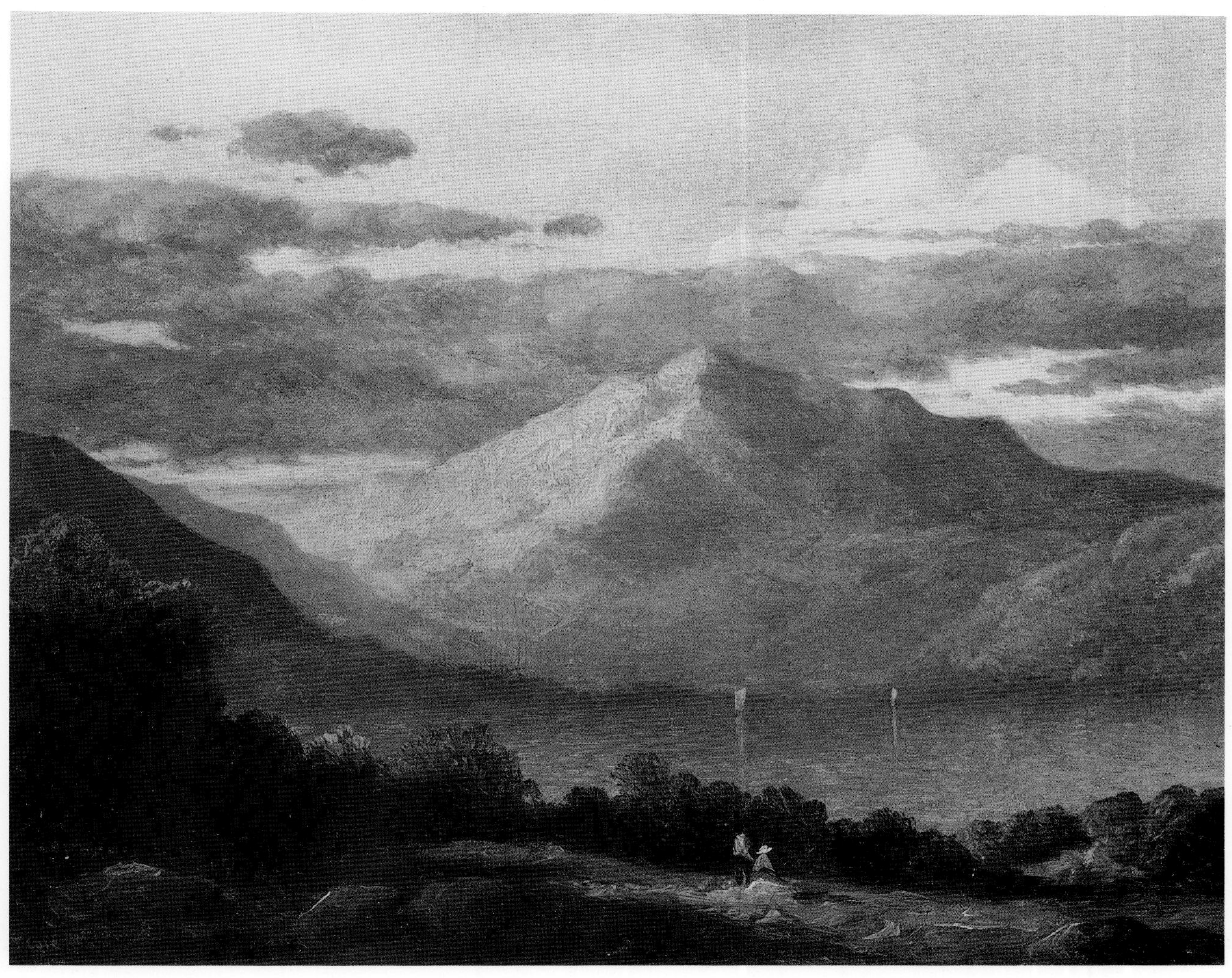

In the Catskills

n.d. Oil on canvas,
10 x 13″
George Walter Vincent Smith
Art Museum,
Springfield, Massachusetts

Cole's ideas of this period were questioned and tested by his most important early patron, Robert Gilmor, Jr., of Baltimore, with whom he began a correspondence in 1825. Gilmor was a wealthy merchant who was highly educated and very well informed concerning matters of art and taste. He eventually acquired four paintings by Cole: *View in the Catskills, Morning*; *Scene from "Last of the Mohicans"*; *Chocorua Peak, N.H., After Sunset*; and *A Wild Scene.* (Merritt, 41) Gilmor favored real scenes in nature as opposed to the composed landscapes that Cole preferred, and his dialogue with Cole on the vocabulary and philosophy of landscape painting is one of the most provocative and fascinating of the period.

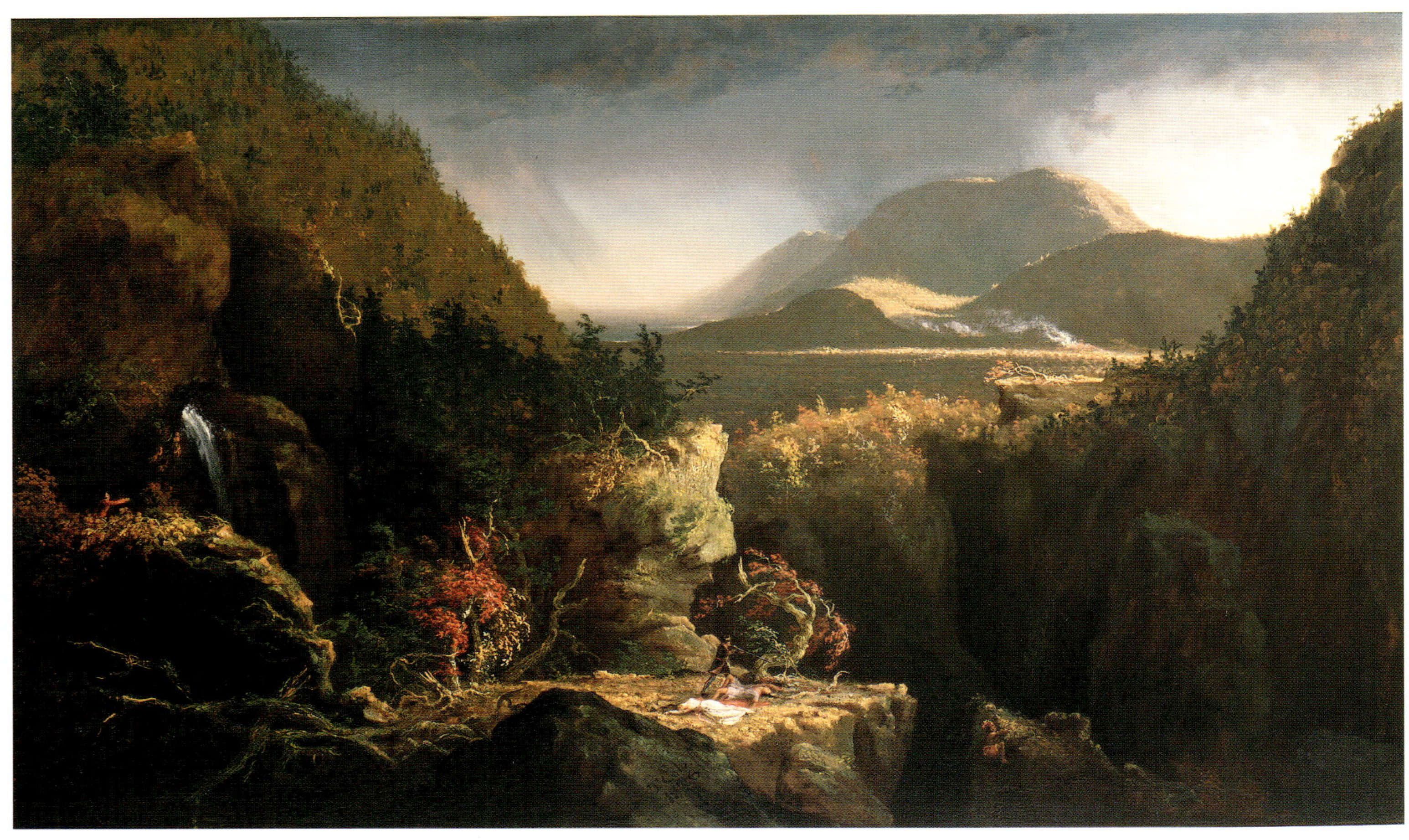

Landscape with Figures: A Scene from "The Last of the Mohicans"

1826. Oil on panel, 26 x 43″
Berry-Hill Galleries, New York

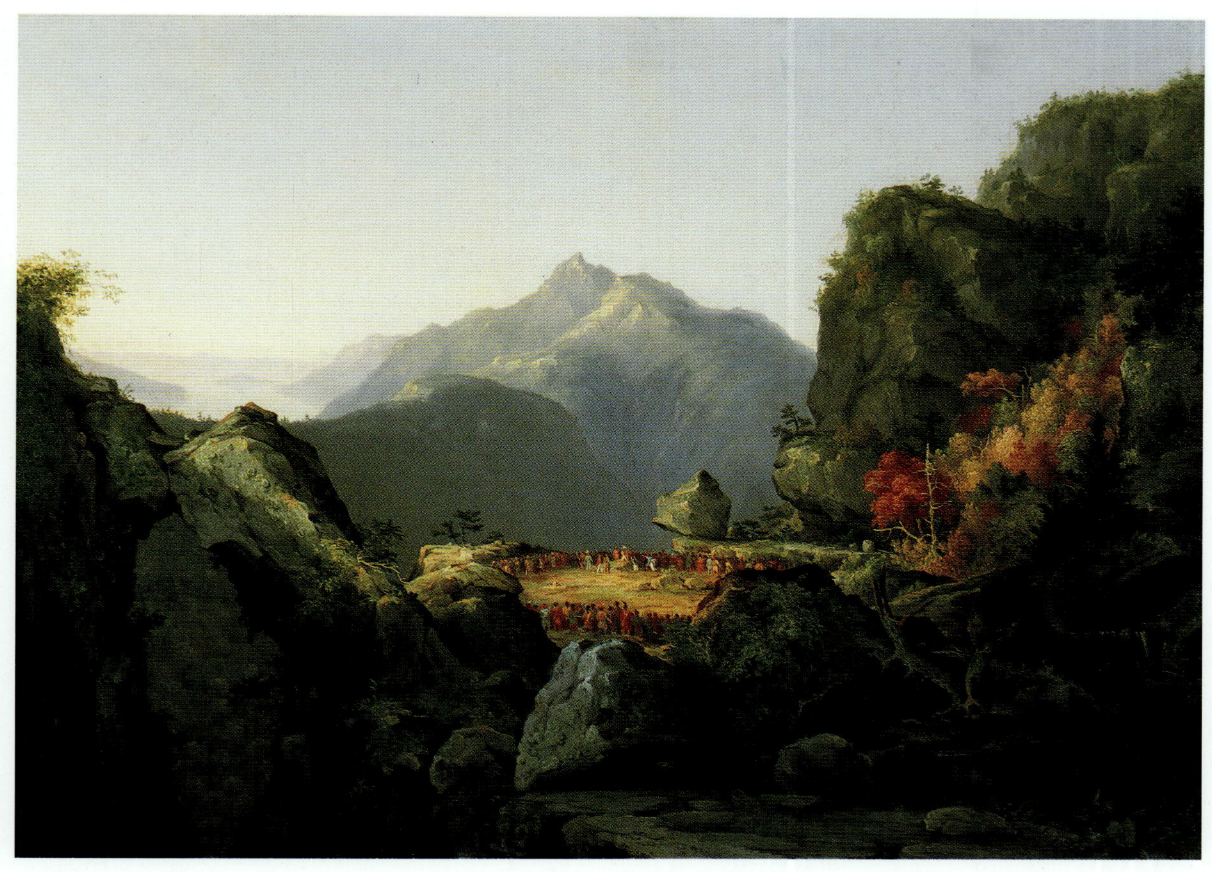

Landscape Scene from "The Last of the Mohicans"

1827. Oil on canvas, 25 x 31″
New York State Historical Association, Cooperstown

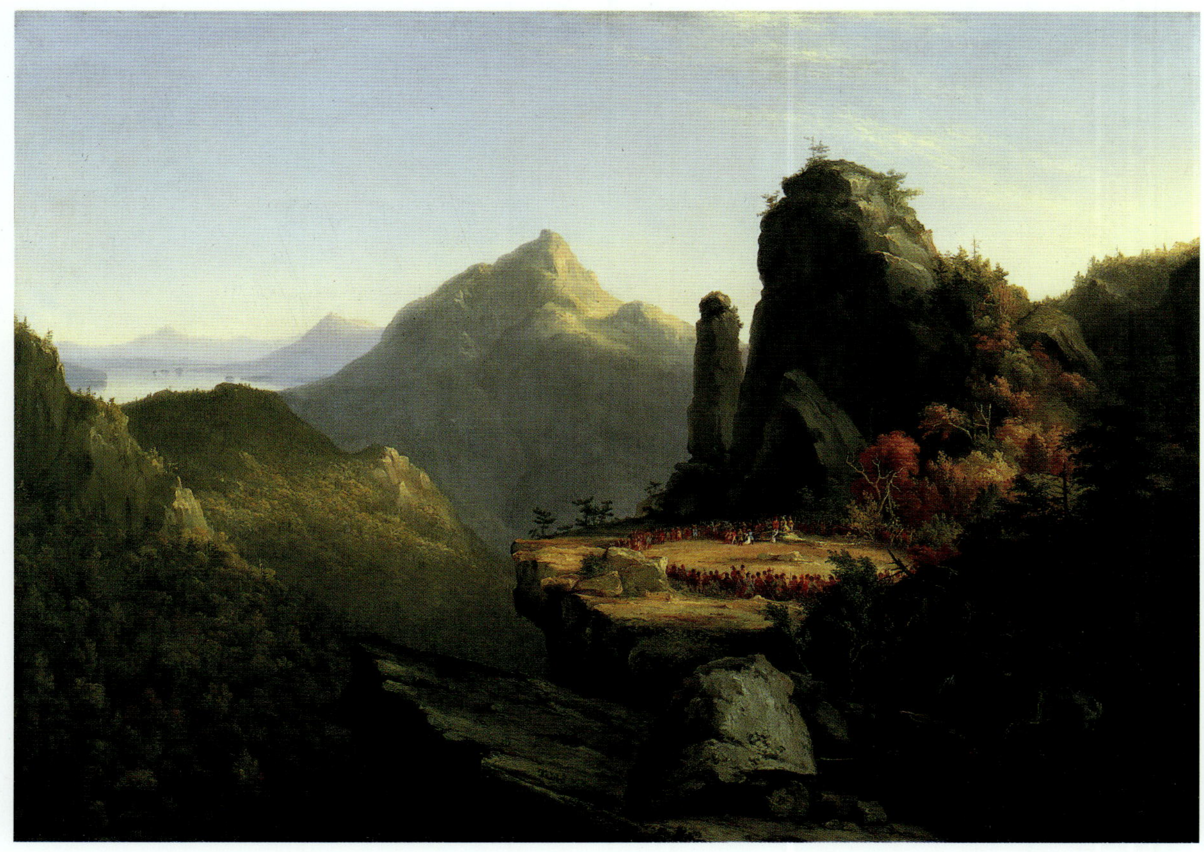

Scene from "The Last of the Mohicans": Cora Kneeling at the Feet of Tamenund

1827. Oil on canvas, 25⅜ x 35 1/16″
Wadsworth Atheneum, Hartford, Connecticut, Bequest of Daniel Wadsworth

Gilmor criticized Cole in a letter of 13 December 1826 in which he discussed his interest in a scene from one of Cooper's novels.

> Above all things however, *truth in colouring* as well as in *drawing* the scenes of our own country is essential, & it is for that reason that I have an objection to your proposal of making your next picture a *composition* to meet my wish of a scene from Cooper in it. As long as Doughty *studied & painted* from nature . . . his pictures were pleasing, because the scene was real, the foliage varied & *unmannered,* and the broken ground & rocks & moss had the very impress of being after *originals,* not ideals. His *compositions* fail I think in all these respects. (Annual II, 45)

Gilmor, the model of a generous patron, went on to comment, "Believing that an artist should be left as much to himself as possible, I will not shackle you in executing your next picture . . . I will only repeat what I formerly said . . . that I prefer *real American* scenes to compositions." (Annual II, 45)

This debate over what was important in the compositional structure of a painting illustrates the level of sophistication of the two men in current landscape theory. The painting about which this dialogue occurred was Cole's composition *Sunrise in the Catskills* of 1826, which clearly illustrates his picturesque working technique. The mists rising against the richly foliated and textured mountain landscape, bathed in a beautiful golden light, were drawn from the natural landscape, but the foreground composition was constructed of natural elements carefully situated to capture the eye most effectively and to present a theatrical stage set for the majesty of the landscape beyond. Gilmor was delighted with the picture and informed Cole of his pleasure in a letter in which he also offered Cole further instructional advice.

> You have misunderstood what I said about compositions. I meant not those you refer to. The finest pictures I will allow are compositions, but they are of experienced artists whose style has been formed, and whose store of natural images are so abundant that they can arrange "real views" from nature in such a manner to form a scene derived in its design from the imagination only. Claude's pictures, though "compositions," are every one of them real views as to the various parts of the landscape. (Annual II, 48)

In the same letter, Gilmor went on to advise the young artist, "Gilpin is worth your studying on this subject. He inculcates fidelity in the view, but very properly leaves the foreground at the disposal of the artist."

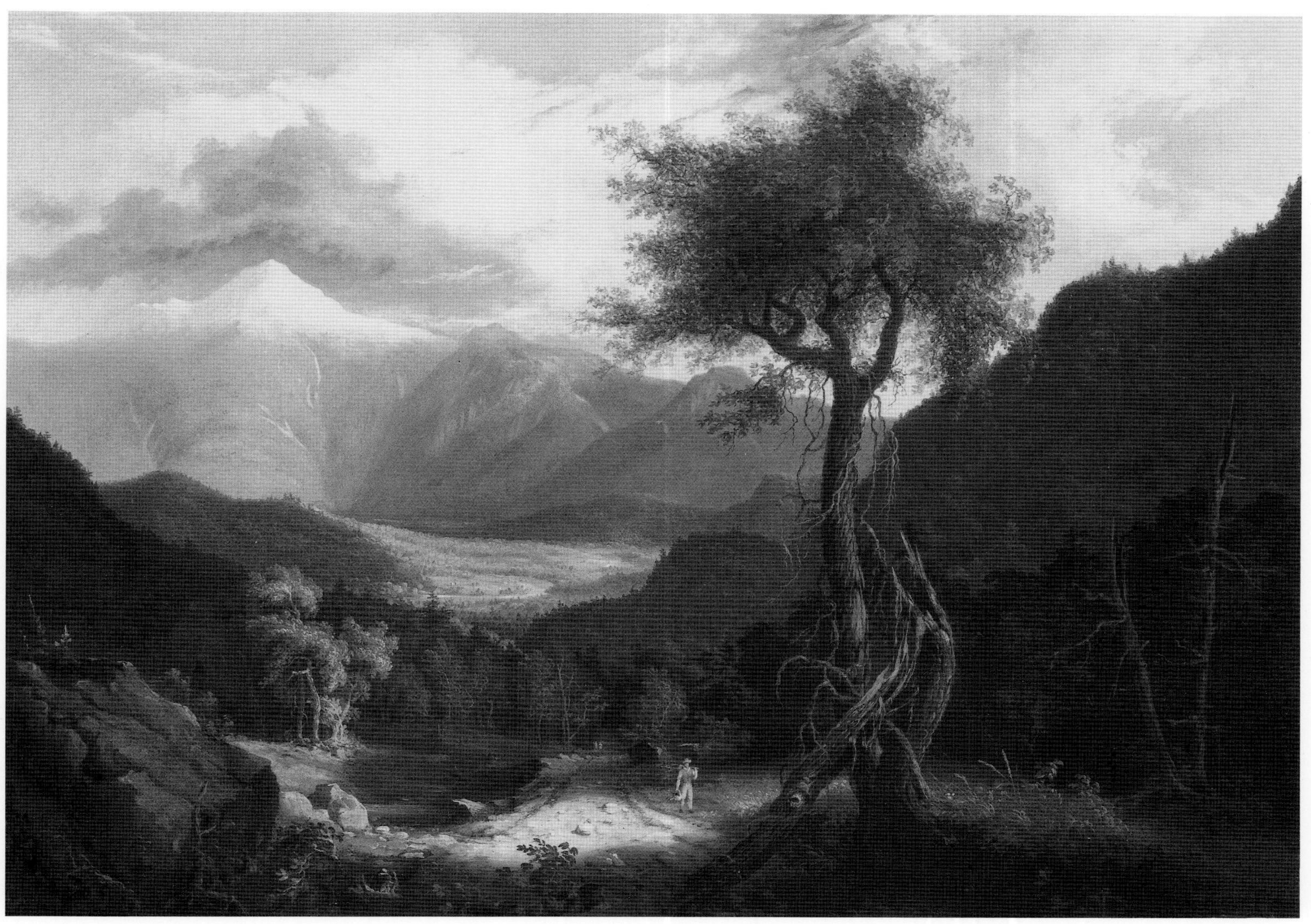

View of the White Mountains

1827. Oil on canvas,
25⅜ x 35³⁄₁₆″
Wadsworth Atheneum,
Hartford, Connecticut,
Bequest of Daniel Wadsworth

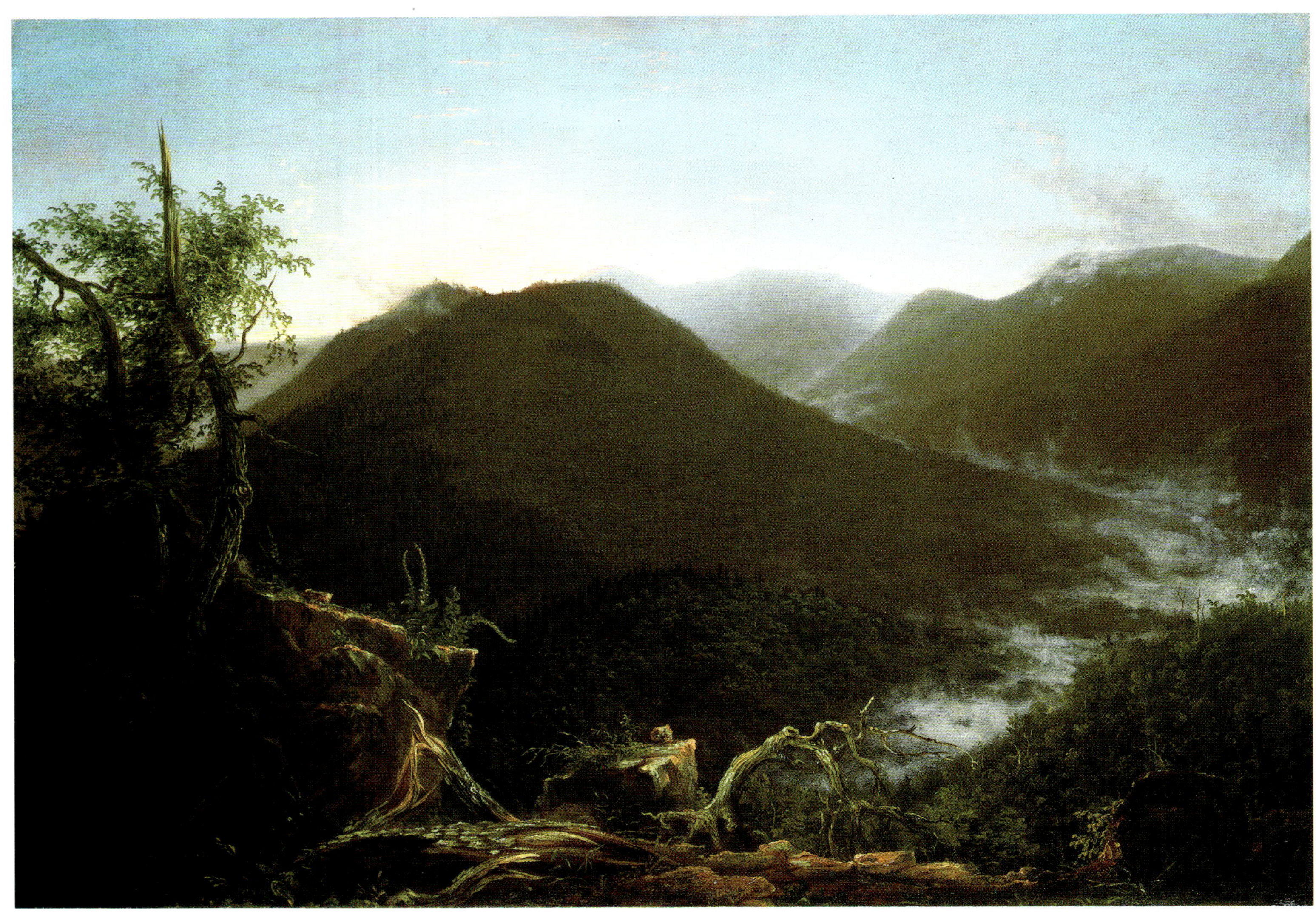

Sunrise in the Catskill Mountains

1826. Oil on canvas,
25½ x 35½"
National Gallery of Art, Washington, D.C.,
Gift of Mrs. John D. Rockefeller 3rd
in honor of the Fiftieth Anniversary
of the National Gallery of Art

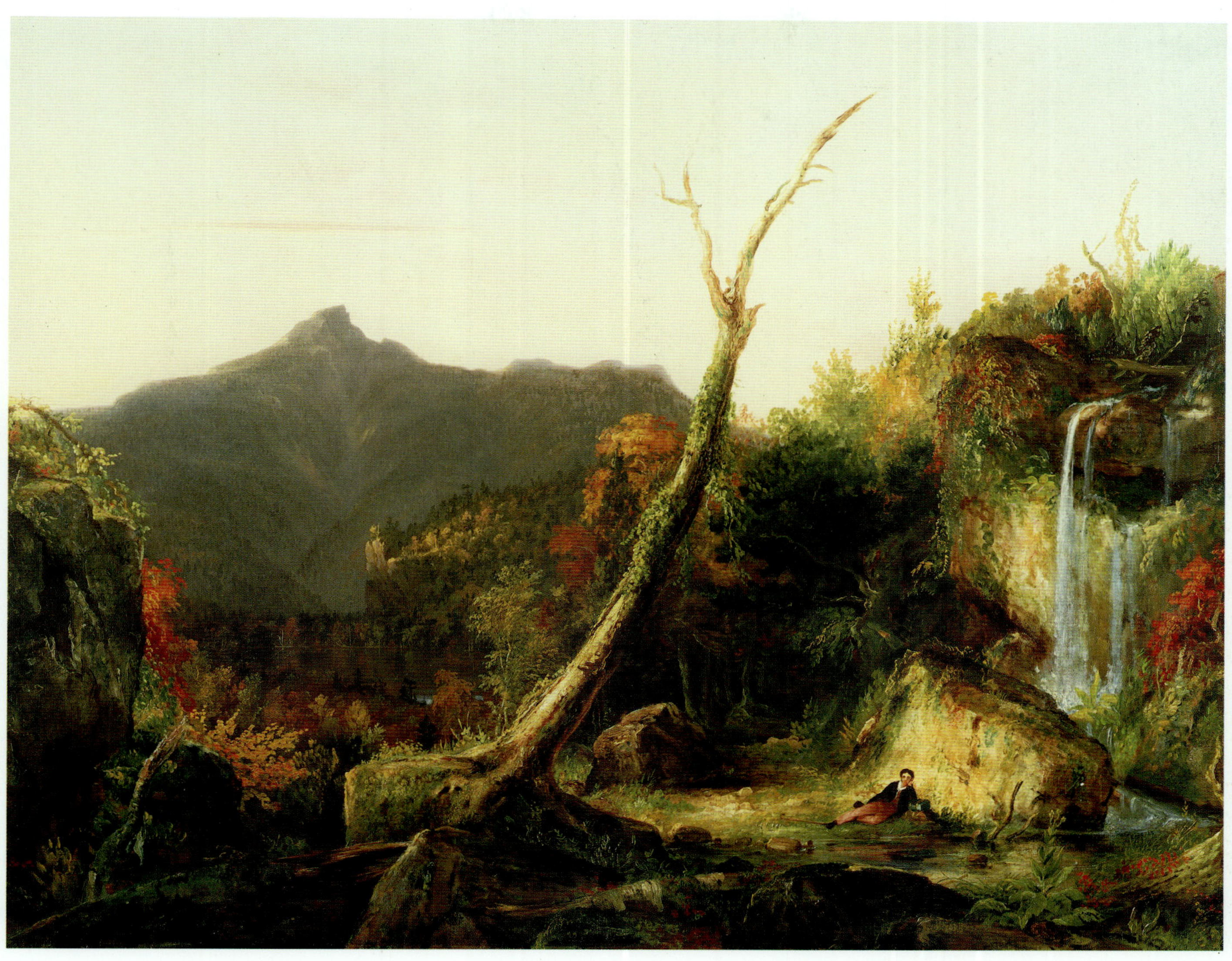

Autumn Landscape (Mount Chocorua)

c. 1827–28. Oil on canvas,
38 x 48″
Courtesy Kennedy Galleries, Inc.,
New York

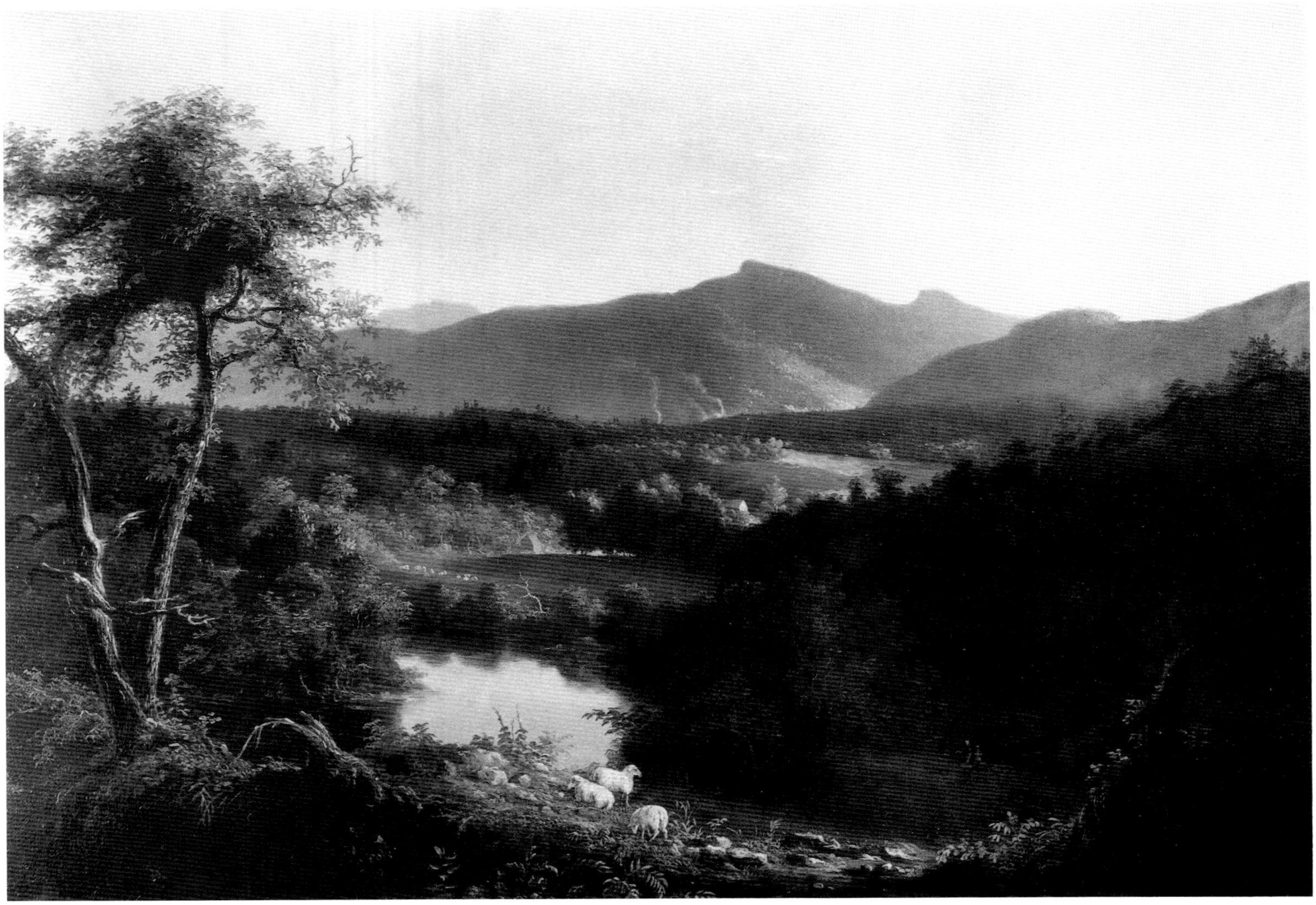

View near Catskill

1827. Oil on canvas,
24½ x 35″
Private collection

It is clear from looking at these lovely early landscapes that Cole not only appreciated the criticism of Gilmor but understood its intent. The exchange of correspondence between the two would last for many years and cover a great deal of aesthetic ground, but the early letters attest to Cole's commitment to and the influence of the picturesque on his formative development. His painting for Daniel Wadsworth, *Last of the Mohicans* of 1827, a companion of the one he produced for Gilmor, articulates the picturesque at perhaps its most baroque. In this work the exaggerations of the landscape for theatrical effect, with the circular stage and vast, looming rock outcroppings, and the aggressive chiaroscuro effects combine to form an amalgam of the real and ideal that delighted both patron and public.

The picturesque would have a continuing interest for Cole, and he would employ its principles in his outdoor landscapes throughout his career. His 1838 painting *Schroon Mountain, the Adirondacks* is a later example of this genre; Cole painted it after visiting the scene with his friend and fellow artist Asher B. Durand on a tour of the picturesque. He was struck by the autumnal beauty, which he described in typical Romantic prose.

> The scenery is not grand, but has a wild sort of beauty that approaches it: quietness—solitude—the untamed—the unchanged aspect of nature—an aspect which the scene has worn thousands of years, affected only by seasons, the sunshine and the tempest. We stand on the border of a cultivated plain, and look into the heart of nature. (Noble, 177)

Autumn was the landscape painter's favorite season, when the eastern landscape surpassed all others in its coloristic richness. Cole's interpretation of Schroon Mountain emphasizes its wildness and the majesty of primeval nature. It is a landscape composition calculated to inspire the viewer with thoughts of the sublime and an associative sense of the Almighty.

Cole and other artists and poets of his time were inspired by the wilderness, and they sought to communicate their ideas concerning it by employing the associationist philosophy of Archibald Alison. The theory that America was the natural remains of the Garden of Eden, of paradise, was subscribed to by Cole and others, and this belief was given impetus by Alison's theories. Associationist doctrine acknowledged the presence of God in the landscape and insisted that this symbolic presence could be seen and experienced particularly in the American landscape because it was untamed. Alison published his *Essays on the Nature*

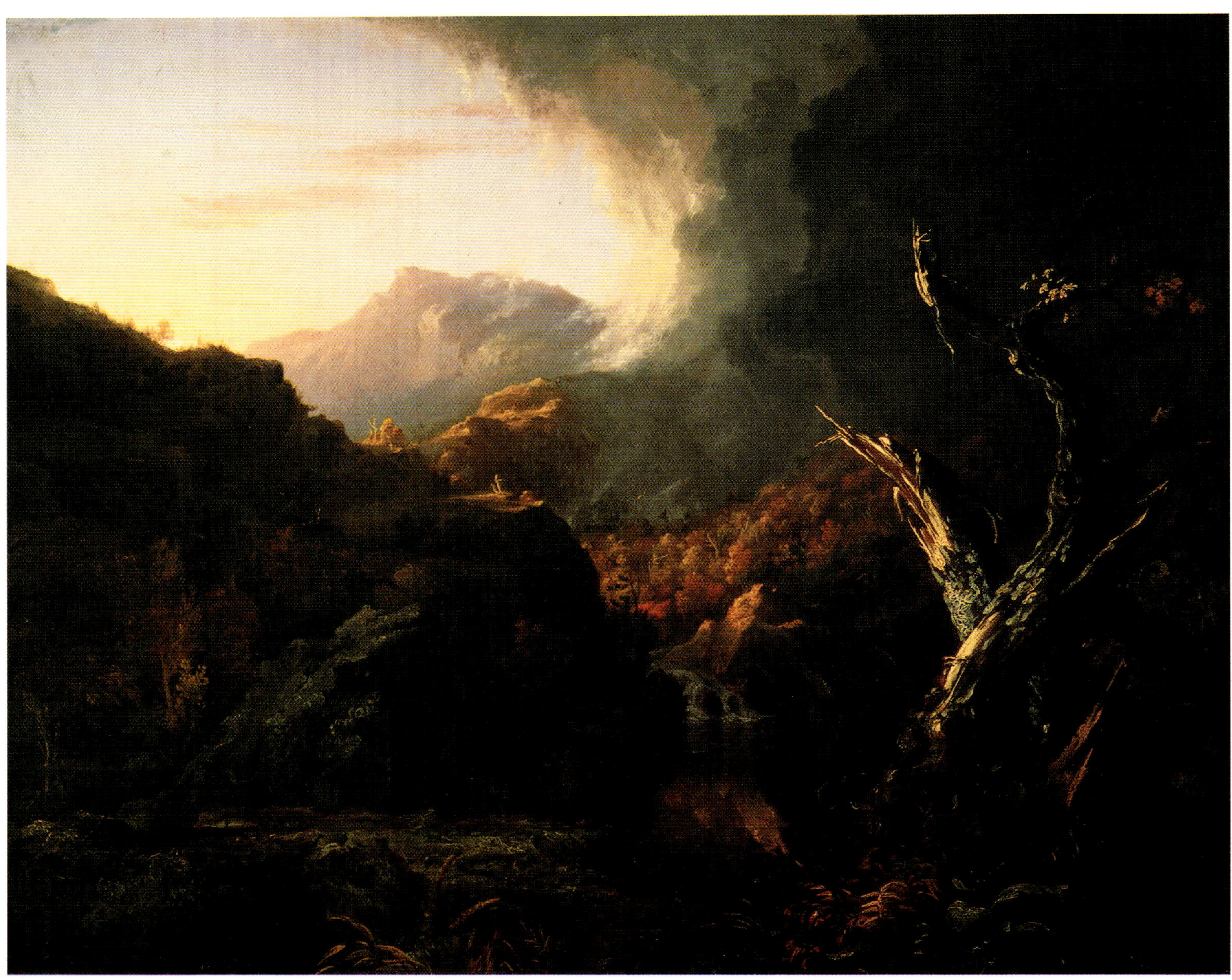

Landscape with Dead Tree

1828. Oil on canvas,
26½ x 32½″
Museum of Art,
Rhode Island School of Design,
Providence,
Walter H. Kimball Fund

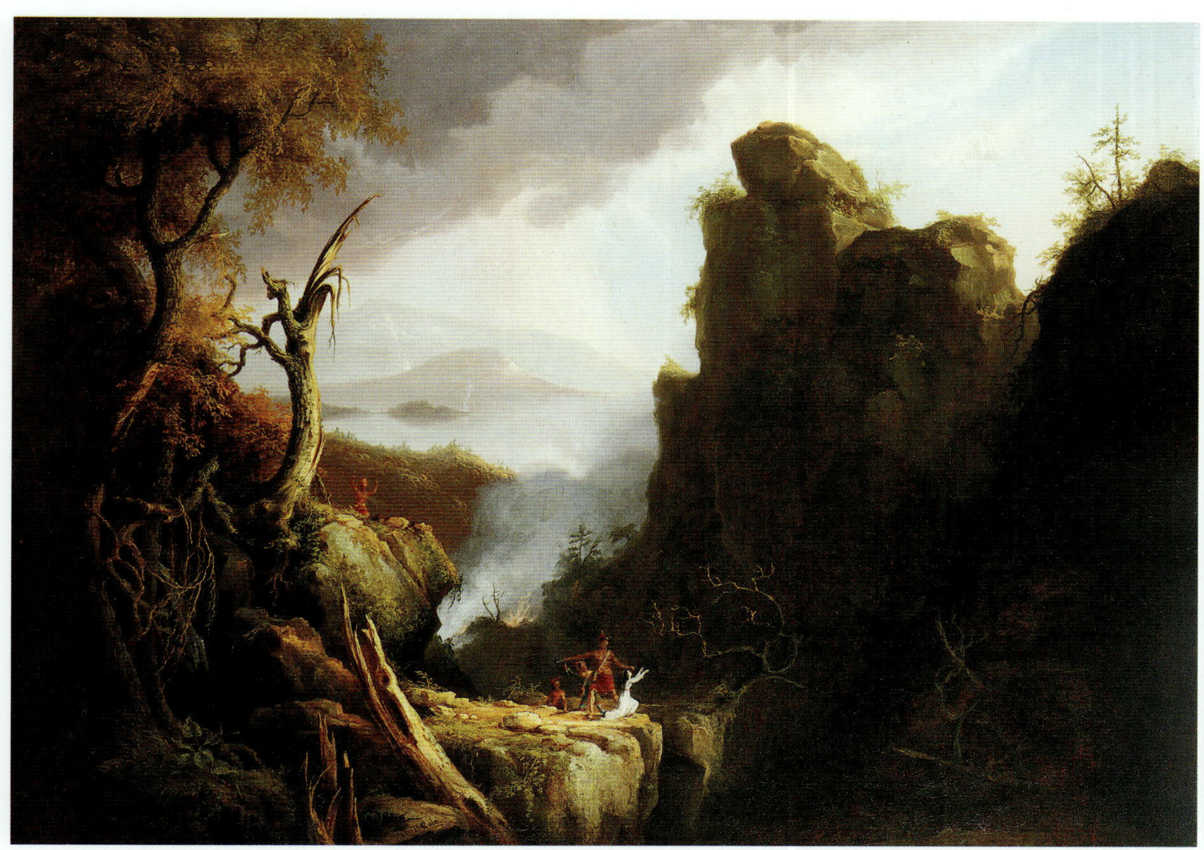

Indian Sacrifice

1827. Oil on canvas,
36 x 48″
University of Pennsylvania,
Philadelphia

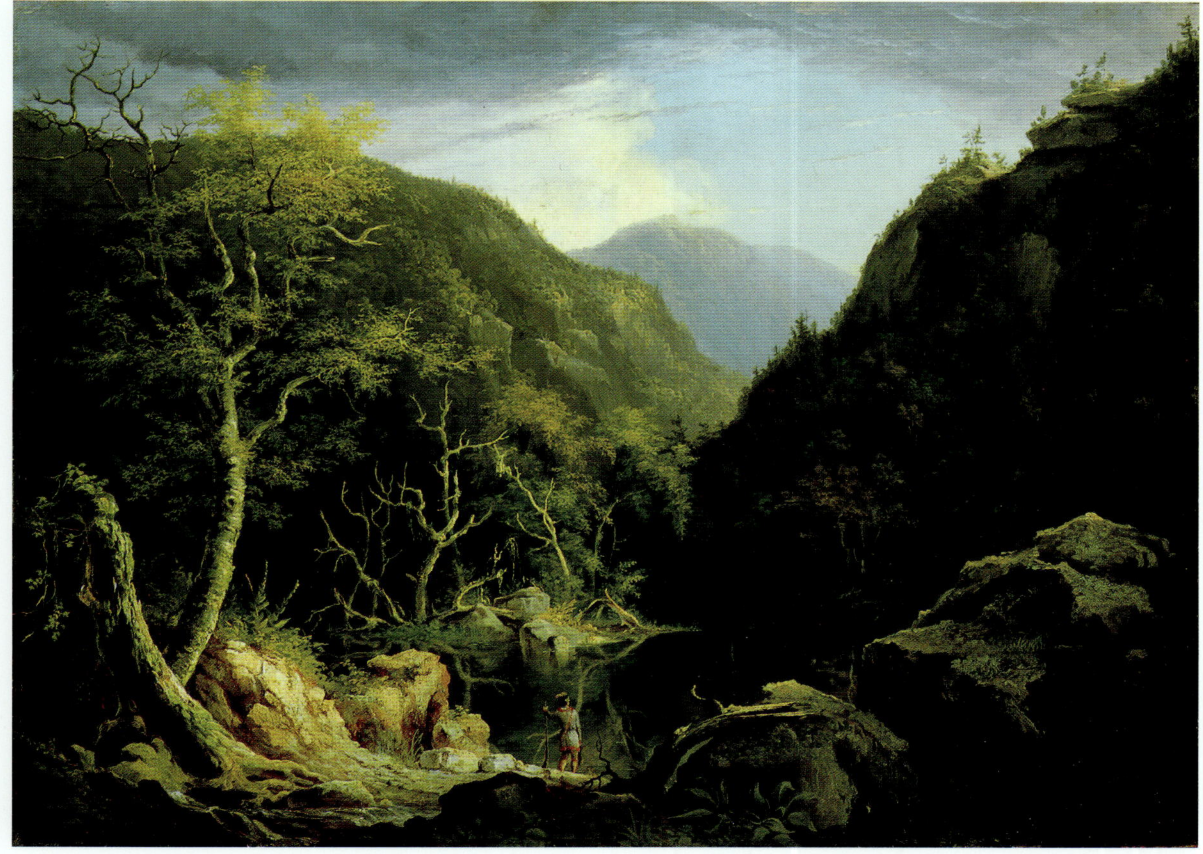

Autumn in the Catskills

1827. Oil on wood panel,
18⅝ x 25 7/16
Arnot Art Museum,
Elmira, New York

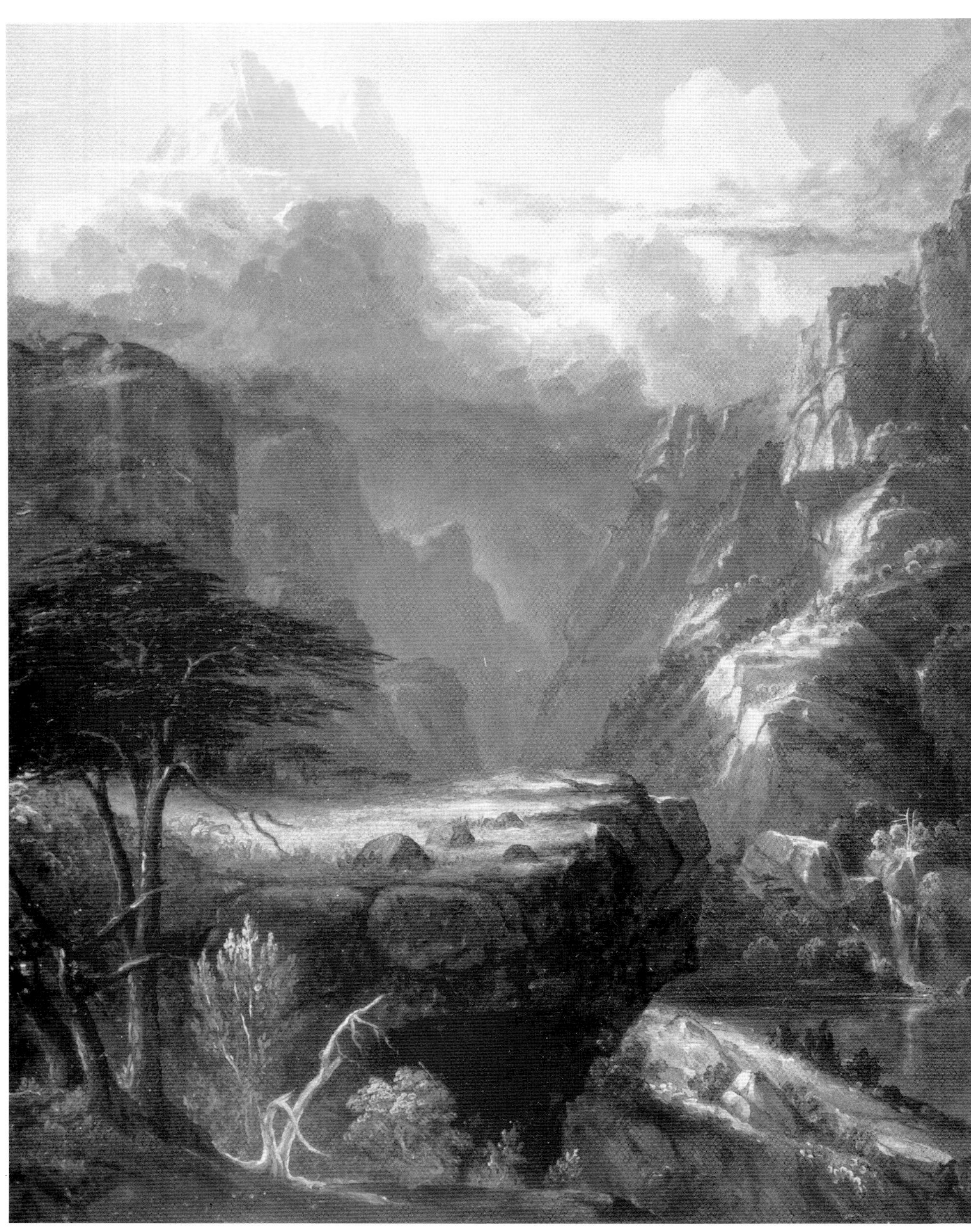

Mountain Scenery
c. 1827. Oil on canvas,
22 x 17"
Courtesy The New-York Historical Society, New York City

and Principles of Taste in 1790, and his philosophy had been well integrated into the aesthetics of the Romantic era by the time Cole commenced his career. Alison's theories complemented feelings of the beautiful and the sublime by associating those feelings of awe and reverence and fear with aspects of the natural landscape. Associationist theory ascribed to every object in the natural world the capacity to evoke trains of thought, and it argued that everyone had the capacity at some level to develop those thoughts. The objects that were alleged to be most capable of provoking associative thoughts were picturesque objects, that is, objects that were rough, tactile, and wild. By contemplating a picturesque landscape, one could develop a series of associations that would lead to a form of spiritual union with the Almighty. In *Schroon Mountain* and other picturesque landscapes Cole attempted to create a landscape expression that would stimulate such feelings. In his famous "Essay on American Scenery," published in 1835, Cole commented on the wilderness of the American landscape in language clearly reflective of associationist doctrine.

> . . . there are those who regret that with the improvements of cultivation the sublimity of the wilderness should pass away: for those scenes of solitude from which the hand of nature has never been lifted, affect the mind with a more deep toned emotion than aught which the hand of man has touched. Amid them the consequent associations are of God the creator—they are his undefiled works, and the mind is cast into the contemplation of eternal things. (Cole, 102)

The principles of the picturesque united with the doctrine of associationism were combined in the early work of Thomas Cole to produce a group of landscape paintings in which the forms and light of the American wilderness lifted landscape expression to a new aesthetic level. The picturesque would continue to have relevance and provide inspiration for Cole, but the fusion of religion and landscape would compel him to attempt more ambitious and larger-scale works of religious significance. In 1826 and 1827 he painted two important and overtly ambitious works: *Saint John the Baptist Preaching in the Wilderness,* a painting for Robert Gilmor, and the *Expulsion from the Garden of Eden,* his first attempt to combine the sublime and the beautiful in a single composition of epic proportion.

Saint John is an almost autobiographical work; Cole had by now developed a deep sympathy for the biblical prophets and identified with them in his own attempts to gain access to a higher spiritual level through the experience and

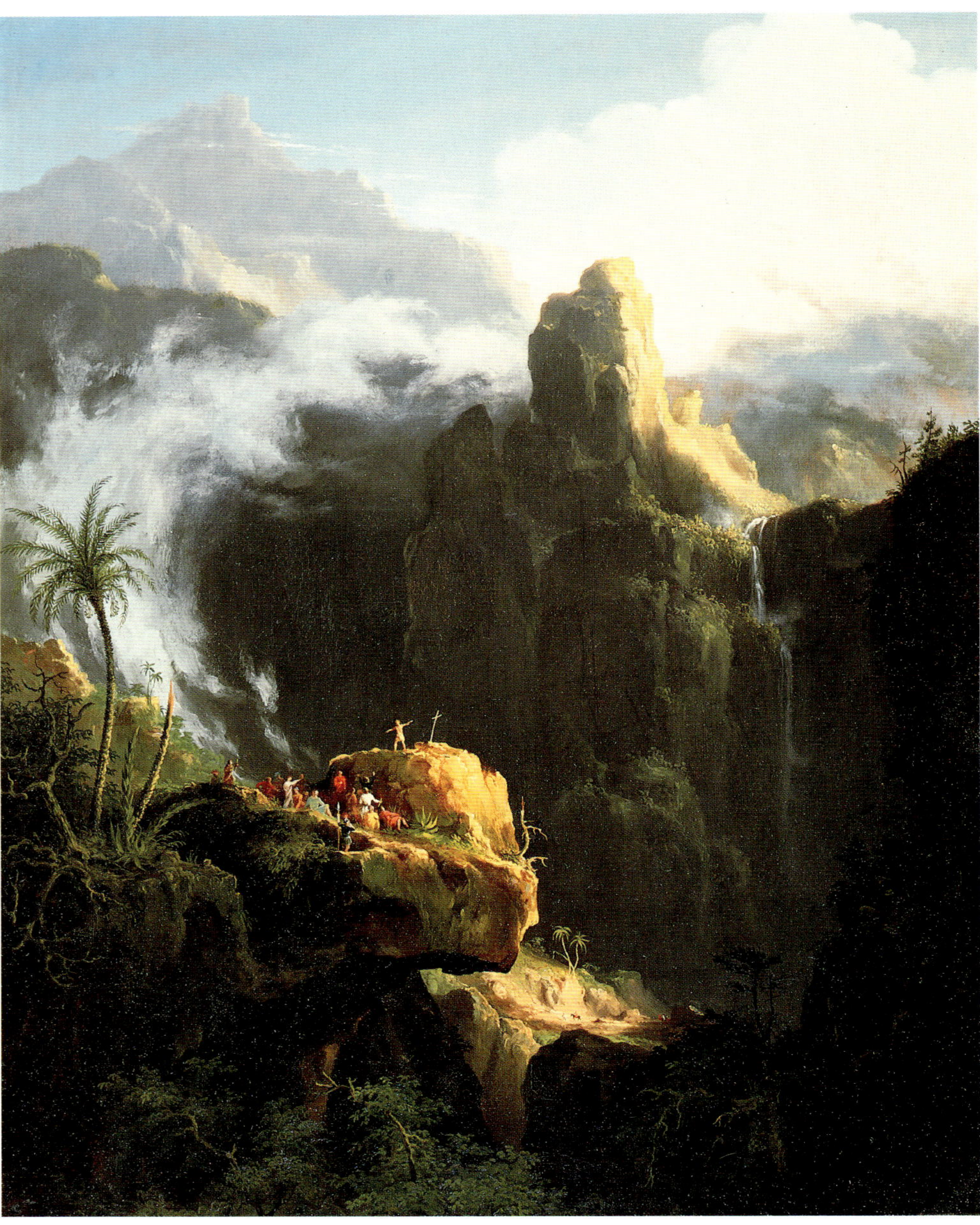

Landscape Composition: Saint John in the Wilderness

1827. Oil on canvas, 36 x 28 15/16"
Wadsworth Atheneum, Hartford, Connecticut, Bequest of Daniel Wadsworth
OPPOSITE: Detail

interpretation of the American landscape. The picture shows evidence of his abiding concern with the picturesque in its dark chiaroscuro effects, but the mere scale of the landscape indicates a more imaginative composition than picturesque principles allowed. Furthermore, the palm trees in the left corner clearly place it outside the experience of American landscape in a literal sense. Indeed, in scale and drama the painting borders on the sublime.

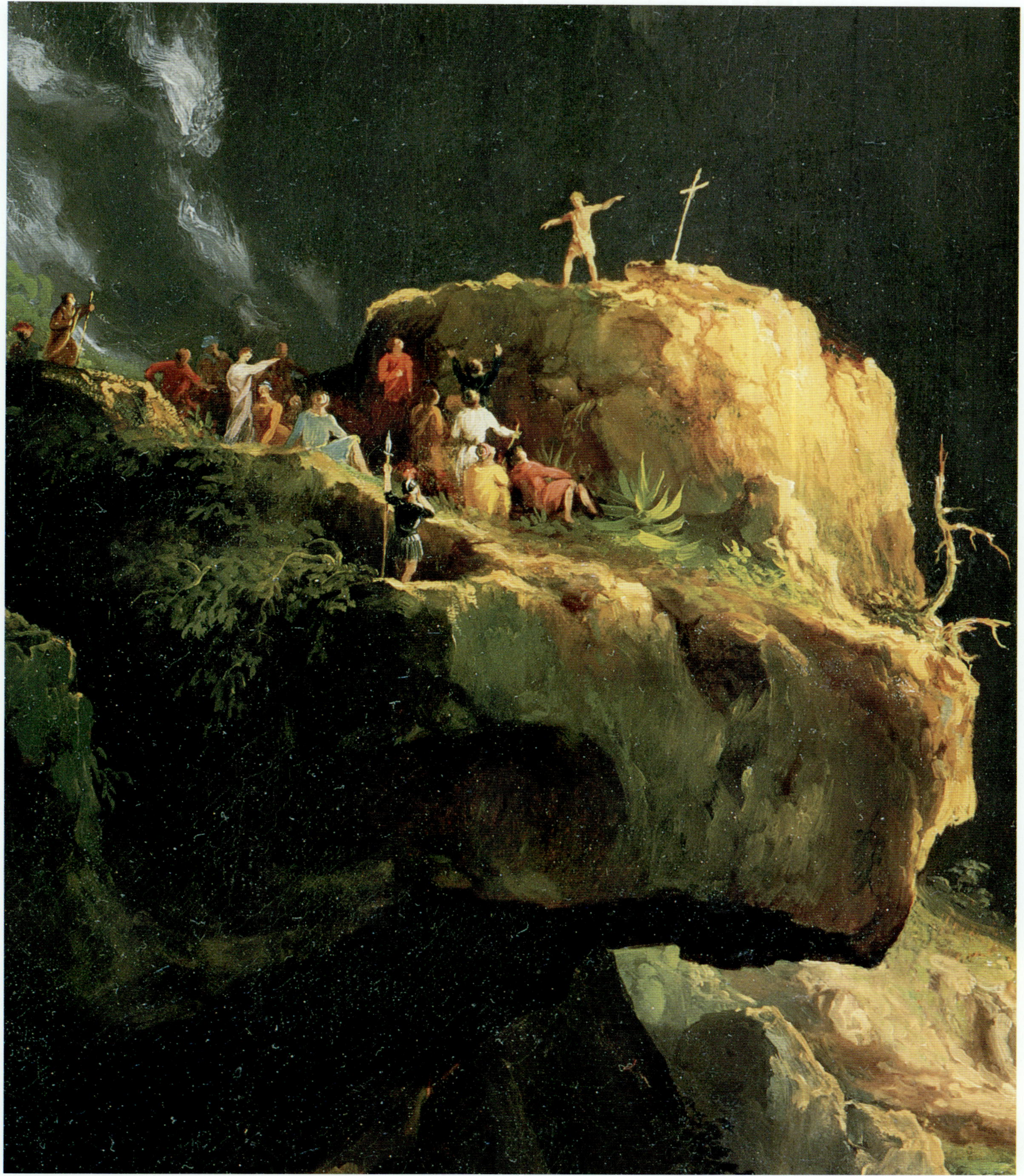

Cole exhibited his two major religious allegories, *The Garden of Eden* and *The Expulsion from the Garden of Eden* in the spring 1828 National Academy of Design exhibition. *The Garden of Eden* is now lost and known only through engravings, but *The Expulsion* is a testament to the soaring ambition of the young artist as well as a major expression of the American Romantic imagination. In a letter to Robert Gilmor, Cole discussed these large allegories, referring to them as "two attempts at a higher style of landscape than I have hitherto tried." (Noble, 64) The pair represented an attempt to unite biblical history with landscape in compositions that were daringly imaginative. They must have startled a public taste that still favored stolid, realist portraits, and they were not well received. Even Cole recognized that his lofty efforts did not result in completely resolved compositions. *The Expulsion,* a fascinating attempt to combine both the sublime and the beautiful in a single work, came in for specific criticism. In the same letter to Gilmor, Cole noted:

> I wish you to consider that I have been speaking of what *I wished* to accomplish in these pictures, rather than what I *have done;* for I may have failed in these efforts. I should, nevertheless, be much gratified if you could see them, even if only to point out wherein I have not succeeded.

These two pictures were Cole's first ambitious attempts to reach beyond the picturesque and conceive of a compositional suite encompassing a theme that required two paintings. It is not surprising that the works, however grand in their compositional scheme, were not critically acclaimed. Their religious iconography, while metaphorically representing the idea of American landscape as a new Eden, was far removed from the picturesque work of the Hudson River Valley and the Catskills upon which Cole had built his success. Imaginative Romantic compositions were difficult for an American audience to accept, particularly since it had only recently begun to appreciate landscape painting itself. Cole's allegorical landscapes were certainly ambitious, but they failed to capture either the imagination or taste of contemporary critics.

The Expulsion was criticized in particular for a lack of originality in the organization of its composition. Cole had rather flagrantly plagiarized the central passage of *The Expulsion* from one of John Martin's engravings for Milton's *Paradise Lost.* Martin, whose reputation for creating sublime biblical landscapes placed him on a par with Turner in England, had published his mezzotints for *Paradise Lost* in 1827, and they achieved a great popular success in both England

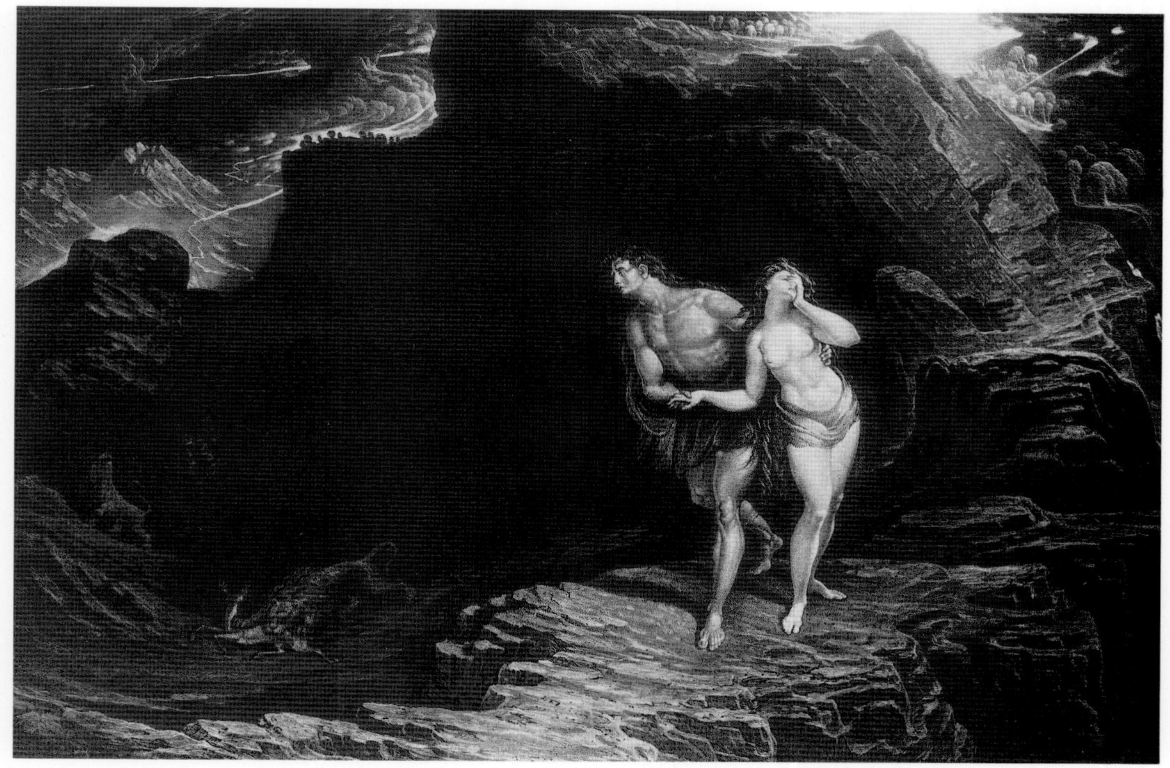

John Martin
The Expulsion

1828. Engraving from:
John Martin, *The Bible,*
London, Charles Tilt, 1828

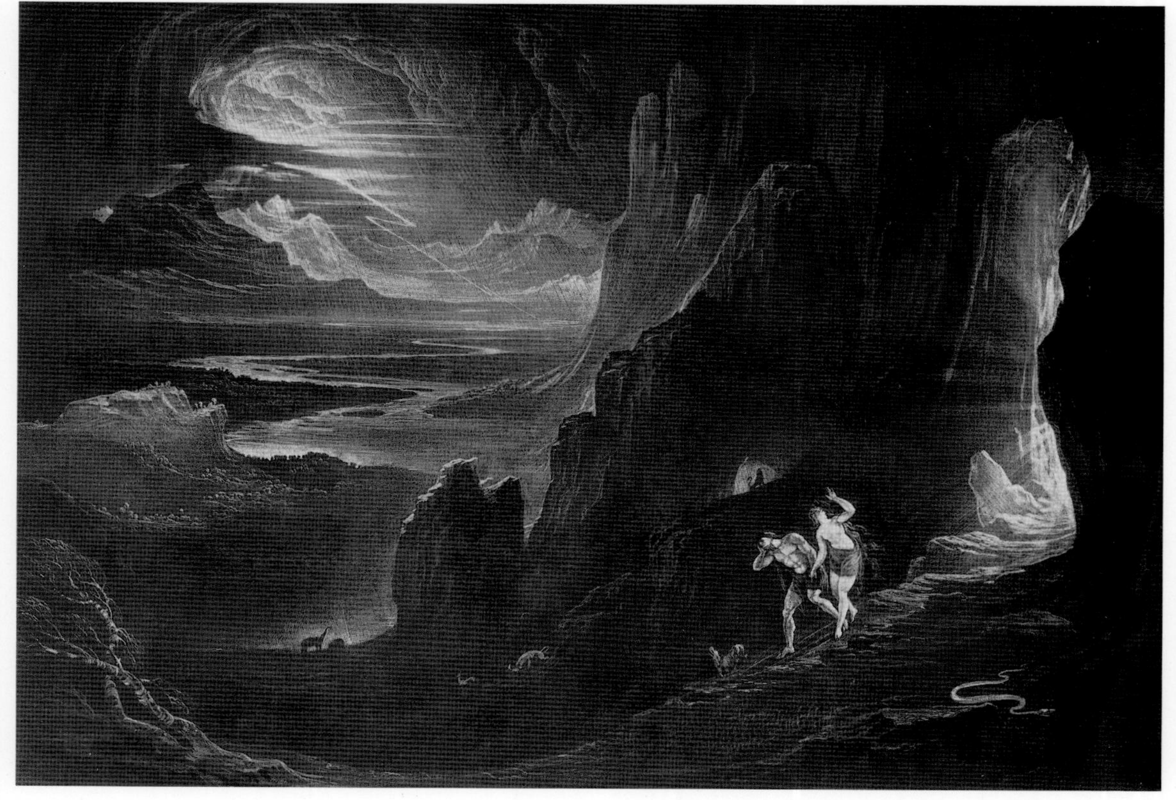

John Martin *Book XII, Line 641*
(The Expulsion from
the Garden of Eden)

1825. Engraving from:
John Milton,
The Paradise Lost of Milton,
London, Septimus Prowett,
February 28, 1827

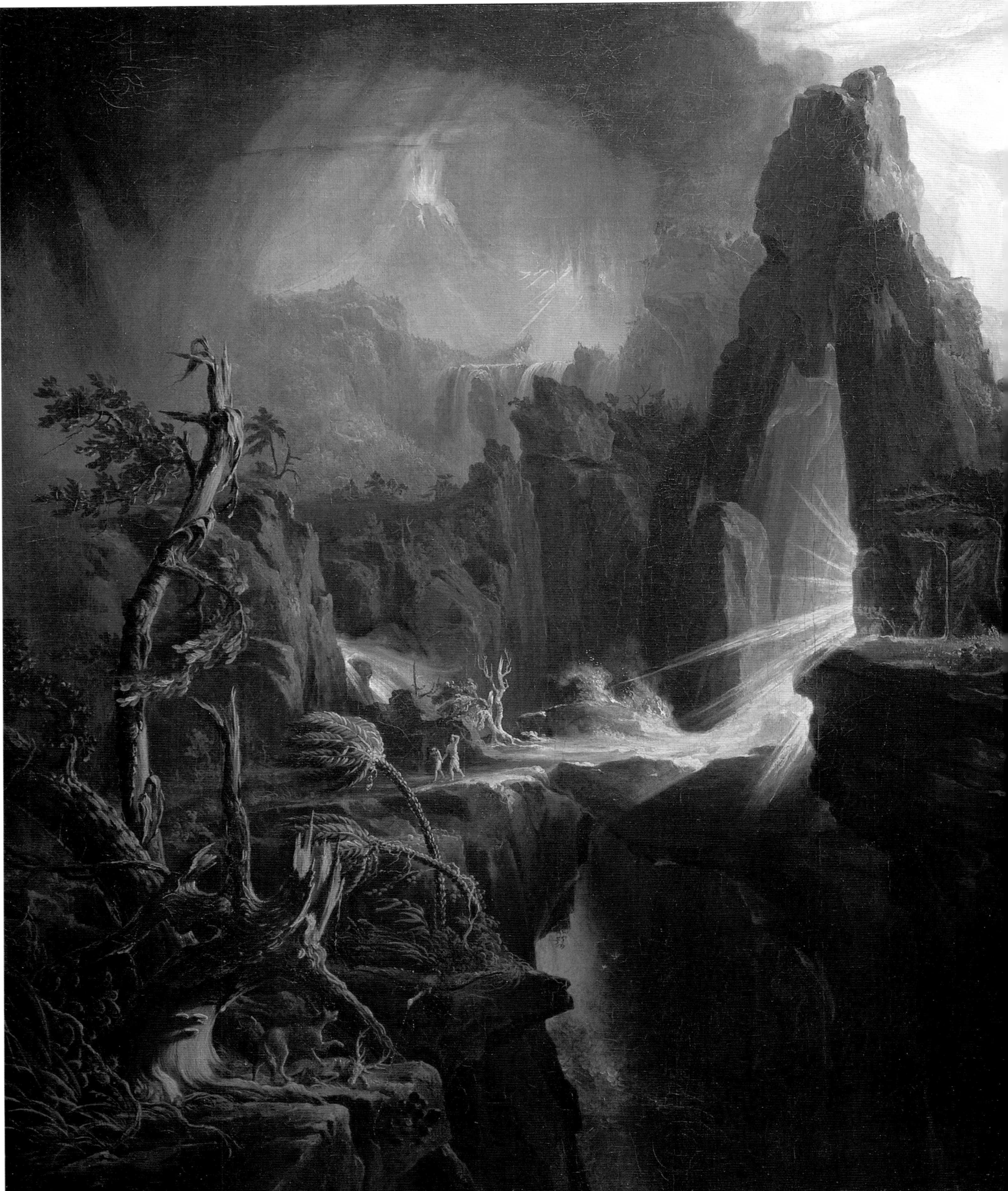

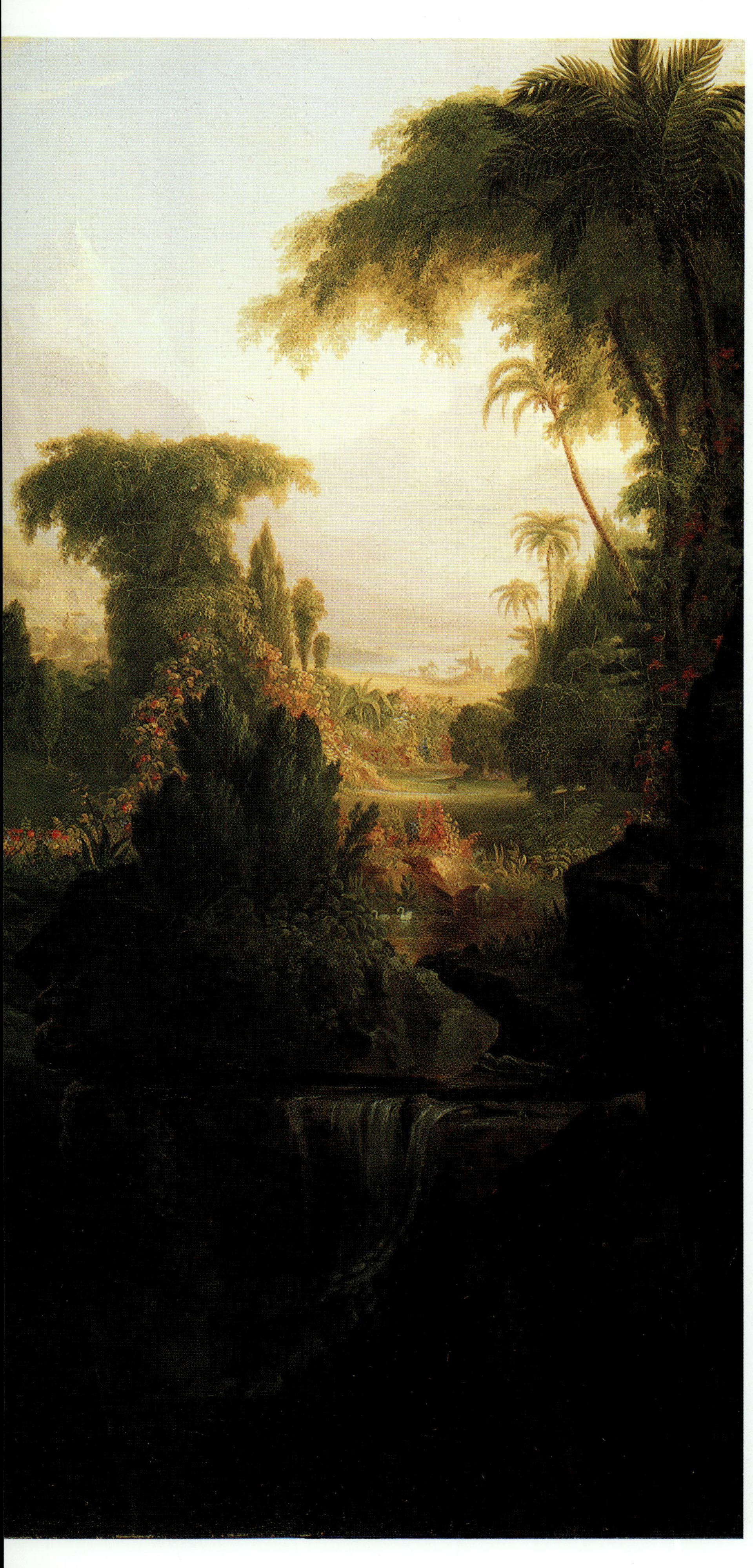

Expulsion from the Garden of Eden

1827–28. Oil on canvas,
39 x 54″
Courtesy, Museum of
Fine Arts, Boston,
Gift of Maxim Karolik for the Karolik
Collection of American Paintings, 1815–1865

and America. Martin had created a pictorial vision of vast scale and infinite, exaggerated spatial vistas, and he employed theatrical chiaroscuro effects to visualize his spectacular definition of the sublime. Cole's reliance on Martin's precedent was perhaps too direct and was commented on by his critics. *The Expulsion* and its companion piece were the largest and most ambitious religious works Cole had produced to date, and their moral and didactic message, while not widely acclaimed, was clear evidence of the level of achievement the young artist set for himself. His interest in uniting history with landscape and the Bible was most clearly manifest in these large paintings. The landscape would always be the common denominator in his art, however, and despite the problems of resolution he encountered in expressing his ideas in *The Garden of Eden* and *The Expulsion,* they shifted the direction of his art for good.

Cole's intentions and goals were carefully delineated in a list of possible subjects he kept in a notebook written at about the same time he began work on the two large allegories. He frequently referred to this list when considering commissions, and it suggested many of his later compositions. What is fascinating is the range of subjects Cole considered. The ideas for pictures traverse the entire landscape of the Romantic imagination; most of the subjects are biblical in source, but there are also American landscape themes and subjects taken from English literature as well as a few from the classics and ancient history. Also listed were ideas for series or companion pieces illustrating historical or natural cycles, such as the ages of man, the seasons, the past and present. These were themes that would occupy Cole throughout his career, particularly after the completion of *The Course of Empire,* when his reputation was such that clients would often permit him to select a subject himself for a commission.

What is particularly interesting about this list is that in it the landscape is the unifying element; in all cases Cole would make the landscape the primary compositional device and from it build a biblical, historical, or moral pictorial argument. He was intent on uniting the American landscape with Old World sources to create a new kind of historical art, one unique to the new nation and inspired by its wilderness, so different from the settled agrarian prospects of England. Cole's *Garden of Eden* and *Expulsion* were not unequivocal artistic successes, but they established a new plateau and direction for his career.

Cole hoped to sell the two pictures, and others, to finance a trip to Europe in order to study the old masters. Robert Gilmor and his close friends in the New York art world encouraged the young artist to undertake such a voyage. The

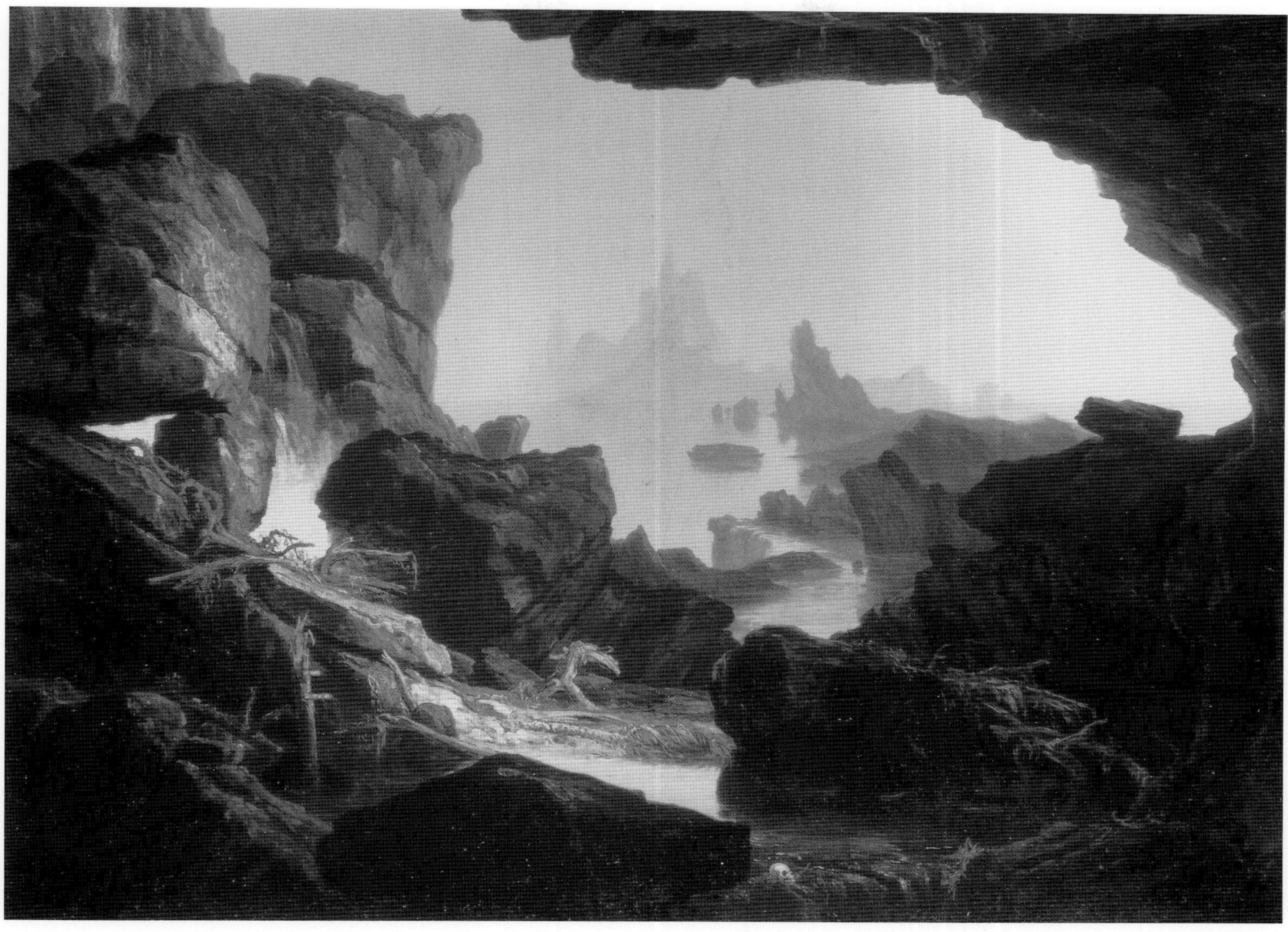

pictures did not sell, however, and in January 1829 Cole wrote to Gilmor to inquire if he would take *The Garden of Eden* and *The Expulsion* and advance him funds against them in order to enable him to finance his trip to Europe. Gilmor did not take the two pictures and proposed instead that Cole raffle them. He did not take up Gilmor's suggestion, but after substantial travail he finally managed to find a buyer for *The Expulsion* and for a scene from the Deluge, and with Gilmor's financial assistance he was finally able to begin plans for his European adventure.

The Subsiding of the Waters of the Deluge

1829. Oil on canvas,
35¾ x 47⅝"
National Museum of American Art,
Smithsonian Institution,
Gift of Mrs. Katie Dean in Memory of
Minnibel and James W. Dean and
Museum purchase through
S.I. collections acquisitions program

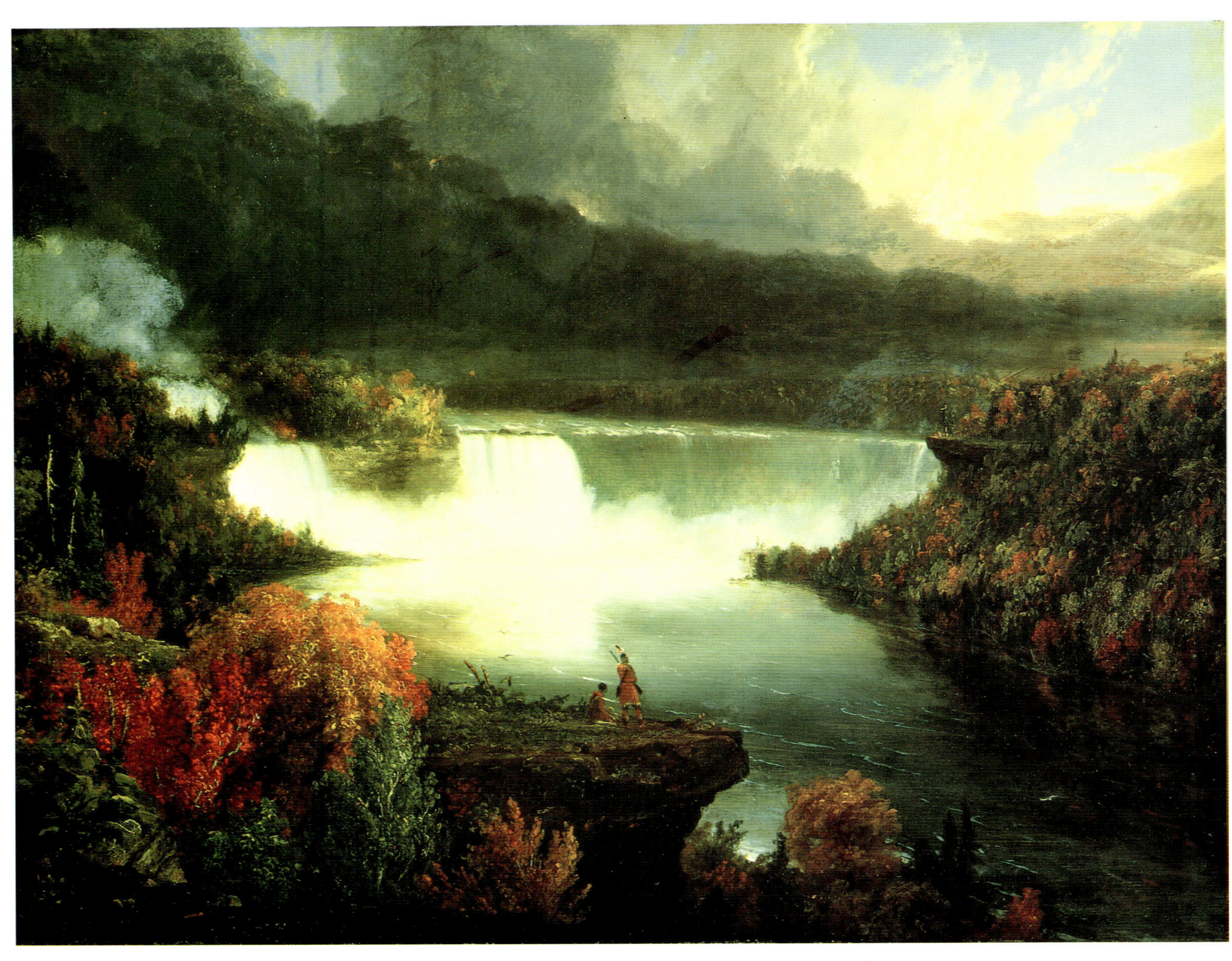

Niagara Falls

1830. Oil on panel,
18⅞ x 23⅝″

Friends of American Art Collection,
1946.396

3. *Europe*

Thomas Cole sailed from New York for London on 1 June 1829 armed with letters of introduction from Robert Gilmor and other important figures in the nascent American art world. He would remain abroad for almost three years, working, traveling, studying the art of the contemporary English and French schools, and, most importantly for Cole, the old masters. Prior to his departure, he wrote to Robert Gilmor to thank him for his support and to tell him that before leaving America he intended to make a first visit to Niagara Falls, one of the quintessential sublime experiences.

> Next Wednesday I intend setting off for the Falls of Niagara. I cannot think of going to Europe without having seen them. I wish to take "a last lingering look" at our wild scenery. I shall endeavor to impress its features so strongly on my mind that in the midst of the fine scenery of other countries their grand and beautiful peculiarities shall not be erased. (Noble, 73)

Cole's visit to Niagara was, according to Noble, less than he imagined it would be. "Niagara to Cole was, by his own declaration, far less than the mountains. They were symbols of the eternal majesty, immutability and repose, which no cataract could ever be." (Noble, 73) Nevertheless, Cole made several sketches of Niagara and took them with him to England in order to paint the scene that most people thought inspired sublimity, even if he did not himself share in the profundity of the experience.

Cole's trip to Europe was much heralded by his peers and associates, and in addition to letters of introduction from Gilmor, he carried letters from Washington Allston and John Trumbull. The trip also inspired William Cullen Bryant to pen one of the most famous poems of the day, which was both an admonition and an acknowledgment that Cole had become a landscape painter uniquely important to his generation.

> To Cole, The Painter, Departing for Europe
>
> Thine eyes shall see the light of distant skies:
> Yet, Cole! thy heart shall bear to Europe's strand
> A living image of our own bright land,

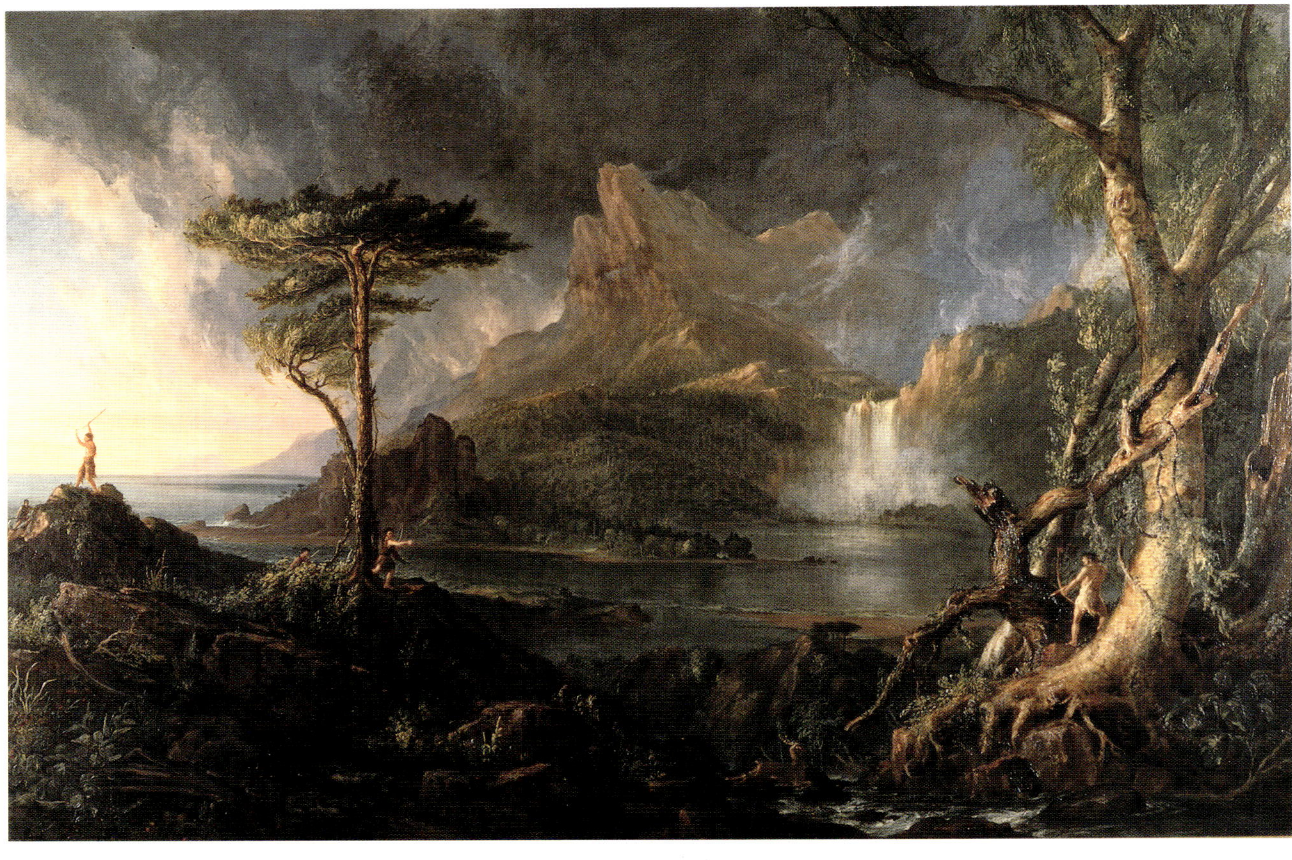

A Wild Scene

1831–32. Oil on canvas, 50¾ x 76¼"
The Baltimore Museum of Art, Leonce Rabillon Bequest Fund, by exchange, and Purchase Fund

Such as upon thy glorious canvas lies.
Lone lakes—savannahs where the bison roves—
Rocks rich with summer garlands—solemn streams—
Skies where the desert eagle wheels and screams—
Spring bloom and autumn blaze of boundless groves.

Fair scenes shall greet thee where thou goest—fair
But different—everywhere the trace of men.
Paths, homes, graves, ruins, from the lowest glen
To where life shrinks from the fierce Alpine air.
Gaze on them, till the tears shall dim thy sight,
But keep that earlier, wilder image bright.

Cole carried a letter of introduction to Sir Thomas Lawrence from Robert Gilmor and other letters of introduction to important figures in the British art establishment. Once landed, Cole traveled first to London, where he made an effort

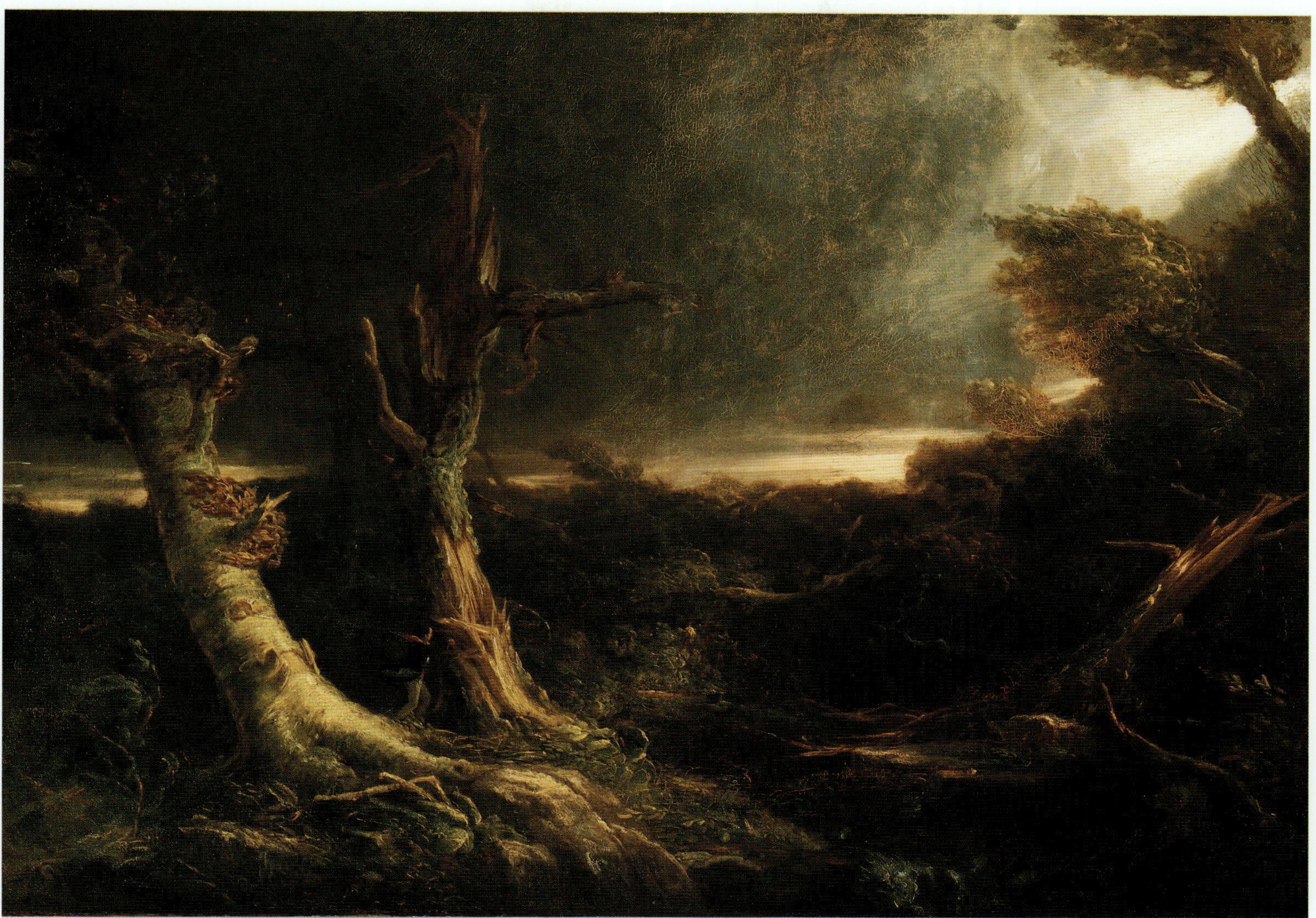

Tornado

1835. Oil on canvas,
46⅜ x 64⅝″
Collection
The Corcoran Gallery of Art,
Washington, D.C.,
Museum Purchase, Gallery Fund

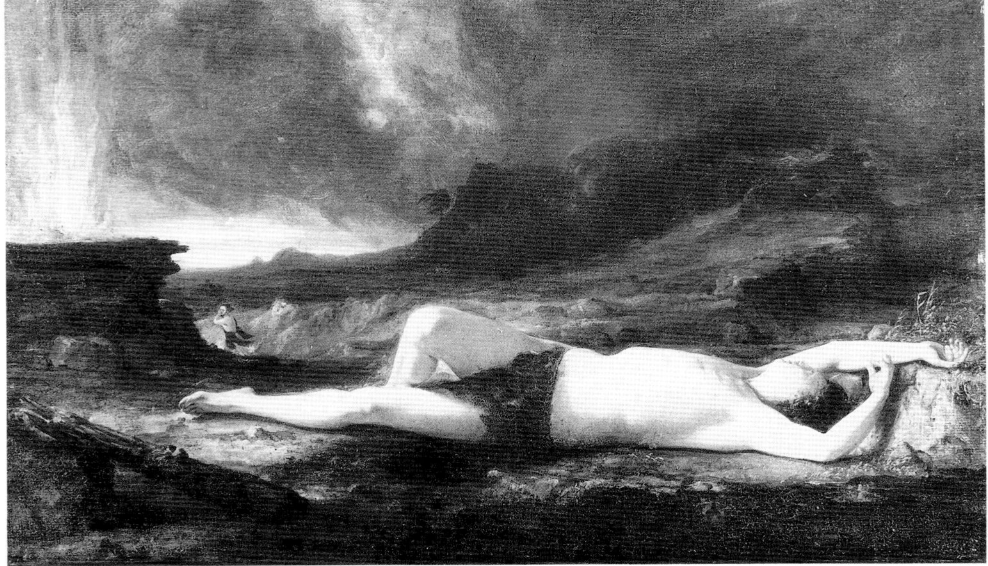

The Dead Abel

1831–32. Oil on paper mounted on wood panel, 17 x 28½″
Collection the Albany Institute of History and Art, Albany, New York

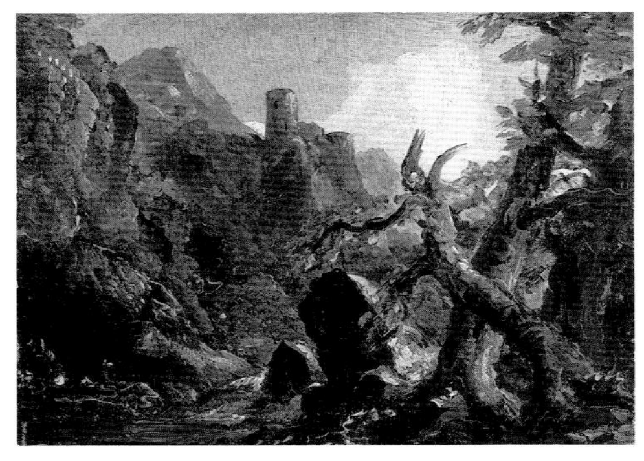

Salvator Rosa Sketching Banditi

1832 or later. Oil on panel, 7 x 9½″
Courtesy, Museum of Fine Arts, Boston, Gift of Maxim Karolik to the Karolik Collection of American Paintings, 1815–1865

to absorb and study English art and the works of its practicing contemporary masters. He visited the Royal Academy and many private collections, and he exhibited his own work in the annual exhibitions of both the Academy and the Gallery of British Artists, but with little apparent success. He carried many sketches with him to Europe, and in London he worked several into finished pictures, including *Niagara Falls, Hagar in the Wilderness,* and *Tornado.* He was displeased with the placement of his pictures at the exhibitions and felt that their location in the galleries was responsible for the limited interest shown by the British public.

He visited the leading artists: Sir Thomas Lawrence, whose work he admired, and J. M. W. Turner, whose work he found both interesting as well as problematic. Cole admired the great landscapist's *Building of Carthage,* which he found poetic, and which would provide later inspiration for his own great series *The Course of Empire.* But Turner's new work was difficult and perplexing to Cole, whose own style was much more literal and dependent on careful study and sketching of subjects taken from nature. Turner had, by this time, embarked on a much different stylistic direction, one that stressed the nuances and effects of light and atmosphere. "They appear to me . . . to have an artificial look. When considered separately from the subject, they are splendid combinations of colour. But they are destitute of all appearance of solidity: all appears transparent and soft, and reminds me of jellies and confections." (Noble, 81)

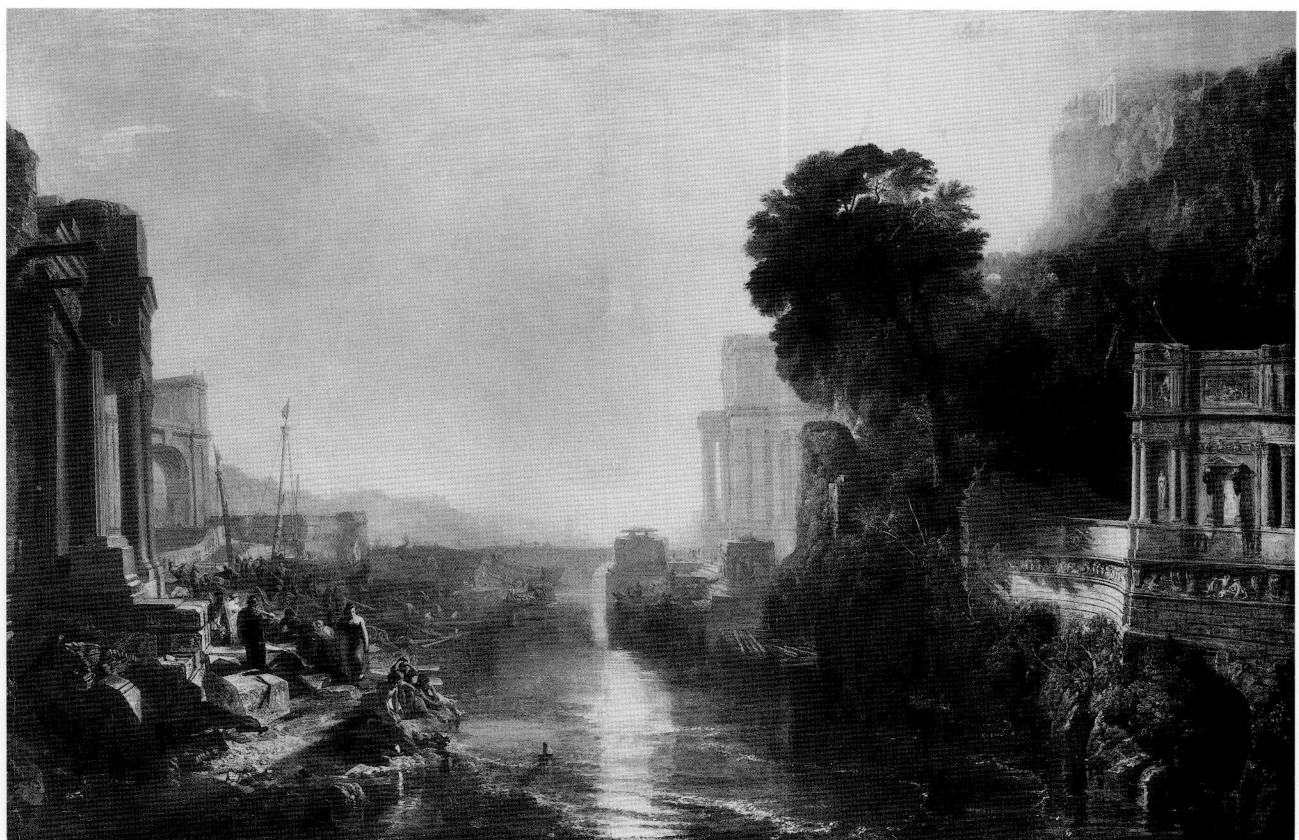

J. M. W. Turner
Dido Building Carthage, or The Rise of the Carthaginian Empire
1815. Oil on canvas, 61¼ x 91¼"
The National Gallery, London

Cole was thus unable to accommodate himself to Turner's turn toward an evanescent expression of light and color and was deeply disturbed at Turner's new and personal form of "impressionism." Cole believed Turner had "forsaken the main object of art for the study of its technicalities." (Noble, 82) Cole would remain an artist whose own work would draw its inspiration and composition from the experience of landscape united with a poetic idea. His heroes were the artists of older generations—Salvator Rosa, Gaspar Poussin, and Claude Lorrain—and his own style was much more indebted to their precedent. Of all the English artists Cole most admired Richard Wilson, the "English Claude," whose work he studied carefully.

In England Cole worked on developing and improving his own style, but he did not follow the conventional routine there of copying the works of the old masters. It was only with some reluctance that, later in his stay, he copied a Wilson. He was instead much more intent on making his own way in the British art world as an equal. He remained in England until May 1831 when he visited

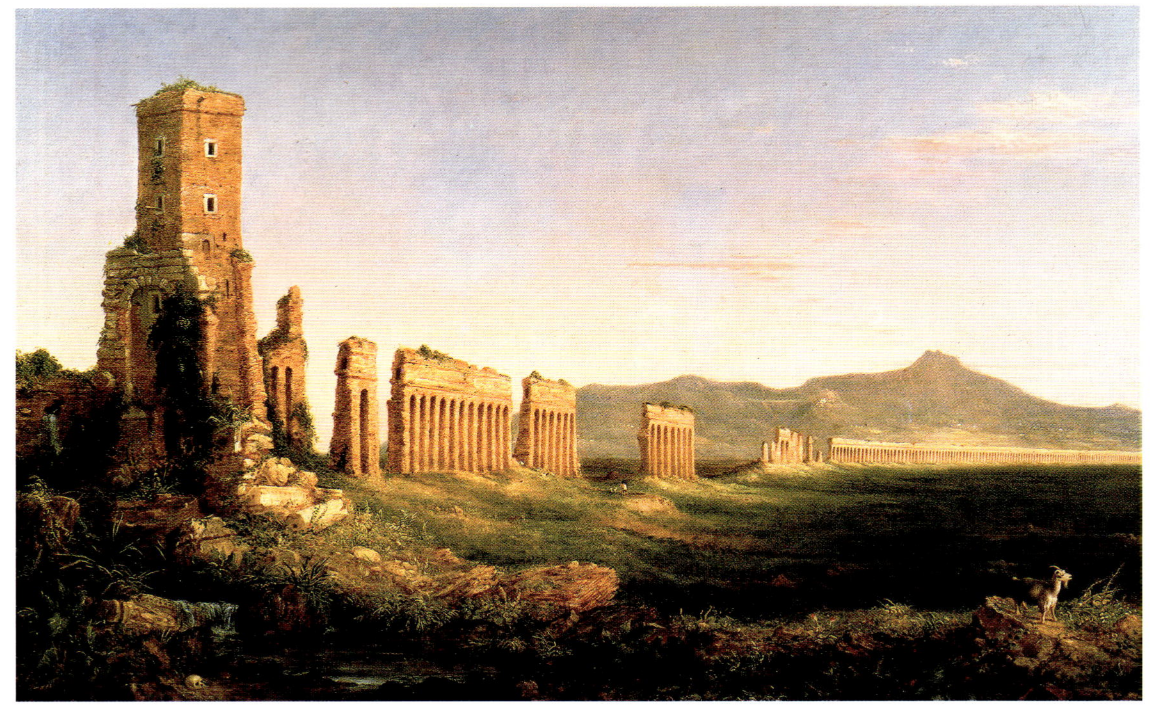

Aqueduct near Rome

1832. Oil on canvas,
44½ x 67½"
Washington University
Gallery of Art, St. Louis,
University Purchase Bixby
Fund, by exchange, 1987

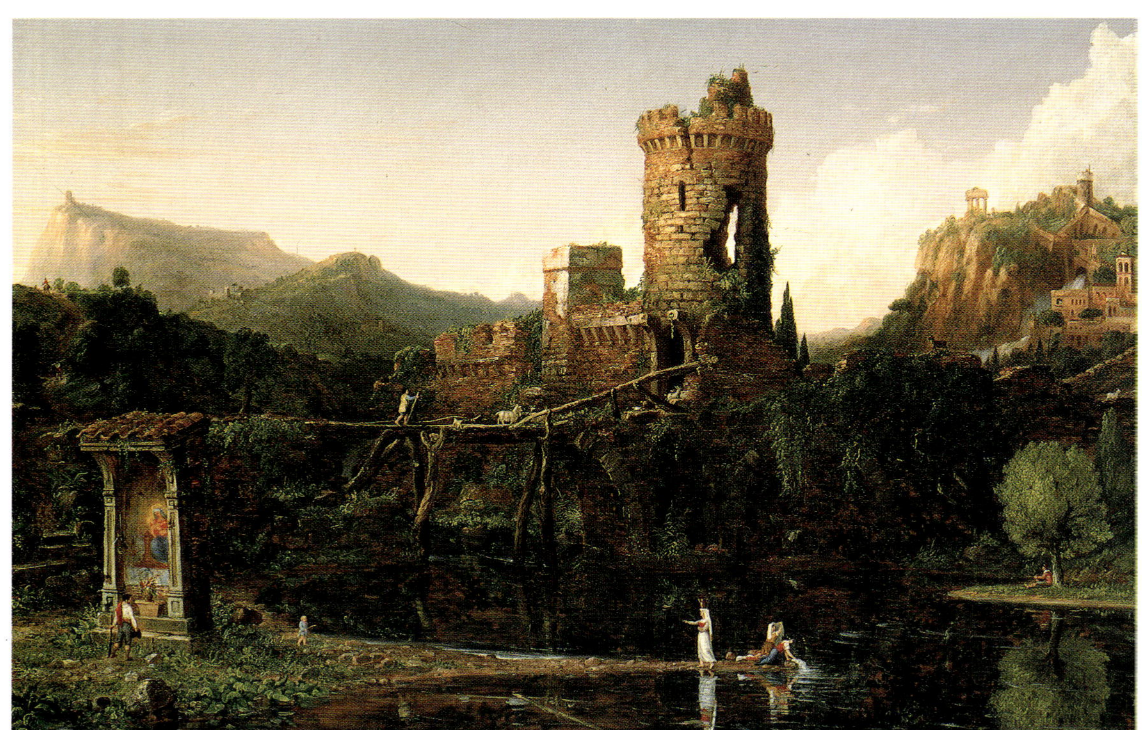

Landscape Composition: Italian Scenery

1831–32. Oil on canvas,
40¾ x 61½"
Memorial Art Gallery of
the University of Rochester,
Rochester, New York,
Purchased through the
Marion Stratton Gould Fund
and with the gift of Mr. and
Mrs. Thomas H. Hawks

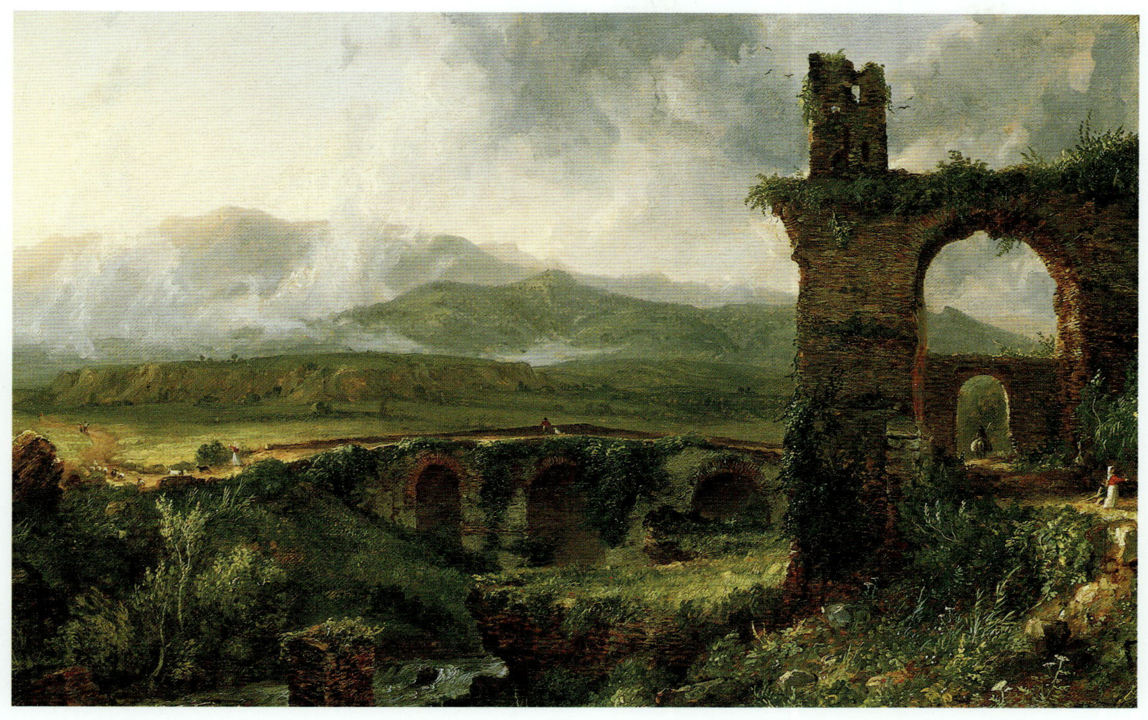

A View near Tivoli (Morning)

1832. Oil on canvas,
$14^{3/4} \times 23^{1/8}$"
The Metropolitan Museum of Art,
New York,
Rogers Fund, 1903

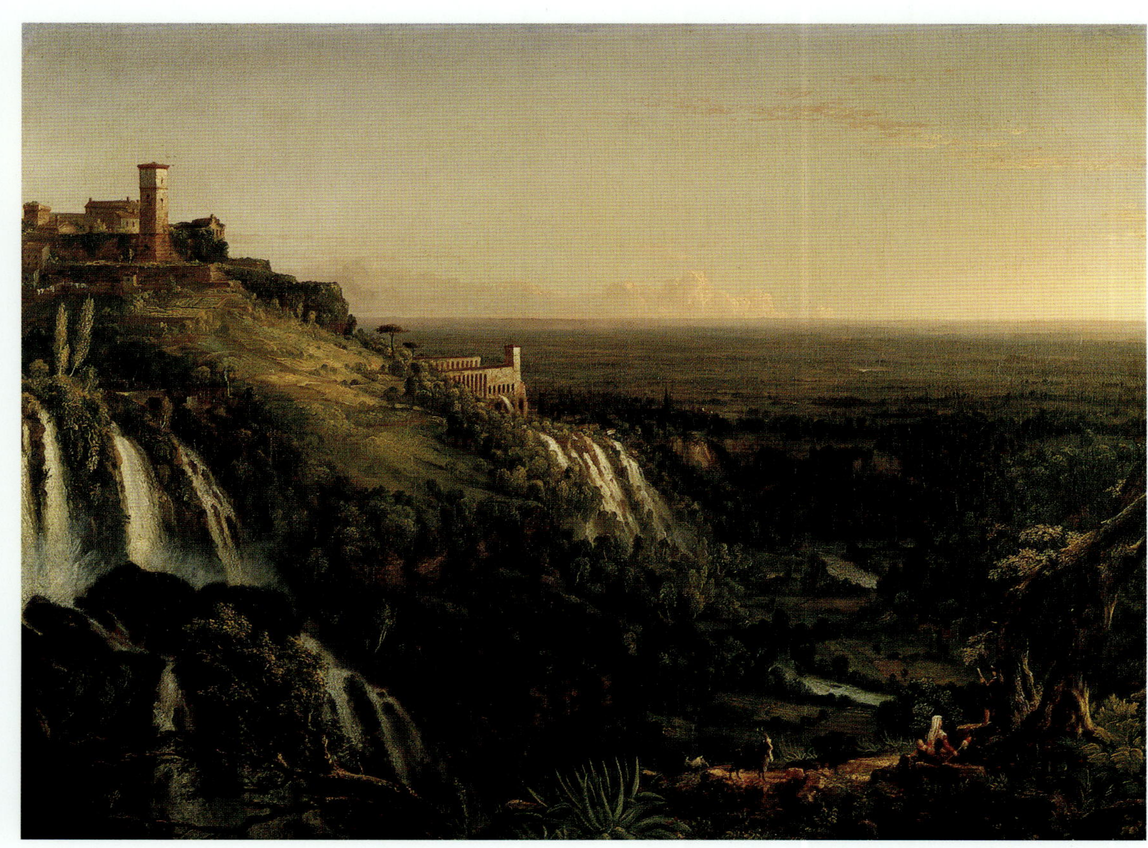

The Cascatelli, Tivoli, Looking Towards Rome

c. 1832. Oil on canvas,
$32^{3/4} \times 44^{1/2}$"
Columbus Museum of Art,
Columbus, Ohio,
on loan from Mr. and Mrs.
Walter Knight Sturges

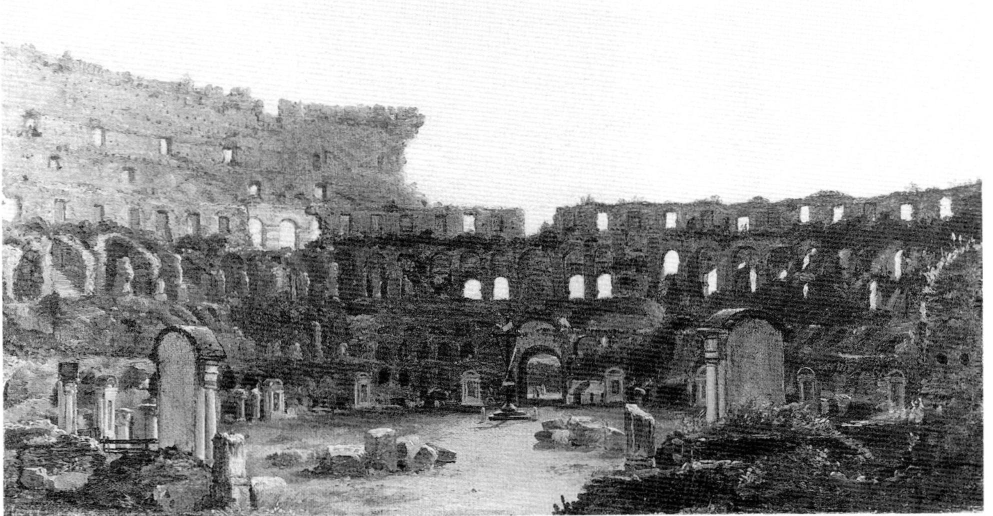

Interior of the Colosseum, Rome
c. 1832. Oil on canvas, 10 x 18″
Collection the Albany Institute of History and Art, Albany, New York

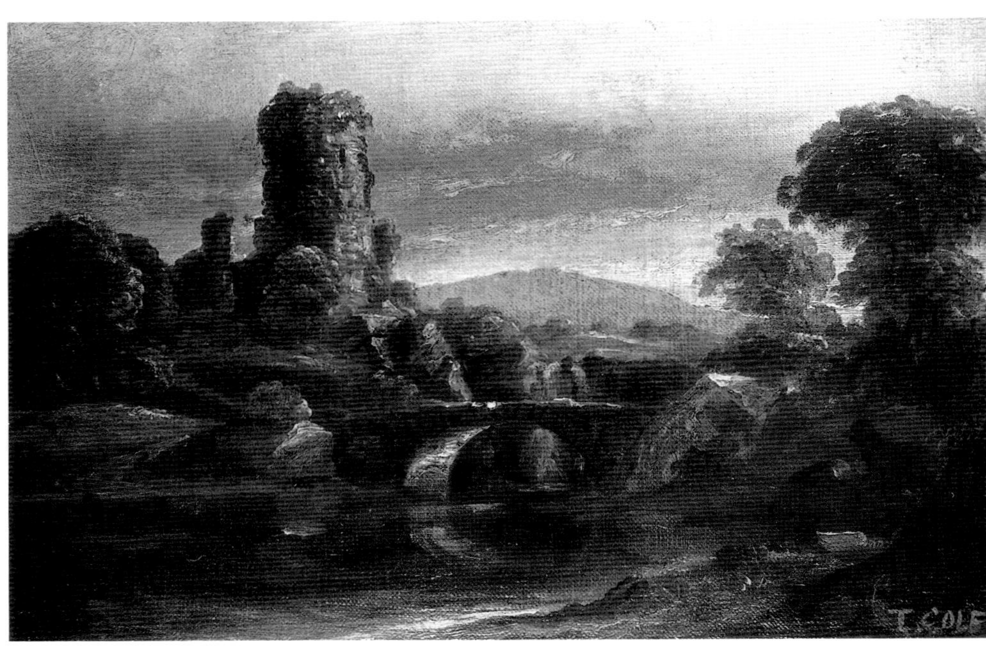

Landscape Composition: Italian Scenery
1832. Oil on canvas, 37½ x 54¼″
Courtesy The New-York Historical Society, New York City

France and made the obligatory pilgrimage to the Louvre. His assessment was that too many old master paintings had been replaced by lesser-quality modern pictures, which he found uninspiring. Cole traveled through France on his way to Florence and seems not to have been genuinely inspired by the landscape until he arrived in Italy. He was enchanted, as were so many generations of artists before him, with the Italian landscape and commented, "I am not surprised that

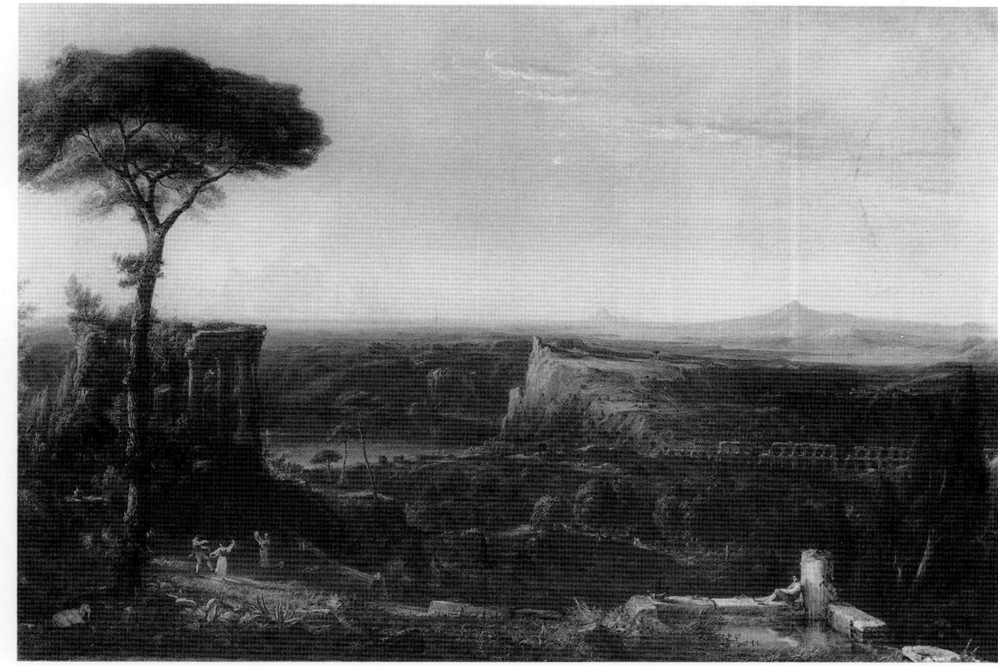

Castle and River

c. 1832. Oil on canvas, 8½ x 13″
The Brooklyn Museum, New York, Bequest of Samuel E. Haslett

the Italian masters have painted so admirably as they have: Nature in celestial attire was their teacher." (Noble, 98)

Cole remained in Florence for several months, painting incessantly on themes that he intended to send back to New York for exhibition. He wrote to J. L. Morton, the secretary of the National Academy of Design, at the end of January, describing his efforts.

> I have several pictures on the easel. One is a large picture representing a romantic country, or perfect state of nature, with appropriate savage figures. It is a scene of no particular land but a general idea of a wild: and when you see it, I think you will give me credit for not having forgotten those sublime scenes of the wilderness in which you know I so much delight; scenes whose peculiar grandeur has no counterpart in this section of Europe. I am also painting a scripture subject, The Angels appearing to the Shepherds. (Noble, 99–100)

The painting Cole describes, *A Wild Scene,* was very important in his career and was intended for Robert Gilmor. It was Cole's first attempt at epic landscape since his earlier efforts on *The Garden of Eden* and *The Expulsion,* and it is interesting that when he returned to epic landscape he would return to the wilderness imagery that had established his reputation. *A Wild Scene* is an imaginative com-

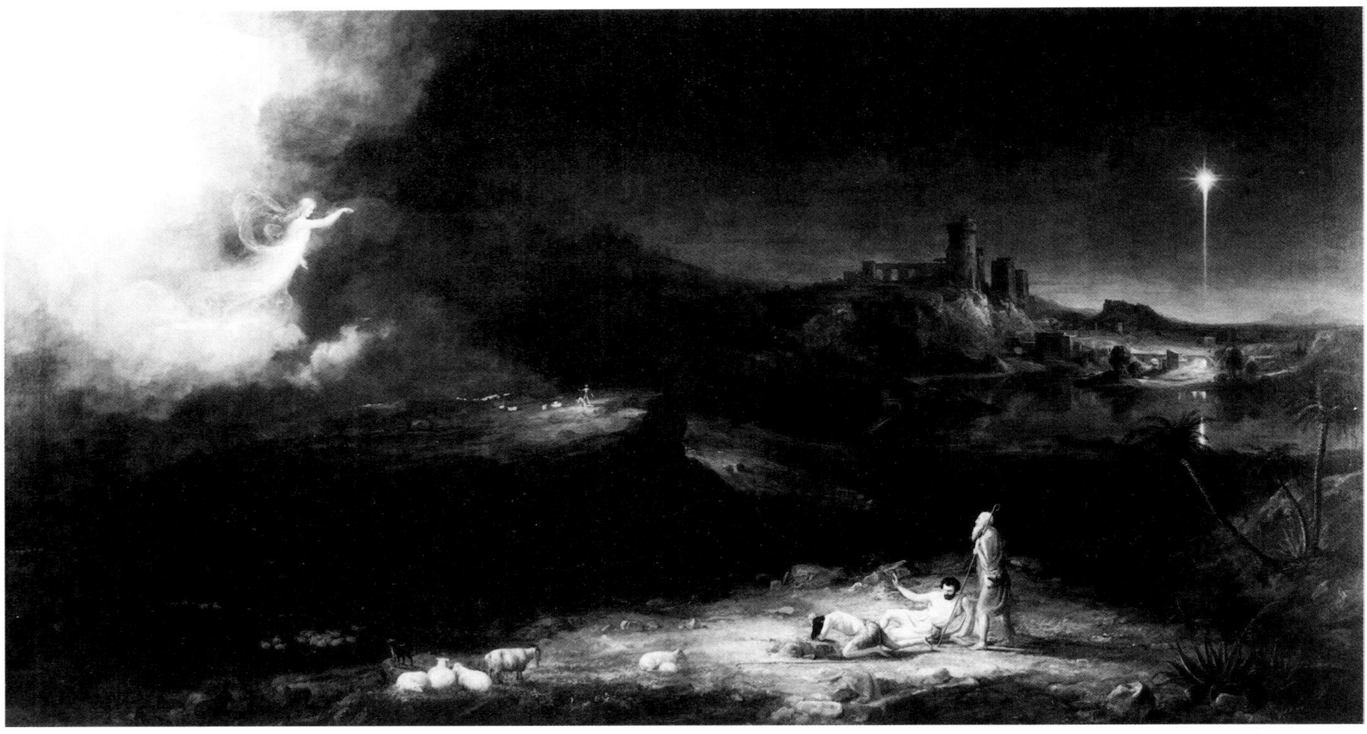

The Angel Appearing to the Shepherds
1833–34. Oil on canvas,
101½ x 185½″
The Chrysler Museum,
Norfolk, Virginia,
Gift of Walter P. Chrysler, Jr.
in memory of Colonel Edgar William
and Bernice Chrysler Garbisch

position in that it represents various aspects of landscape and chiaroscuro effects united by Cole's creative imagination to form a coherent whole. This large painting, whose size left Gilmor frustrated in his attempt to find a place to display it, anticipated *The Course of Empire.*

Cole worked for the better part of seven months on this picture and offered it to Gilmor for three hundred dollars as a settlement for the advance he had provided for Cole's trip to the Continent. In his correspondence on the subject Cole acknowledges that the painting was intended as the first of a series, which he had long contemplated, but he wished Gilmor to have this work if it pleased him, in gratitude for his commitment to his work. Gilmor, on his part, was delighted with the picture and wrote Cole of this fact, noting, "I have been much pleased with it as of the genuine Salvator school." (Annual, I, 77)

The picture captures and unites Cole's continuing interest in the wild landscape with his concern for the epic and historical. It is more original in conception than his *The Garden of Eden* or *Expulsion* and more fully resolved in its composition. The beautiful light of dawn illuminates the scene and irradiates the center of the composition, the opalescent waterfall and the vast mountain, and it

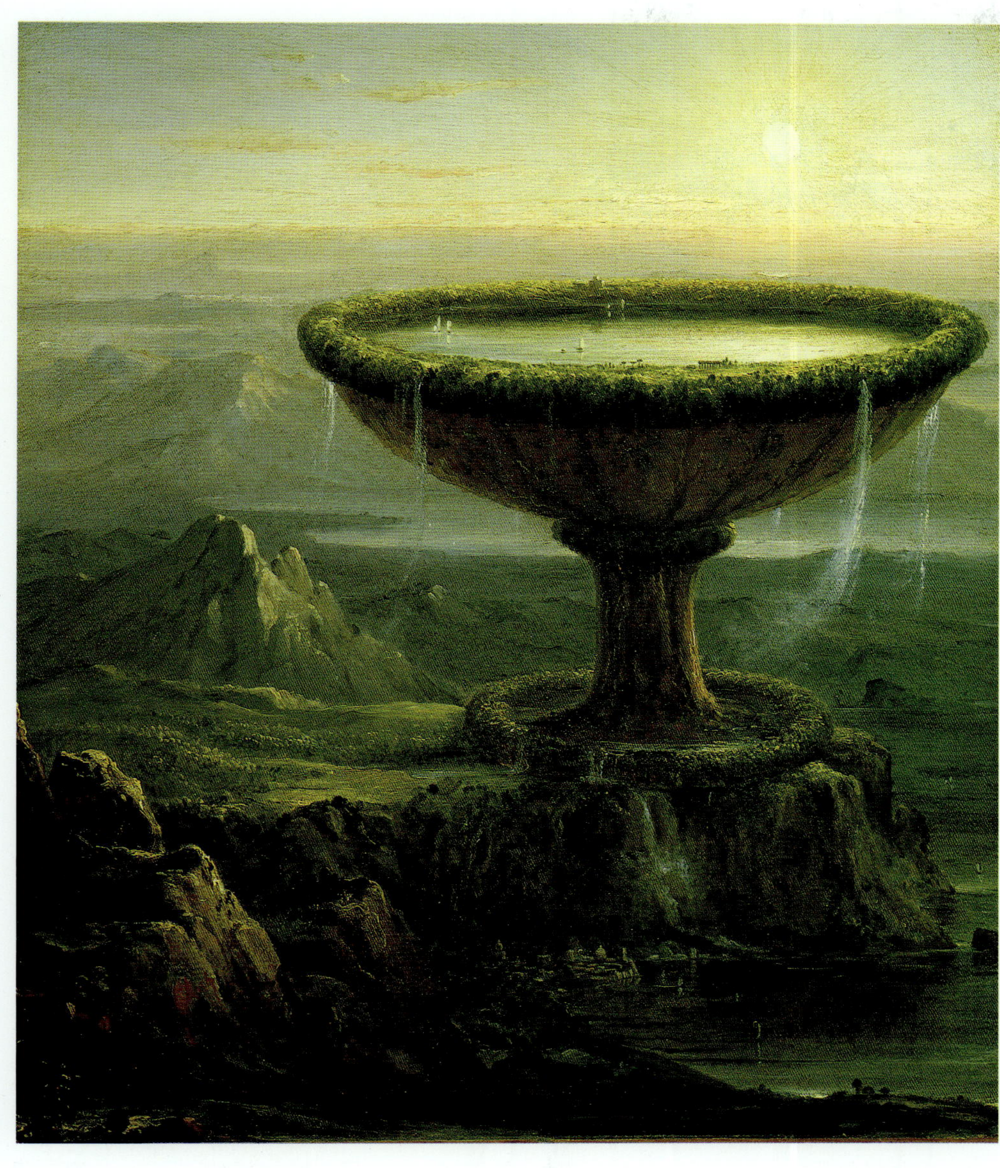

The Titan's Goblet

1833. Oil on canvas,
19⅜ x 16⅛"
The Metropolitan Museum of Art,
New York,
Gift of Samuel P. Avery, Jr.,
1904

reflects across the expanse of water against the counterpoint of the trees and rocks in the foreground. In this work Cole succeeded in creating a composition whose organization and structure would serve as a precedent for Church, Cropsey, and the other American landscape painters who followed him. This picture was successful, and Gilmor appreciated it because its subject matter was not biblical and because it concentrated on depicting a wilderness landscape, just as Cole had done in his earlier picturesque work. Imaginative landscapes of biblical subjects had not yet found an audience in the United States.

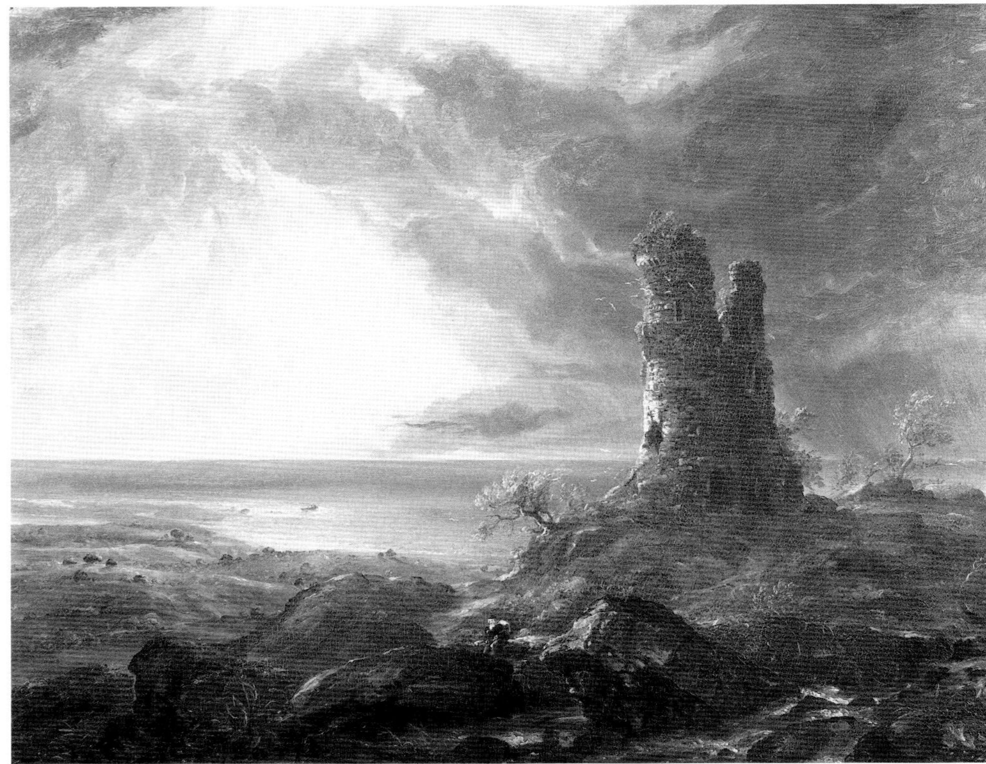

Ruined Tower

c. 1832. Oil on composition board, 27 x 34″
Collection the Albany Institute of History and Art, Albany, New York, Bequest of Edith Cole Hill;

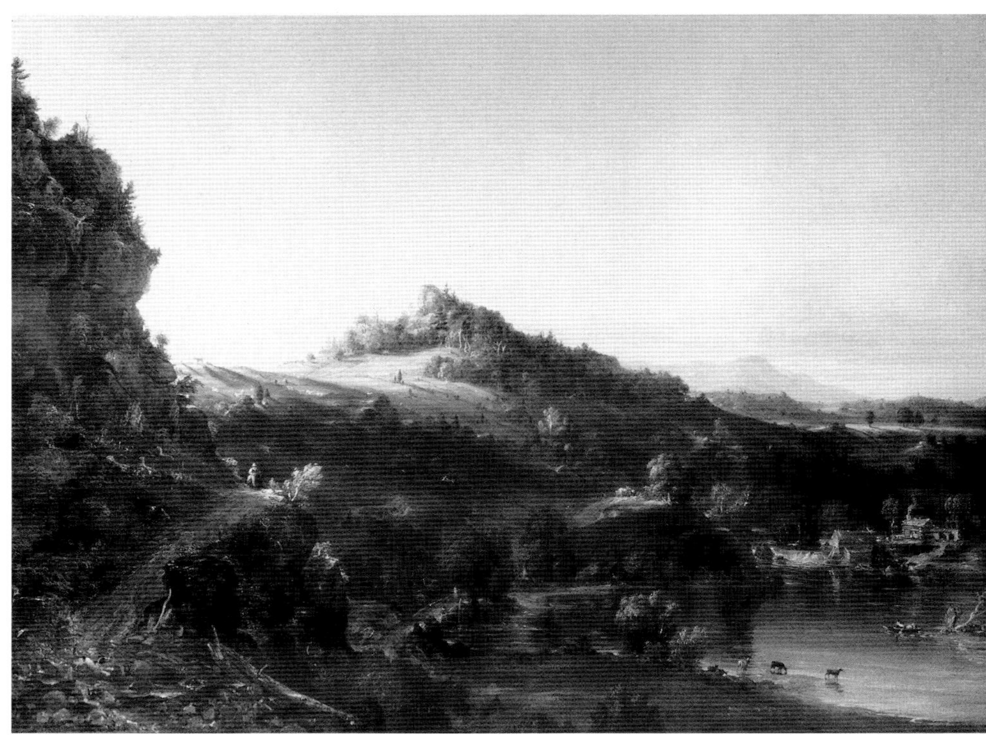

Catskill Scenery

1833 (?). Oil on canvas, 24¼ x 32¼″
The St. Louis Art Museum. Museum Purchase, Friends Fund, Eliza McMillan Fund and Gift of Mrs. John S. Ames and Miss Elizabeth Green by exchange

Cole departed for Rome the following February, where he took lodgings on the Pincian Hill in rooms that were alleged to have been used as a studio by Claude. It was in the environment of Rome, a city redolent with history, that Cole began seriously to consider the formal development of *The Course of Empire.* No city could have provoked more personal or profound thoughts regarding this theme than could Rome. Cole had long been fascinated with the idea of the cycle of life and the cycles of history, and in its decaying grandeur Rome represented in both symbol and reality the old edifice of Europe. Against this could be compared the New World's pristine wilderness, a new Eden as against a fallen civilization.

The experience of Rome stimulated Cole's imagination, and although he painted few pictures of Italian scenery, he sketched continuously and upon his return used these drawings to paint commissioned works for American patrons. Among the many ruined antiquities, he was particularly fascinated with the Colosseum, and in 1832 he painted an interior scene of this space as an aide-mémoire.

Cole responded to the experience of Italy much as did other sophisticated visitors, in particular the English painters, and he followed closely in their paths. Paintings such as *The Cascatelli, Tivoli*; *Italian Scenery*; and *Aqueduct near Rome*, all completed in 1832, were not necessarily unusual compositions, but Cole's rendering of the light and the subtle textures of his surfaces show that he had developed a masterful and carefully calculated technique. This is shown to great advantage in his *View of Florence from San Miniato,* painted in 1837 but clearly inspired by his earlier sketches and a nostalgic memory of the suffusive, warm light of Italy. Like many of Cole's landscapes, this is a view down into space with mountains in the distance.

Cole continued to find the ruins of antiquity fascinating, and he was greatly moved by a visit to Paestum. As he began the preparations for his return voyage, he wrote to Gilmor that he was "now engaged in a picture that is a view of the Campagna of Rome—broken aqueducts, etc. But I long for the wild mountains of the West." (Noble, 123) It was obvious that his identity as an American landscape painter remained of the highest importance to him and that he was now ready to return to America, having experienced the art of Europe but without having succumbed to contemporary artistic styles in either England or France. He had gained confidence and he had matured, and now he reaffirmed his commitment to painting historical landscape.

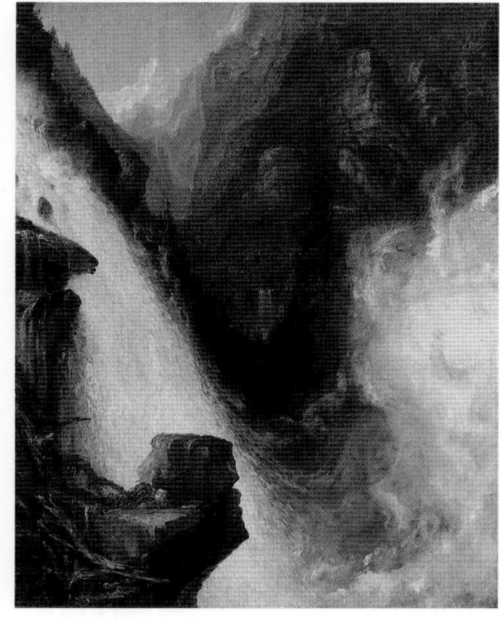

Scene from Byron's "Manfred"

1833. Oil on canvas,
50 x 38″
Yale University Art Gallery,
New Haven, Connecticut,
John Hill Morgan Fund

4. *The Course of Empire*

Thomas Cole returned to New York in the fall of 1832 and took rooms on the corner of Wall Street and Broadway. Soon thereafter he had the great good fortune to make the acquaintance of Luman Reed. Reed was the most important patron of the arts in his day; a wealthy merchant, he would assume major importance for Cole and would eventually commission ten paintings from him, the most important being *The Course of Empire*.

Reed was interested in creating a private picture gallery, and Cole's work was to be the centerpiece. He also acquired important work by Cole's contemporaries, including Asher B. Durand and William Sidney Mount, but it was to Cole's work that he was most profoundly attracted. Unlike Robert Gilmor, whose correspondence with Cole represented a unique historical dialogue on technique, aesthetics, and composition and obviously influenced the young artist in an important way, Reed had little interest in debating the merits of composition or discussing aspects of the picturesque and the sublime. He was more specifically a connoisseur, and his first commission from Cole was an Italian landscape, which initiated their artist-patron relationship.

In 1833 Cole settled in the upstate New York village of Catskill on the Hudson, and in his cherished landscape he began a correspondence with Reed concerning the proposed gallery. He obviously thought deeply about the matter and forwarded Reed some drawings of the arrangement of the rooms in his home in accordance with the subjects he wished to paint, broaching the subject of painting a historical series. Cole had discussed the subject at length in previous correspondence with Robert Gilmor during his visit to Europe when he was working on *A Wild Scene,* drawing on his list of ideas of contemplated subjects. In a letter to Reed of 18 September 1833 in which he discussed the details of Reed's galleries, Cole went into great detail on the subject of his proposed series.

> In the drawings you will perceive that I have taken one side of the room for this subject; and, as my description to you of my plan was very imperfect, I will now take the liberty of making an extract from my memorandum book of what I have conceived about it.

The Course of Empire: The Savage State

1836. Oil on canvas, 39¼ x 63¼″
Courtesy The New-York Historical Society, New York City

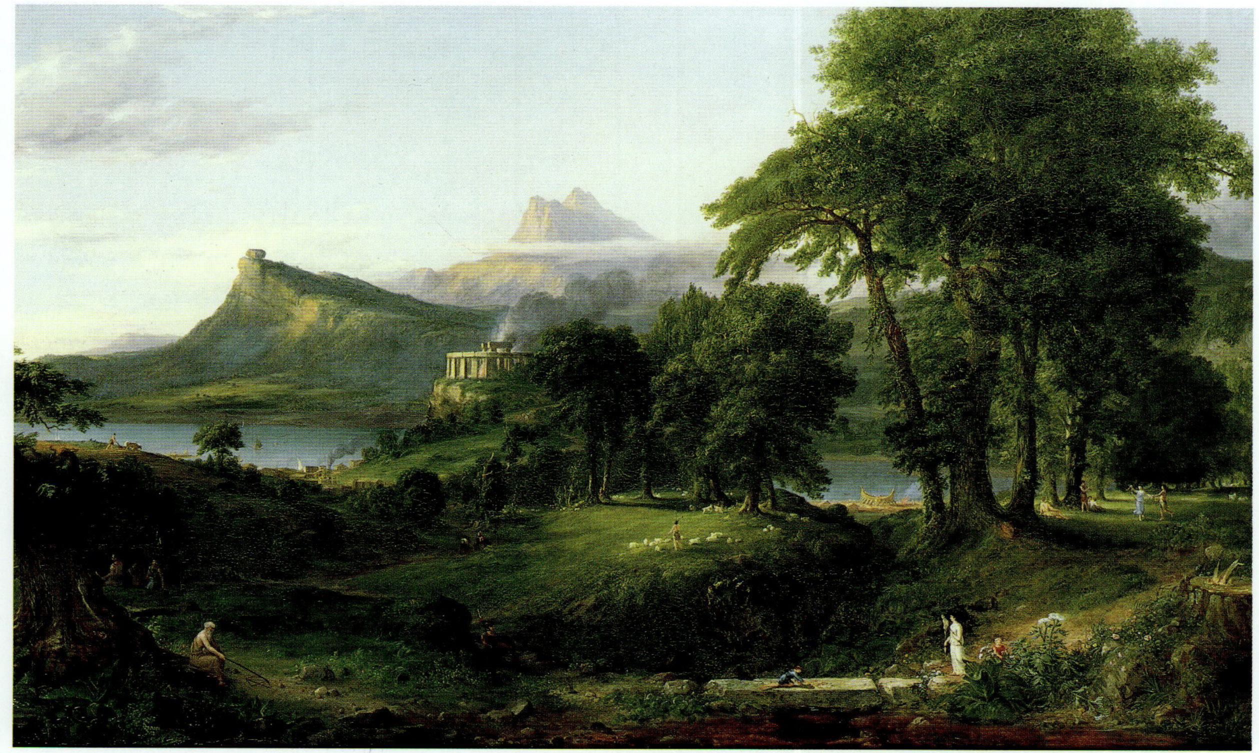

The Course of Empire: The Arcadian or Pastoral State

1836. Oil on canvas, 39¼ x 63¼″
Courtesy The New-York Historical Society, New York City

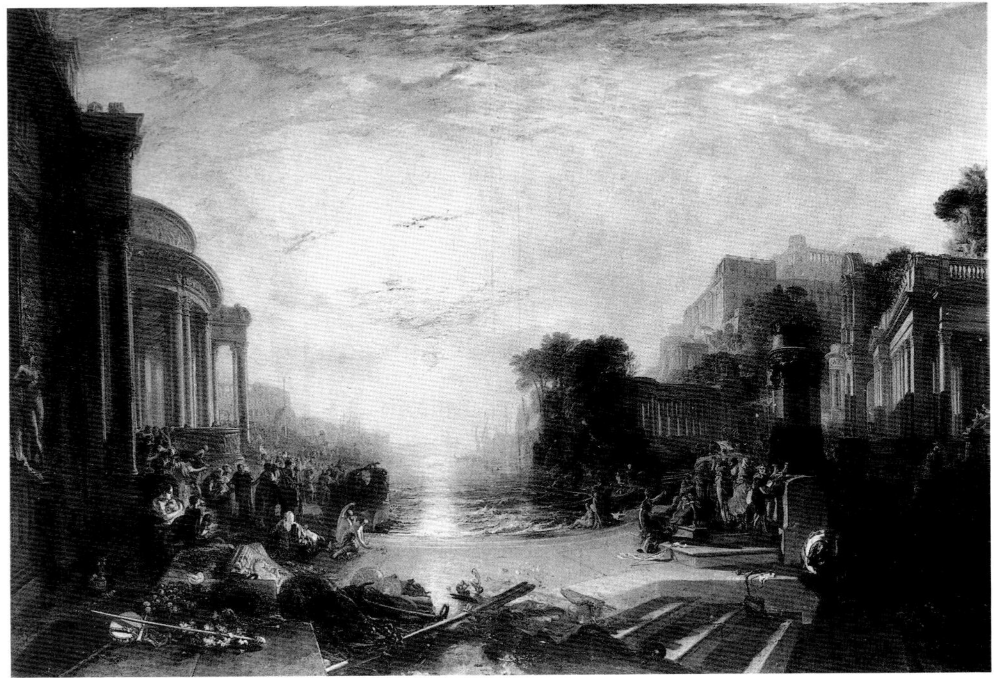

J. M. W. Turner
Decline of the Carthaginian Empire
1817. Oil on canvas, $67\frac{1}{2}$ x 95"
Tate Gallery, London

> A series of pictures might be painted that should illustrate the history of a natural scene, as well as be an epitome of Man—showing the natural changes of landscape, and those effected by man in his progress from barbarism to civilization—to luxury—the vicious state, or state of destruction—and to the state of ruin and desolation.
>
> The philosophy of my subject is drawn from the history of the past, wherein we see how nations have risen from the savage state to that of power and glory, and then fallen, and become extinct. Natural scenery has also its changes—the hours of the day and the seasons of the year—sunshine and storm: these justly applied will give expression to each picture of the series I would paint. It will be well to have the same location in each picture: this location may be identified by the introduction of some striking object in each scene—a mountain of peculiar form, for instance. (Noble, 129)

Cole continued to describe at length each of the five scenes that would form the series, these being the savage state, the pastoral state, the consummation of empire, destruction, and desolation. Together the group would constitute the most ambitious artistic undertaking yet conceived by an American artist.

During this time Cole continued to develop other ideas and work on other canvases as well. He completed a large picture, *The Angels Appearing to the Shep-*

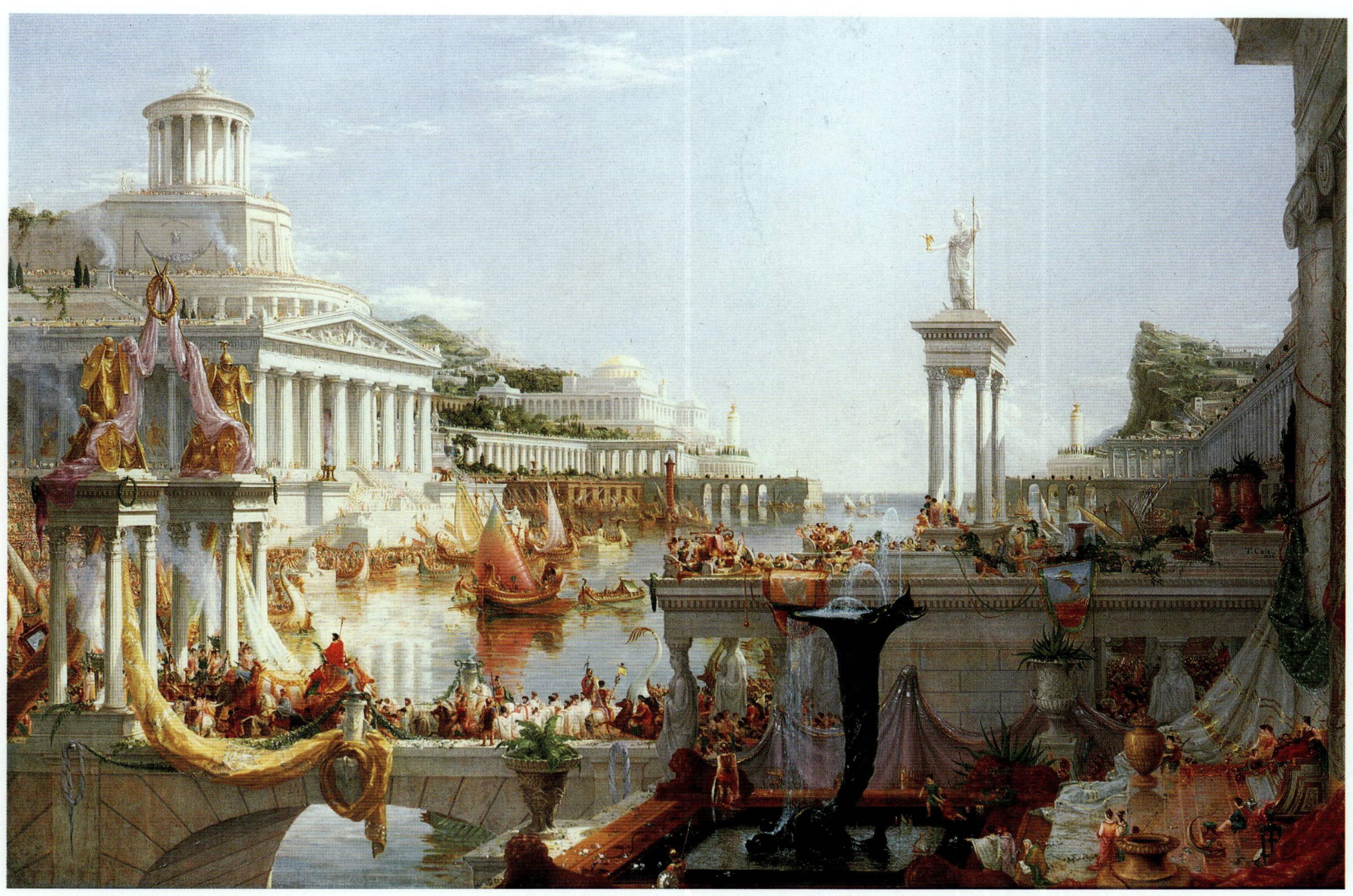

The Course of Empire:
The Consummation of Empire

1836. Oil on canvas,
51¼ x 76″
Courtesy The New-York
Historical Society,
New York City

herds—a large, dark, scriptural painting, vast in scale but somewhat empty in content—but *The Course of Empire* was foremost on his mind.

These years were difficult for Cole; he had assumed the financial responsibility for his family, which added pressure to his personal life, and he was attempting to resolve the compositional difficulties associated with *The Course of Empire*. His correspondence reveals the heavy melancholy that pervaded the literature and art of the Romantic era, and in this sense Cole was certainly characteristic of the artists of his generation. But it was indeed a difficult time in his career as he challenged another artistic frontier with his series. He was recognized, however, as the foremost landscapist of his time and was securely placed at the head of his profession, and despite his complaints this was one of the most fertile and creative periods in his life.

At the same time he was grappling with the issues presented by *The Course of Empire,* he also continued to write, and in 1835 he went down to New York from Catskill to the annual meeting of the National Academy of Design and read his lecture on American scenery before the New York Lyceum. This lecture was one of the most moving pieces of its time, important not only for its defense of the wild landscape but also as a document that reflected the complex agony of the Romantic imagination. Cole and other artistic and literary figures of his generation were witnessing a momentous historical transformation: the passing of the age-old wilderness era and the birth of the new world of industrialization and urbanization. Nature in a wilderness condition, and its consequent associations with God, was fast disappearing. There was a special urgency to Cole's message:

> . . . the most distinctive, and perhaps the most impressive, characteristic of American scenery is its wildness.
>
> It is the most distinctive, because in civilized Europe the primitive features of scenery have long since been destroyed or modified—the extensive forests that once overshadowed a great part of it have been felled—rugged mountains have been smoothed, and impetuous rivers turned from their courses to accommodate the tastes and necessities of a dense population . . .
>
> And to this cultivated state our western world is fast approaching; but nature is still predominant, and there are those who regret that with the improvements of cultivation the sublimity of the wilderness should pass away: for those scenes of solitude from which the hand of nature has never been lifted, affect the mind with a more deep toned emotion than aught which the hand of man has touched. Amid them the consequent associations are of God the cre-

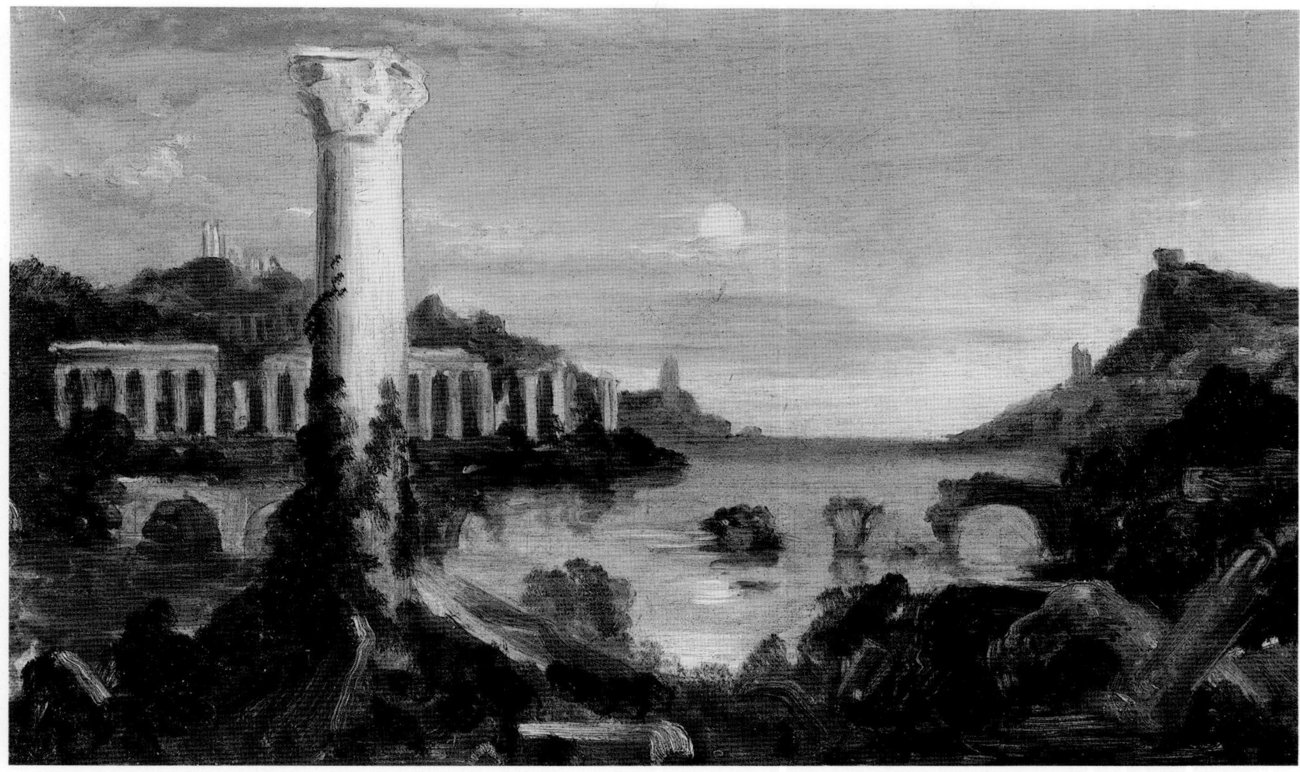

Study for *Desolation,*
fifth of *The Course of Empire* series
1836. Oil on panel,
9½ x 15½″
Collection Hirschl
and Adler Galleries, Inc.,
New York

> ator—they are his undefiled works, and the mind is cast into the contemplation of eternal things. (McCoubrey, 102)

This lecture, formulated at the same time that Cole was preparing to begin *The Course of Empire,* underscores the importance of the theme for him. It would be a moral history lesson for a young government and country, which would emphasize and symbolize America's unique place in world history.

Throughout his life Cole would use the warm weather as an opportunity to venture forth on picturesque tours of the landscape, and the sketches that resulted from these excursions were turned into a landscape vocabulary of poetic richness. As he was working on *The Course of Empire,* he continued this practice, heeding Bryant's advice to keep his eyes focused on the beauty and sublimity of the wilderness. A prescient remark Cole noted after one of his picturesque tours reveals how closely he identified with the source of his inspiration, the wild landscape, and what separated the American landscape from all others: "The painter of American scenery has, indeed, privileges superior to any other. All nature here is new to art." (Noble, 148)

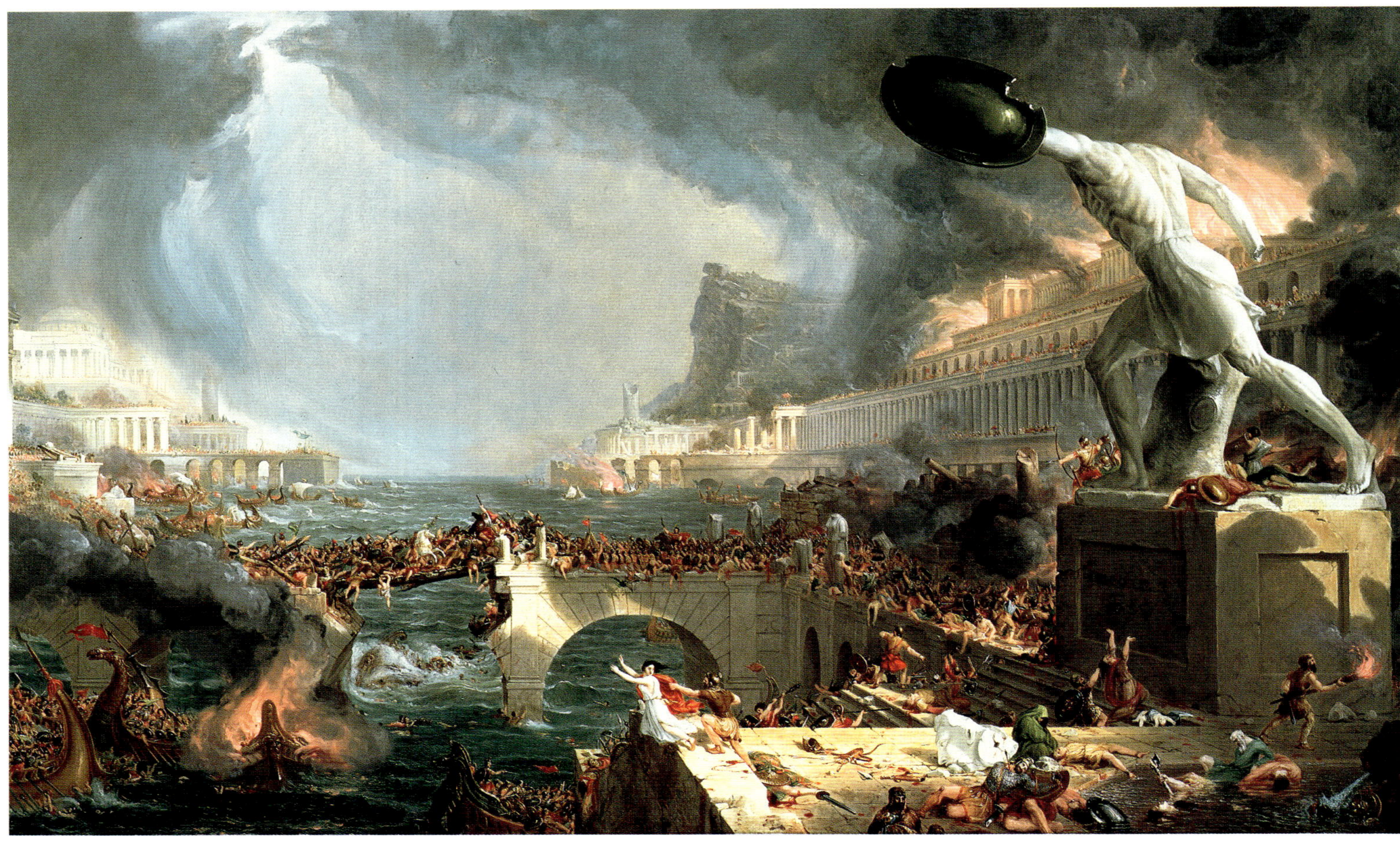

The Course of Empire: Destruction

1836. Oil on canvas,
39¼ x 63½″
Courtesy The New-York
Historical Society,
New York City

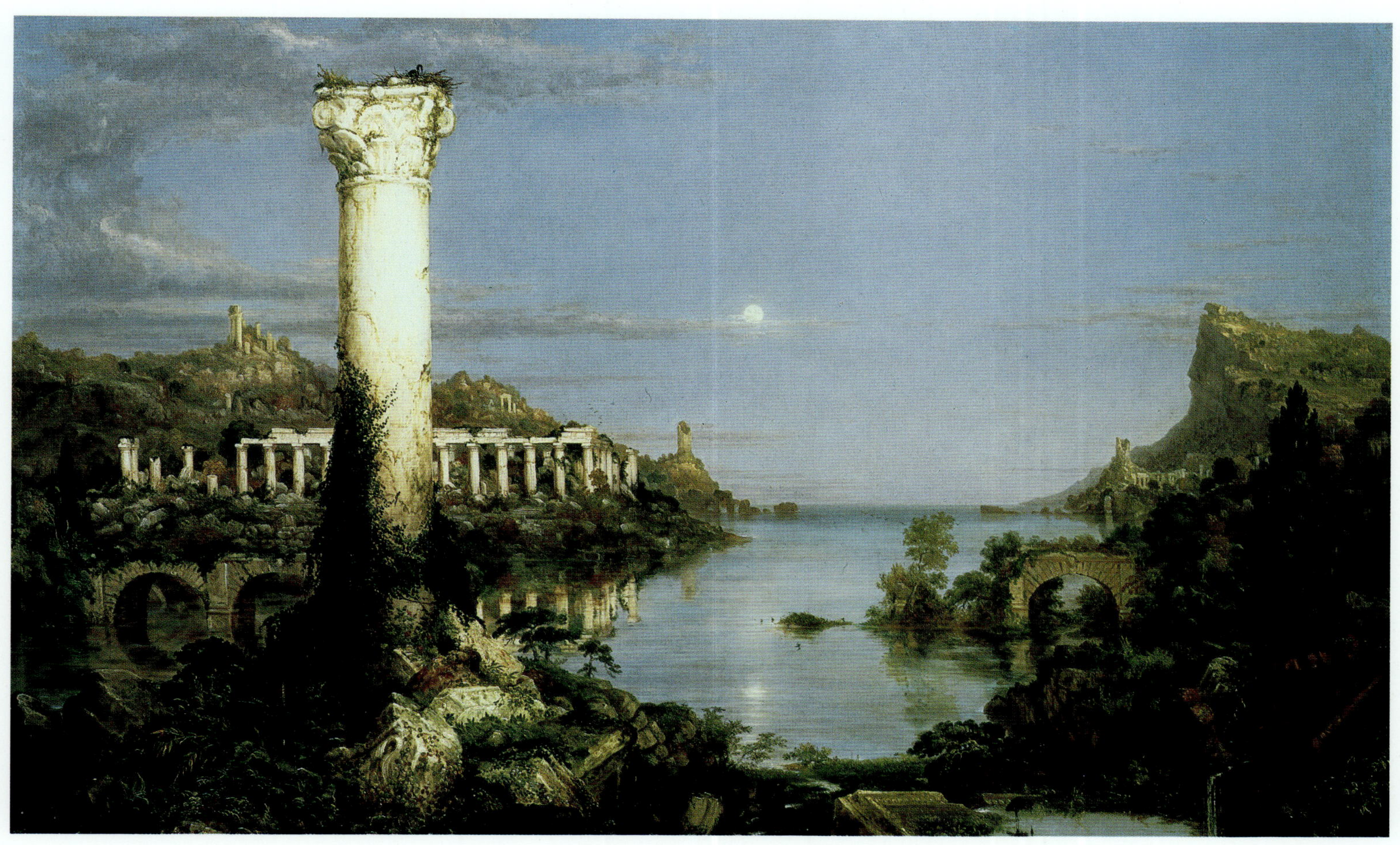

The Course of Empire: Desolation

1836. Oil on canvas,
39¼ x 63¼″
Courtesy The New-York
Historical Society,
New York City

Cole labored, in continuous self-doubt, on the large central picture of the series in January 1836, while Reed's gallery, under Cole's architectural consultancy, began to take final form. Asher B. Durand, and George W. Flagg, the nephew of Washington Allston and an accomplished portrait painter, were also working on commissions for Reed. Reed, however, would not see the completed project; he took ill and died in June 1836. His death was a bitter blow to Cole and the other artists he patronized, for he was an enlightened and benevolent patron. Cole persevered, nevertheless, and by October he had completed the series and exhibited it in New York to great approbation. James Fenimore Cooper called it "a great epic poem" and concluded that *The Course of Empire* was "the work of the highest genius this country has ever produced"; he predicted that the day would come when the series would fetch $50,000!

The five pictures are superb manifestations of the Romantic spirit and imagination. Noble, concurring with Cooper, pronounced *The Course of Empire* "a grand epic poem, with a nation for its hero, and a series of national actions and events for his achievement." (Noble 168) In this series Cole achieved artistic maturity and independence in compositions of his own. The theme of the march of civilization unfolds against a natural landscape with a mountain in the far distance, beneath which the panorama of events occurs.The theater of time is emphasized by its passage as the sun rises with the birth of civilization and sets in the concluding frame of *Desolation*.

There are certainly precedents for these compositions; Turner's *Decline of the Carthaginian Empire,* 1817, might easily have served as inspiration for Cole's *Consummation of Empire,* and the exaggerated architectural perspective and scale in *Destruction* certainly bring to mind the work of John Martin, whose mezzotint engravings after Milton's *Paradise Lost* had earlier been used by Cole as a source for his composition *The Expulsion from the Garden*. But the earlier work of these two artists served more as a point of reference, which Cole subsumed beneath his own ideas. In its totality, *The Course of Empire* represents a truly heroic moment both in Cole's career and in the history of American painting. It was a paradigm of the Romantic spirit—melancholy, grand in conceptual scope, and didactic and moralizing—and it succeeded in delighting its audience. Noble discussed the sense of finality and hopelessness of the theme in an interesting passage, commenting that the development of the subject lies "wholly within the bounds of time, with no living, actual relation, any more than the Iliad, to a life hereafter—to the world of Christian revelation . . . " (Noble, 168) But for all its melancholy, it is not mournful. The series was a triumph for Cole, whose wish to transcend the picturesque and elevate landscape to the level of history painting had finally been accomplished to public acclaim.

The artistic success of *The Course of Empire* was also reflected in Cole's personal life. He was married in the fall of 1836 to Maria Bartow, and his career took a new turn. Other subjects and artistic interests stimulated his imagination, and he was able to continue to work in other genres at the same time he was immersed in *The Course of Empire.*

The Course of Empire did not shackle his creative initiative, and he did not become preoccupied with completing it as had Washington Allston with his *Belshazzar's Feast.* Cole continued to work on other themes, notably the picturesque, to engage his interest and to pay the bills, and he painted some of his most interesting and successful work coincidentally with *The Course of Empire. The Oxbow* is an example of his ability to shift successfully from one mode of expression to another. Painted in 1836, it depicts a famous scene in New England using the picturesque formal conventions so characteristic of Cole's style. The roughly textured and heavily built-up surface of the foreground provides a stage against which is shown a landscape of great depth and majesty, almost sublime in its scale. It is an actual view, and as such it is removed from the moral allegory represented in *The Course of Empire.* This would have been considered only appropriate by Cole, who believed in hierarchies of subjects, with history painting at the pinnacle. This large picture was exhibited at the spring exhibition of the National Academy and was bought by Charles Talbot of New York for $500.

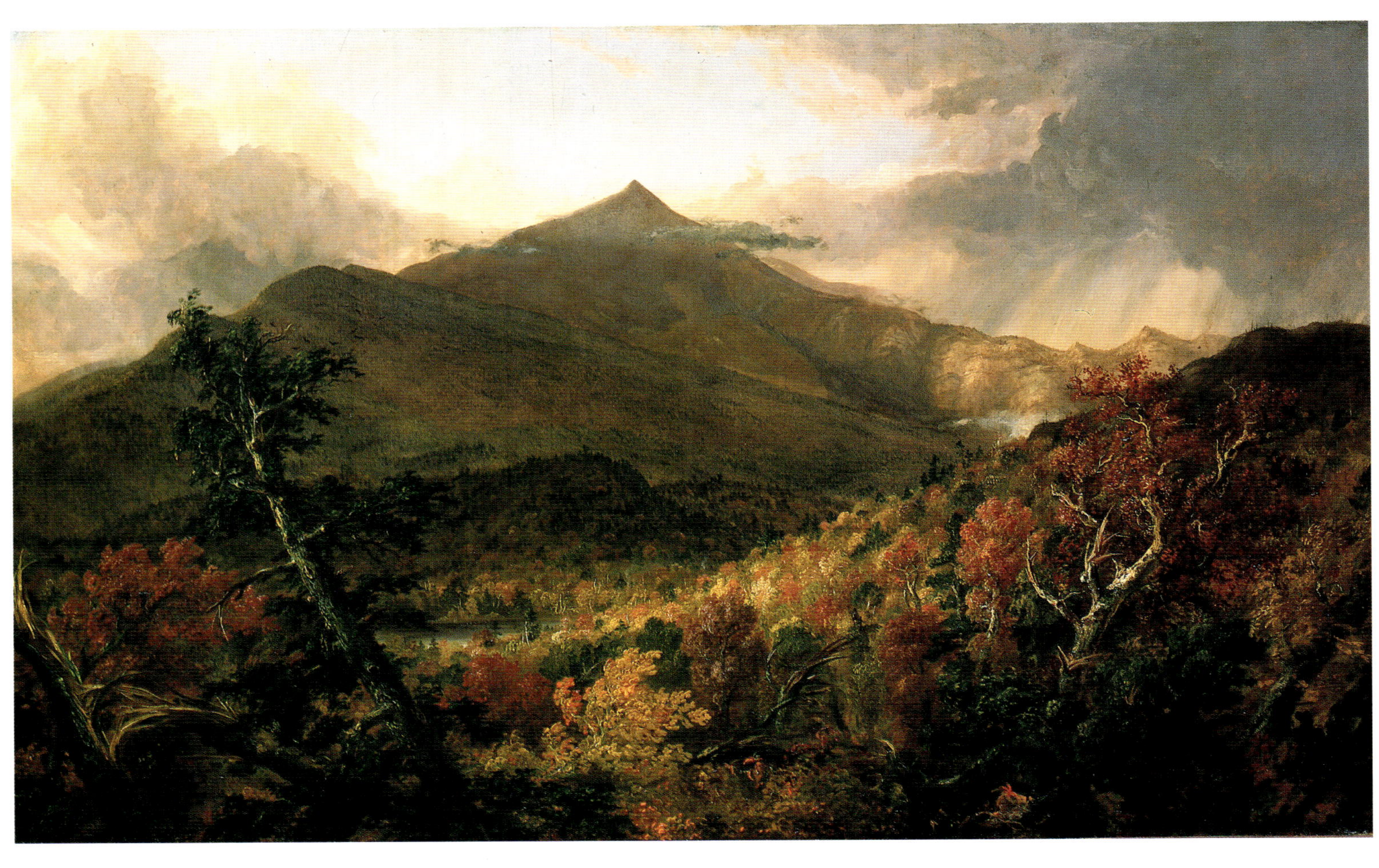

Schroon Mountain, Adirondacks

1838. Oil on canvas,
39⅜ x 63″
The Cleveland Museum of Art,
Hinman B. Hurlbut Collection

5. *Maturity and Success*

The success of *The Course of Empire* led to several new commissions, and in the winter of 1837 Cole was rewarded with an important one from William P. Van Rensselaer of Albany for two pictures to be entitled *The Departure* and *The Return*. Cole also noted that he painted at the same time *A View on the Catskill* for Jonathan Sturges, the partner and son-in-law of Luman Reed and likewise an important and generous patron of Cole and others. He painted an autumnal scene for a Mr. Inman and *View of Florence* for a Mr. Cooke. It was also at this time, which followed the death of his father, that he made a tour of the picturesque to explore the scenery around Schroon Lake with his wife and Asher B. Durand.

Schroon Mountain was a major picturesque composition of a scene that greatly inspired the artist. He commented on the landscape of this area, which he painted as an autumnal composition, "I do not remember to have seen in Italy a composition of mountains so beautiful or pictorial as this glorious range of the Adirondack." (Noble, 177) This picture and *The Oxbow* are in their manner picturesque equivalents to the high level of ambition represented in *The Course of Empire*. They relate in this way to *A Wild Scene,* the large painting that went to Robert Gilmor and was intended to have been the first in the series for *The Course of Empire*. In *Schroon Mountain* Cole expanded the scale of the picturesque and emphasized not only the beauty of an autumn landscape but the sublimity of the experience of the wilderness. This expanded and enlarged view of nature would have been consistent with the scale of his vision as articulated in *The Course of Empire*. In recounting the experience of the landscape around Schroon Lake in correspondence with Durand, Cole described in general the working method that governed his approach to the landscape.

> Have you not found?—I have—that I never succeed in painting scenes, however beautiful, immediately on returning from them. I must wait for time to draw a veil over the common details, the unessential parts, which shall leave the great features, whether the beautiful or the sublime, dominant in the mind. (Noble, 185)

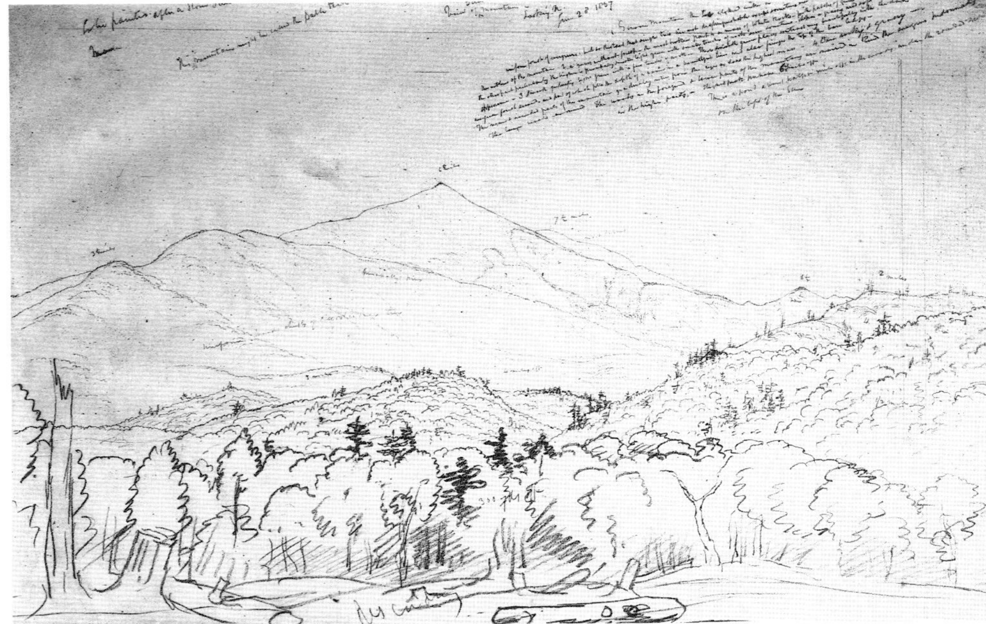

View of Schroon Mountain Looking North, June 28, 1837

1837. Pencil on paper, 9⅞ x 15"
The Detroit Institute of Arts, Founders Society Purchase, William H. Murphy Fund

The commission for Van Rensselaer was to be his next major work, and Cole was particularly gratified to have been given the freedom to select the subject. In a letter written in July 1837 to his patron, Cole noted that he wished to make fresh studies from nature for the Van Rensselaer pictures and commented, "Sunrise and Sunset will be the seasons of the pictures. I shall endeavor to link them in one subject through means of story, sentiment and location." (Noble, 180) By October, however, the subject had expanded, and Cole wrote to apologize for the delay and to explain the concept.

> The story, if I may so call it, which will give title, and, I hope, life and interest to the landscapes, is taken neither from history nor poetry: it is a fiction of my own, if incidents which must have occurred very frequently can be called fiction. It is supposed to have happened in the 13th or 14th century.
>
> (Noble, 181)

The medieval theme of this pair, which were entitled *The Departure* and *The Return,* was inspired by the novels of Sir Walter Scott, and Cole hoped that his patron would appreciate the richness and the picturesque qualities of the two pictures. William Cullen Bryant placed these works among Cole's noblest efforts. Bryant said, with great justice, "There could not be a finer choice of cir-

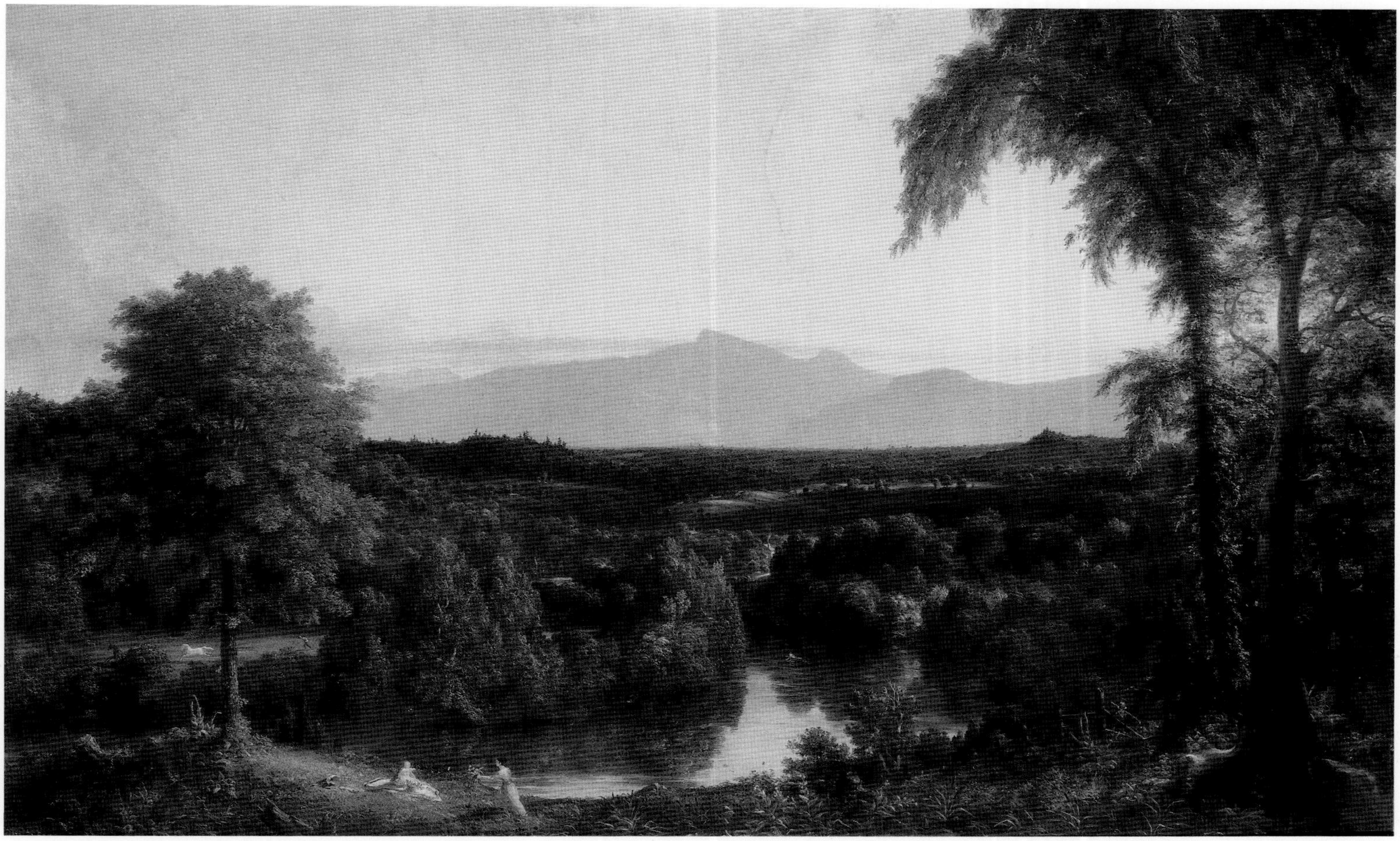

View on the Catskill, Early Autumn

1837. Oil on canvas,
39 x 63″
The Metropolitan Museum of Art,
New York,
Gift in memory of Jonathan Sturges
by his children, 1895

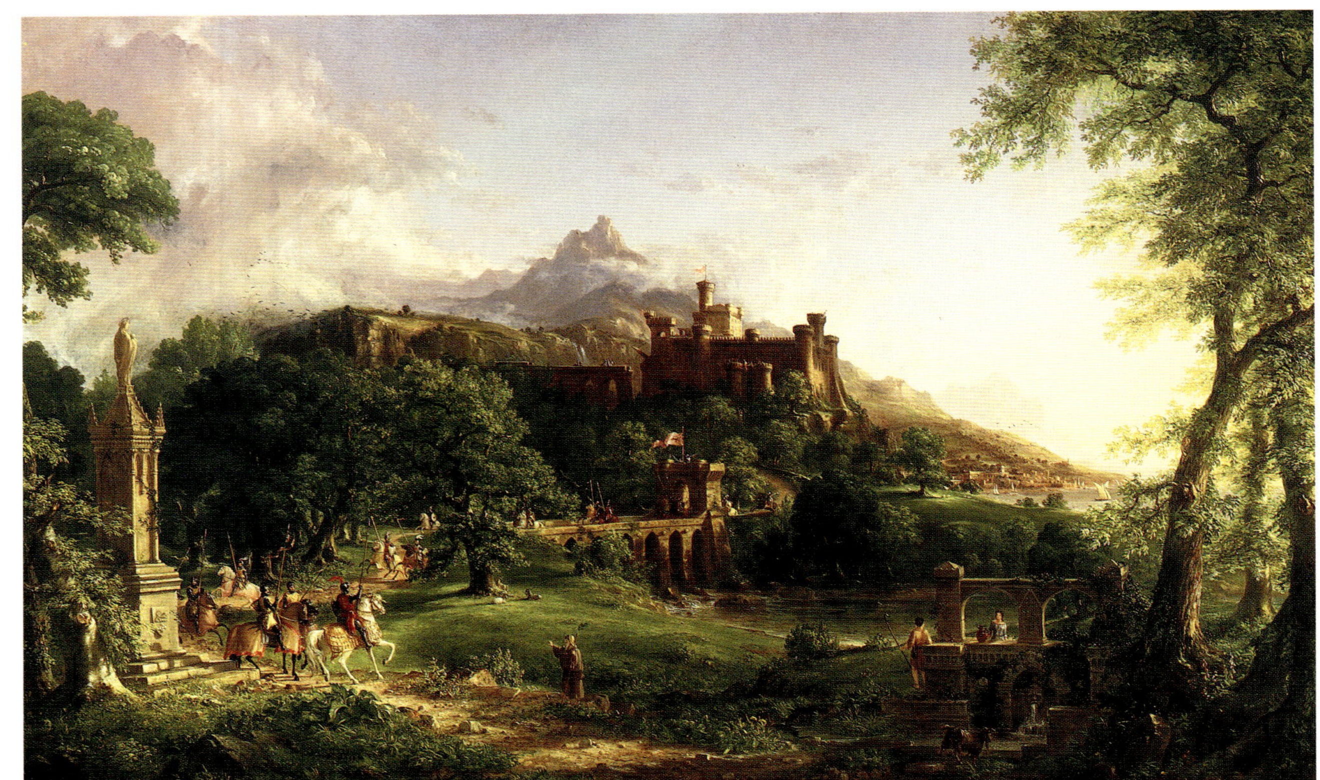

The Departure

1838. Oil on canvas, $39\frac{1}{2} \times 63''$
Collection The Corcoran Gallery of Art, Washington, D.C. Gift of William Wilson Corcoran

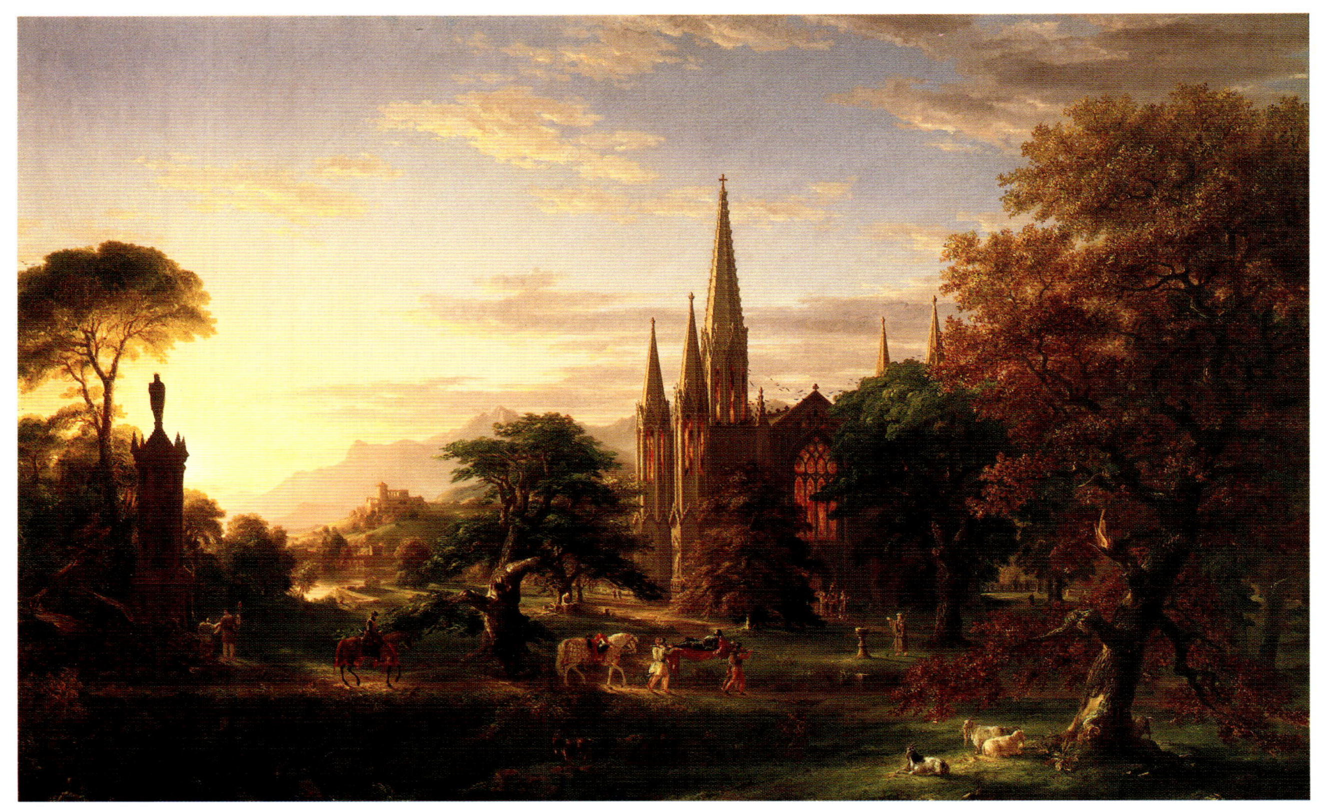

The Return

1838. Oil on canvas, $39\frac{3}{4} \times 63''$
Collection The Corcoran Gallery of Art, Washington, D.C. Gift of William Wilson Corcoran

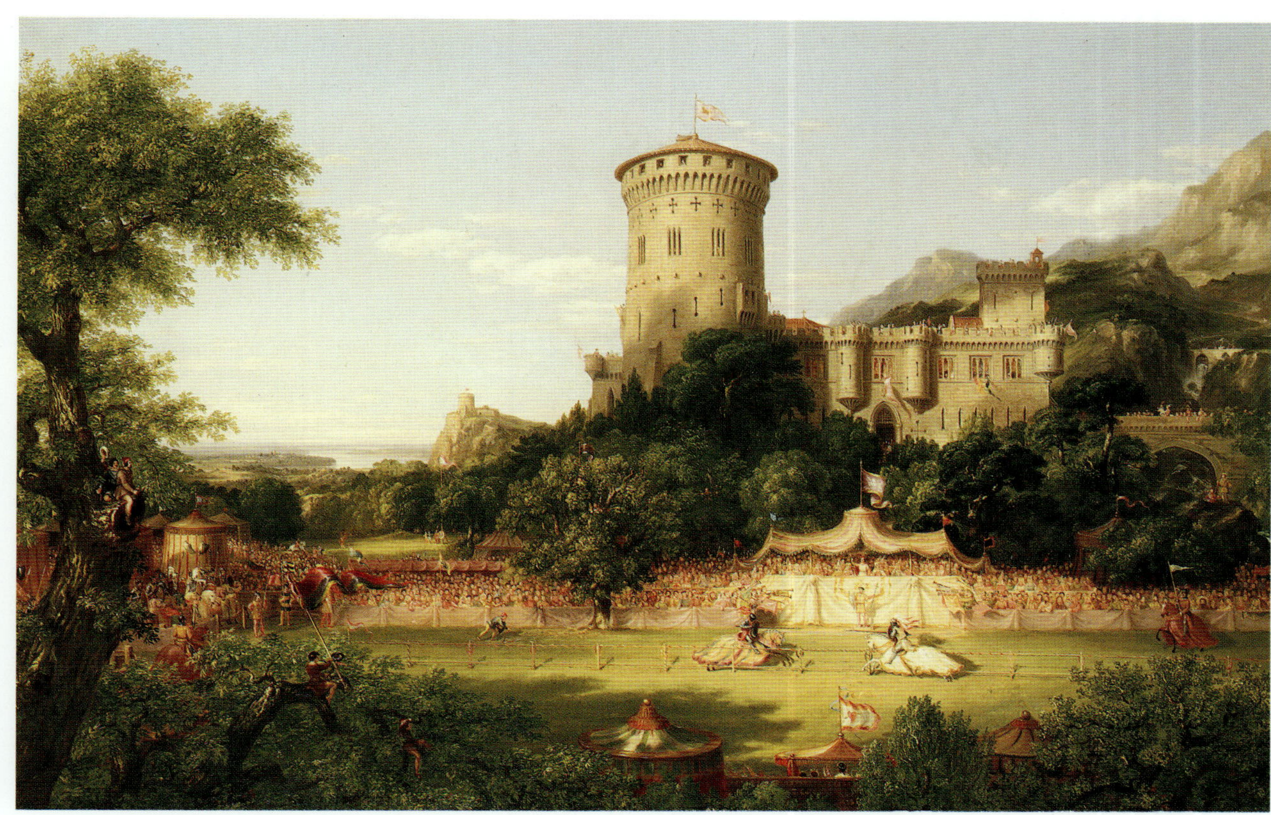

The Past

1838. Oil on canvas,
40 x 61″
Mead Art Museum,
Amherst College,
Amherst, Massachusetts,
Museum Purchase

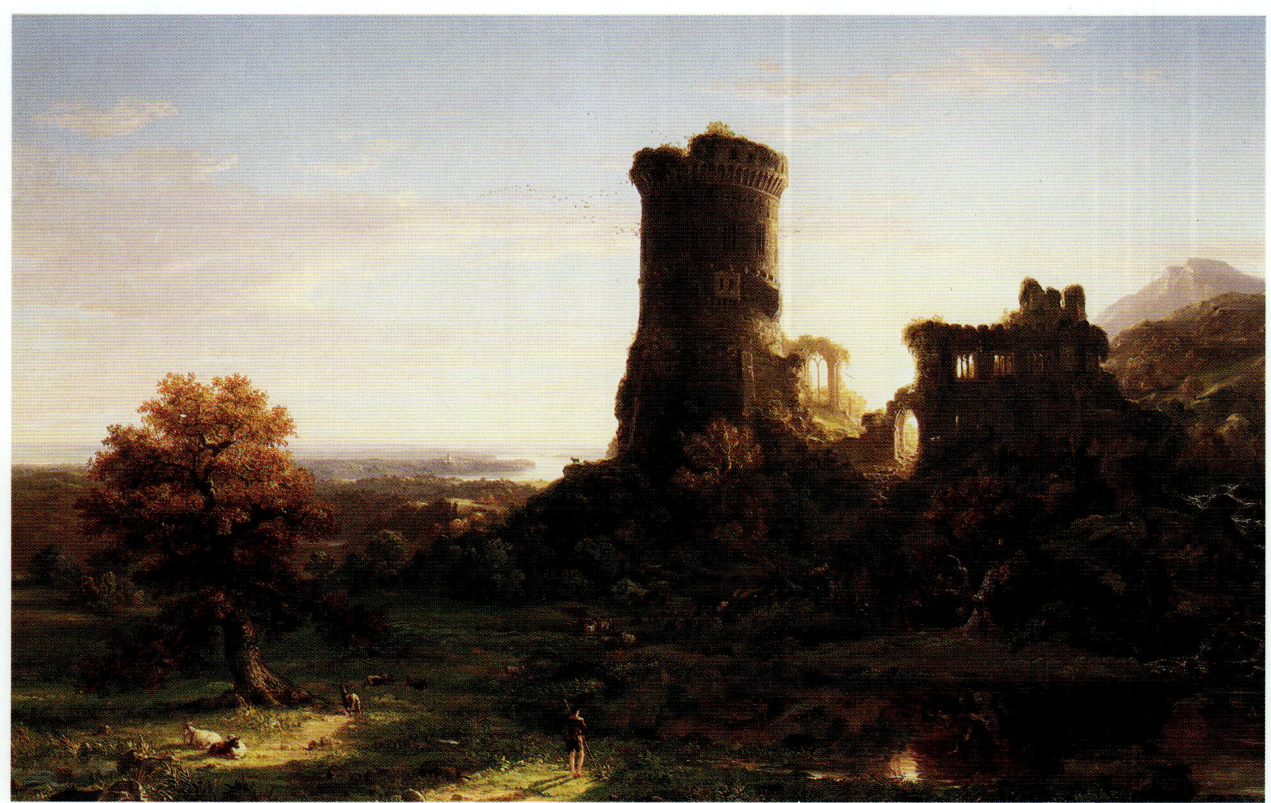

The Present

1838. Oil on canvas,
40 x 61″
Mead Art Museum,
Amherst College,
Amherst, Massachusetts,
Museum Purchase

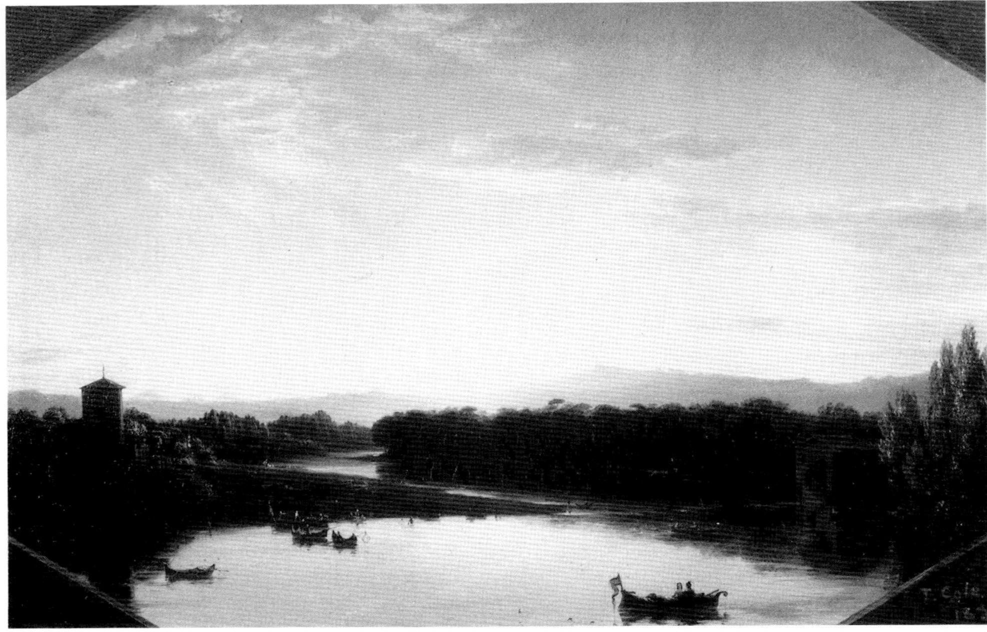

View on the Arno
1838. Oil on wood panel, 17 x 25¼″
Shelburne Museum, Shelburne, Vermont

cumstances, nor a more exquisite treatment of them than is found in these pictures. In the first, a spring morning, breezy and sparkling, the mists starting and soaring from the hills, the chieftan in gallant array, at the head of his retainers, issuing from the castle. In the second, an autumnal evening, calm, solemn—a church illuminated by the beams of the setting sun, and the corpse of the chief borne in silence—these are but a meagre epitome of what is contained in these two pictures." (Noble, 183) The rendering of the light in both paintings is particularly beautiful, and the melancholy theme, which Cole believed might give his patron concern, was nevertheless a popular Romantic interest.

Cole also received several commissions for Italian themes at this time and produced no less than three views on the Arno for collectors in Boston. His most important work in this genre was *View of Florence from San Miniato,* which he exhibited in the 1837 National Academy exhibition.

In February Cole received another important commission from Peter G. Stuyvesant, a descendant of the Dutch governor of New Amsterdam, who had been impressed with the Van Rensselaer paintings and wanted his to be of the same size. Cole responded to Stuyvesant:

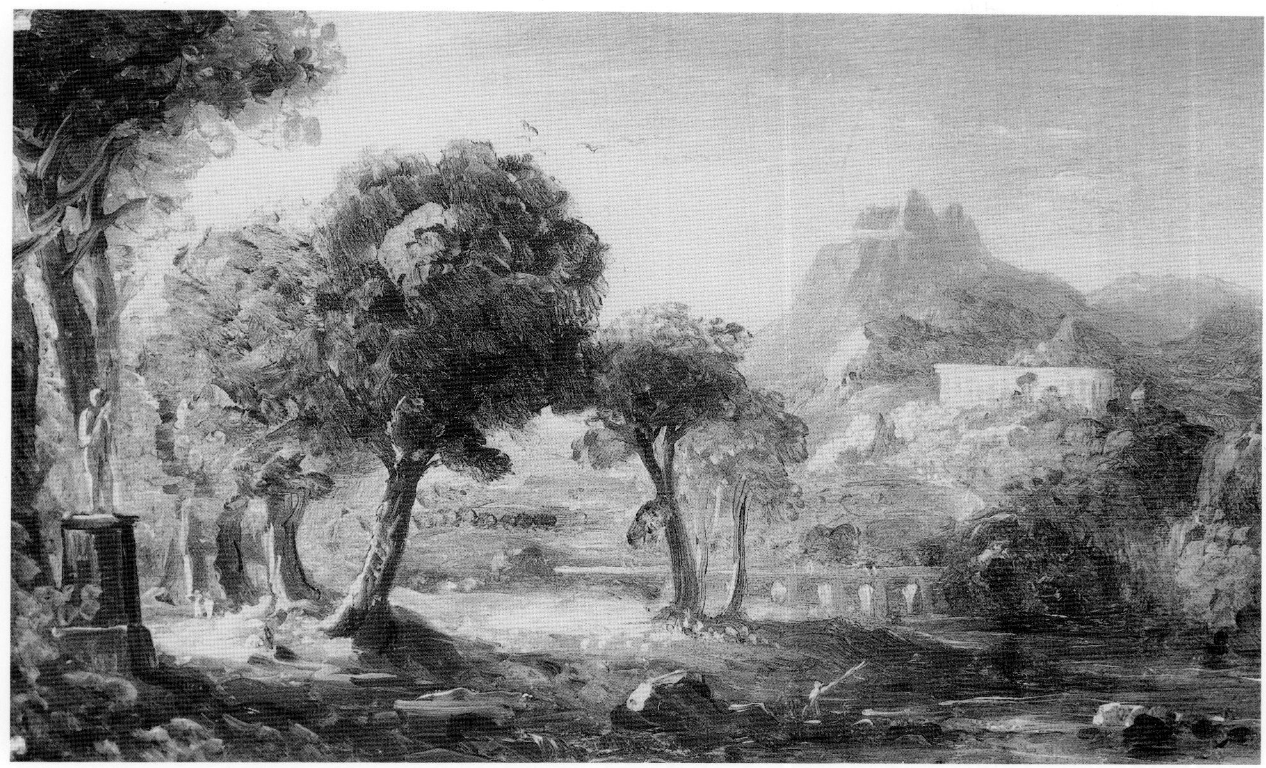

Study for
Dream of Arcadia

1838. Oil on wood panel, $8^{3}/_{4}$ x $14^{1}/_{2}$"
Courtesy The New-York Historical Society, New York City

> You express a desire to have a subject that will embrace two pictures. I am happy to find subjects of this kind attractive. They give more scope for poetical invention, and are, perhaps, more capable of sentiment than subjects requiring only a single canvas. (Noble, 187)

The two pictures that resulted from this commission were originally listed in Cole's notebook as possibly American scenes, but he obviously changed his mind in favor of a medieval theme, which reveals his continuing preoccupation with historical and moral subjects and with the passage of time. The vine-encrusted ruin of a tower in *The Past,* with its picturesque echoes, contrasts sharply with its counterpart, *The Present.*

In the spring 1838 exhibition of the National Academy Cole exhibited *The Dream of Arcadia,* a fascinating painting that caused Noble to credit Cole as being the parent of pastoral painting in America. Cole described this picture in an amusing letter to Durand, and it was very favorably received by the public and

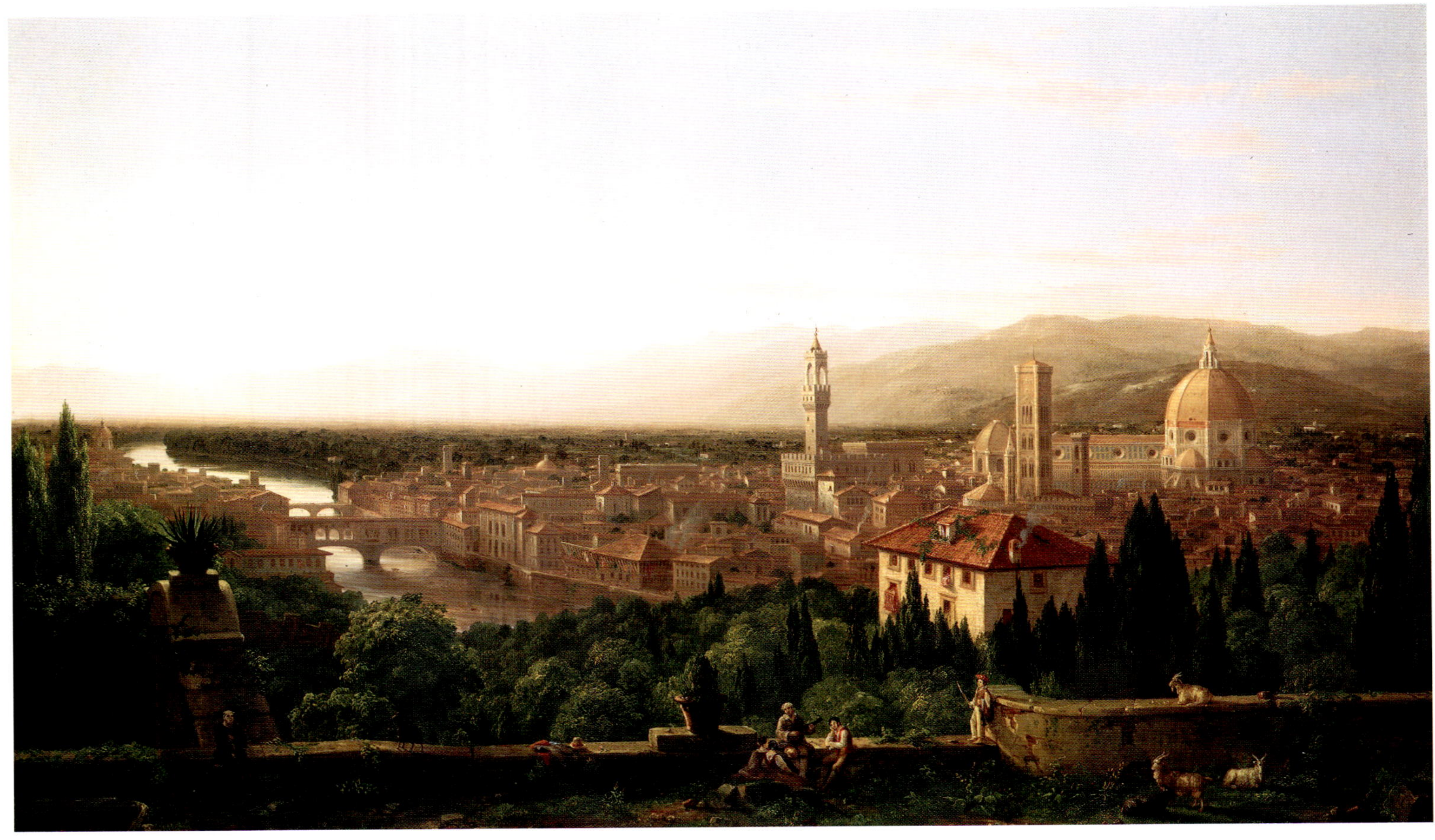

View of Florence from San Miniato

1837. Oil on canvas,
39 x 63⅛″
The Cleveland Museum of Art,
Mr. and Mrs. William H. Marlatt Fund

critics alike. In a letter to Durand of 20 March 1838, he discussed the painting and his interest in the theme at length and in a light-hearted manner unusual for the artist, whose writings are generally very sober.

> I took a trip to Arcadia in a dream. At the first start the atmosphere was clear, and the traveling delightful: but just as I got into the midst of that famous land, there came a classic fog and I got lost and bewildered. I scraped my shins in scrambling up a high mountain—rubbed my nose against a marble temple—got half suffocated by the smoke of an altar, where the priests were burning offal by way of sacrifice (queer taste the gods had, that's certain). (Noble, 188)

The picture is unique in Cole's oeuvre. It is interesting to compare this work with the picturesque *Schroon Mountain,* painted at approximately the same time, to see how Cole could develop two separate styles of landscape painting with equal facility. *Schroon Mountain* celebrates the American wilderness and the natural frontier, while *Dream of Arcadia* dwells in an ancient past and draws its inspiration from literature and poetry. *Dream of Arcadia* was widely reproduced and was engraved in 1850 by James Smillie for distribution to the membership of the American Art Union. Cole would have interpreted the two subjects in the context of the academic hierarchy of genres in which epic and historical subjects were considered more elevated as themes than picturesque landscape. But in America the association of wilderness imagery with God elevated landscape to a level with history painting, as seen by Cole.

Cole found 1838 to be an eventful and interesting year for him as his latent interest in architecture manifested itself with his entry for the design of the State Capitol of Ohio. He was eventually awarded third prize for his efforts and complained that the winner had merely adapted his design.

In March of 1839 Cole received his next important commission, to paint *The Voyage of Life* for Samuel Ward, an important New York banker who, like Luman Reed, had a gallery of paintings in his home. While *The Course of Empire* had represented the emergence of Cole as a mature artist, *The Voyage of Life* would be the creative enterprise dominating his mature years.

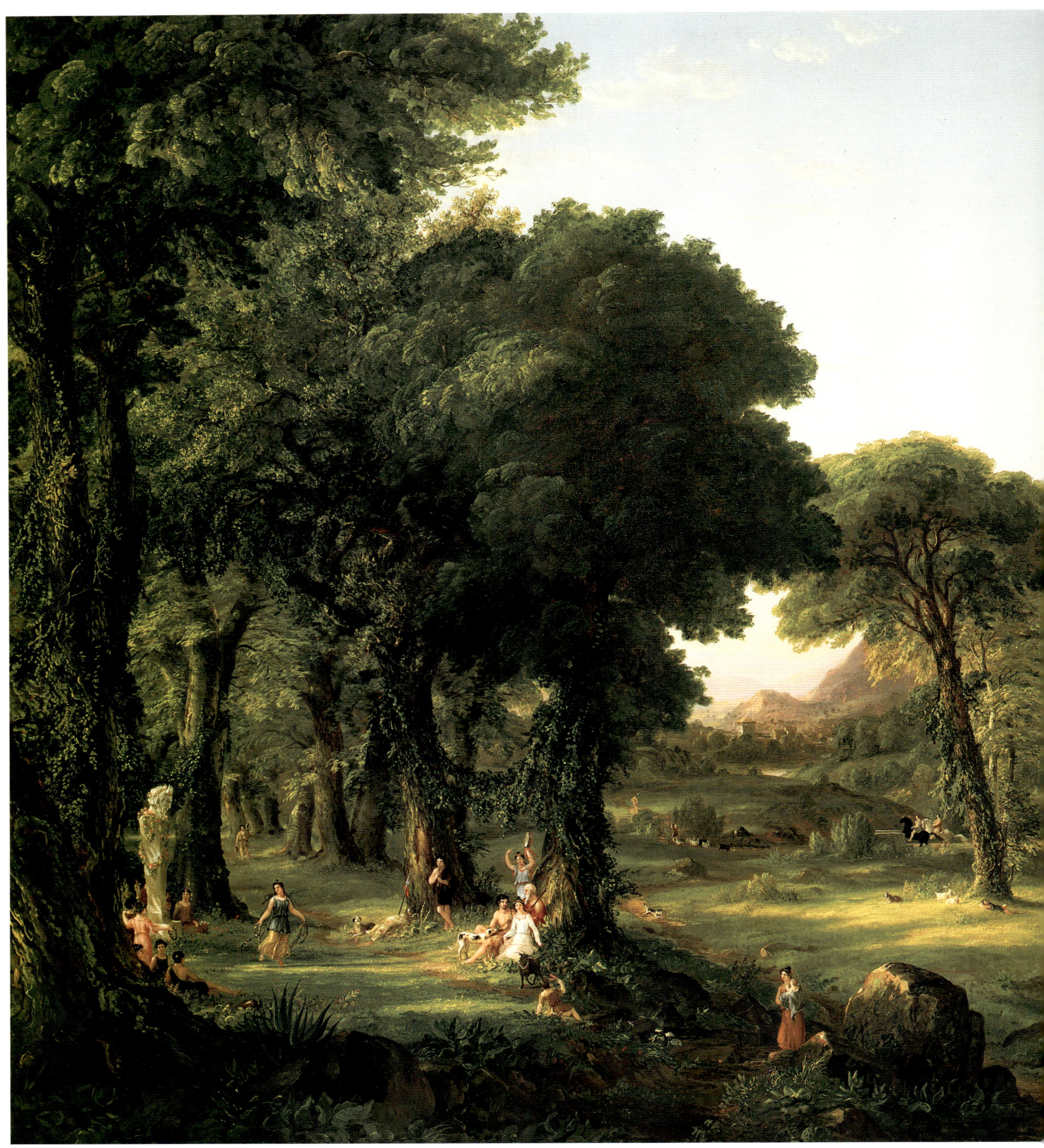

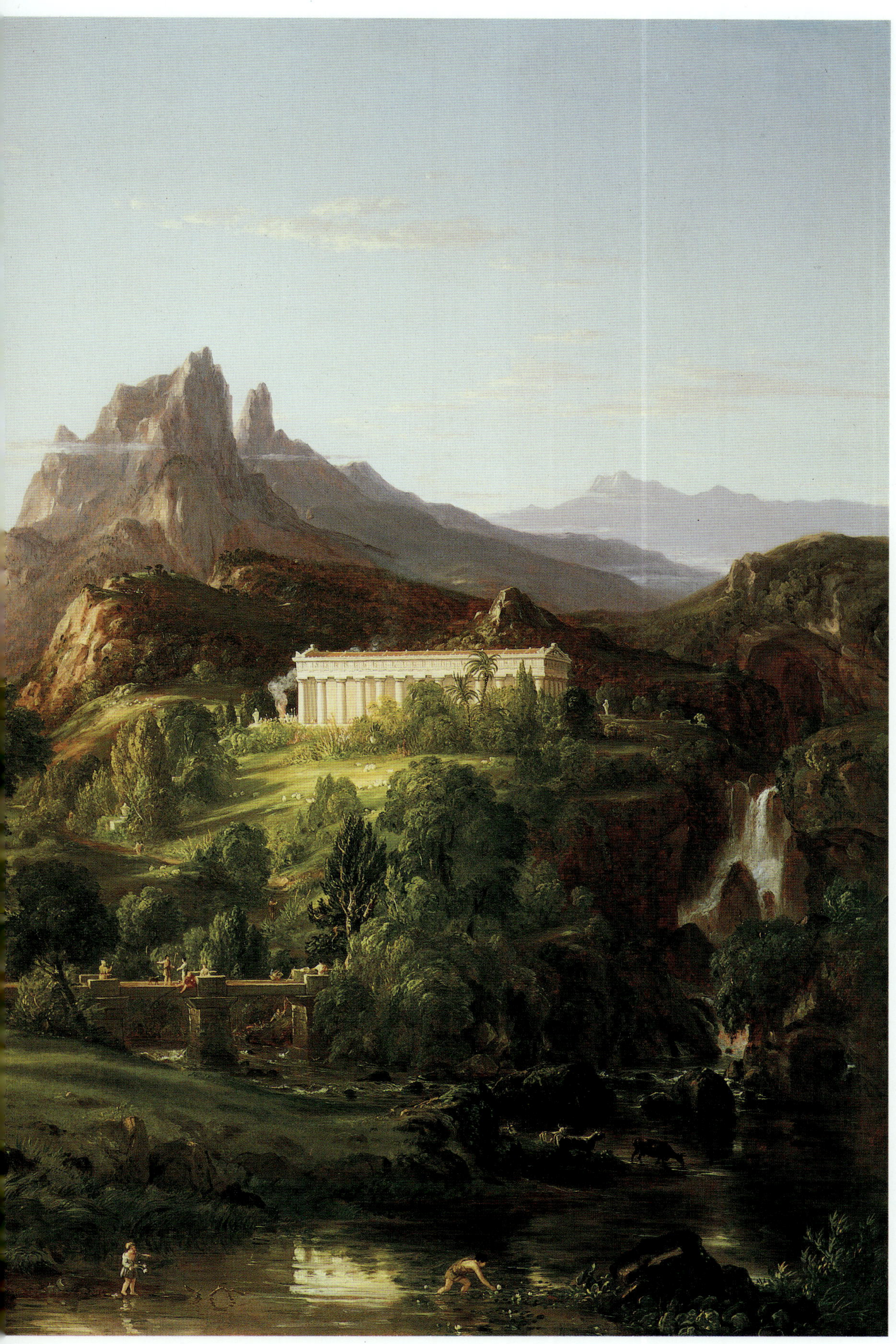

Dream of Arcadia

1838. Oil on canvas,
$39\frac{1}{4}$ x $63\frac{1}{16}''$
Denver Art Museum,
Gift of
Mrs. Katherine H. Gentry

6. *The Voyage of Life*

The commission for *The Voyage of Life* was Cole's most important since *The Course of Empire* and was to be based on an idea Cole had entertained for some time. Ward, a deeply religious man, had modeled his domestic gallery after Luman Reed's, but unlike Reed, Ward did not intend this series to be a course in moral instruction for the public. This was a commission for a private home on a theme whose program was far more personal than the High Romantic sentiment that had inspired the grandiloquent *Course of Empire*. *The Voyage of Life* offered a simple, straightforward, and conventional Christian allegorical message. The four pictures, *Childhood, Youth, Manhood,* and *Old Age,* depict the pilgrim's path through life, concluding in the final work with the promise of eternal salvation. The two series contrast the historical with the allegorical, the latter resembling both John Bunyan's *Pilgrim's Progress* and the biblical imagery of the river of life. In his later years Cole himself became much more religious, and that sentiment shows in the pictures for this series.

As with all his major commissions, Cole did not begin work immediately; instead he used the summer months of 1839 to make a picturesque tour of the White Mountains. It was a pleasant trip and one that would produce sketches and studies for future landscapes, but he was obviously mentally composing his new series. He painted a picturesque view, *Portage Falls on the Genesee*, as a result of this trip, but at the end of the summer he was prepared to begin work in earnest, and he wrote to Ward:

> . . . I hope you will not infer that I have allowed so many months to pass without making some progress towards their completion . . . the poetical conception of a subject may not be difficult, for it is spontaneous; but to imagine that which is to be embodied in light, and shadow, and color—that which is strictly pictorial—is an accumulative work of the mind. (Noble, 205)

By October he had begun work on *Childhood,* and his hopes and enthusiasm for the success of the series were high. The next month he was crushed when he

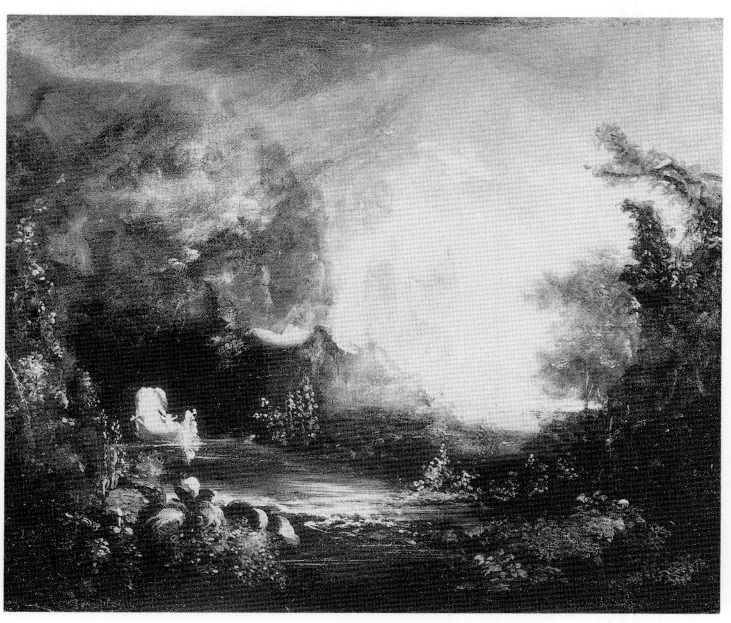

Study for *The Voyage of Life: Childhood*

c. 1837–39. Oil on wood panel,
11⅝ x 14″
Collection the Albany Institute of
History and Art, Albany, New York

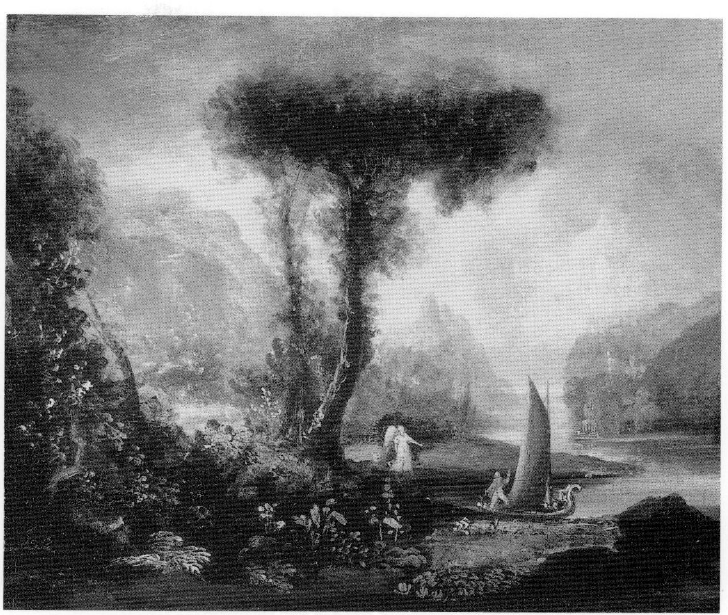

Study for *The Voyage of Life: Youth*

c. 1837–39. Oil on wood panel
12 x 13⅝″
Collection the Albany Institute of
History and Art, Albany, New York

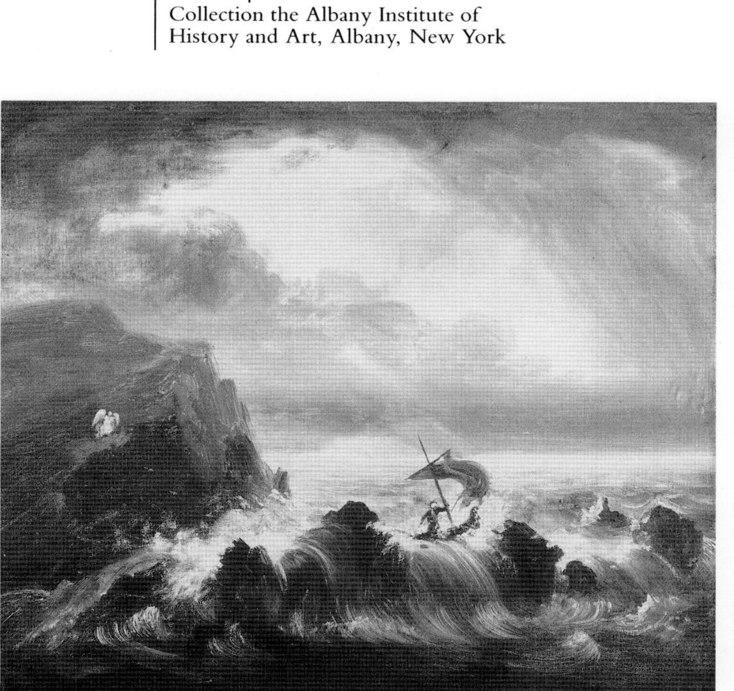

Study for *The Voyage of Life: Manhood*

c. 1837–39. Oil on wood panel,
12 x 13⅝″
Collection the Albany Institute of
History and Art, Albany, New York

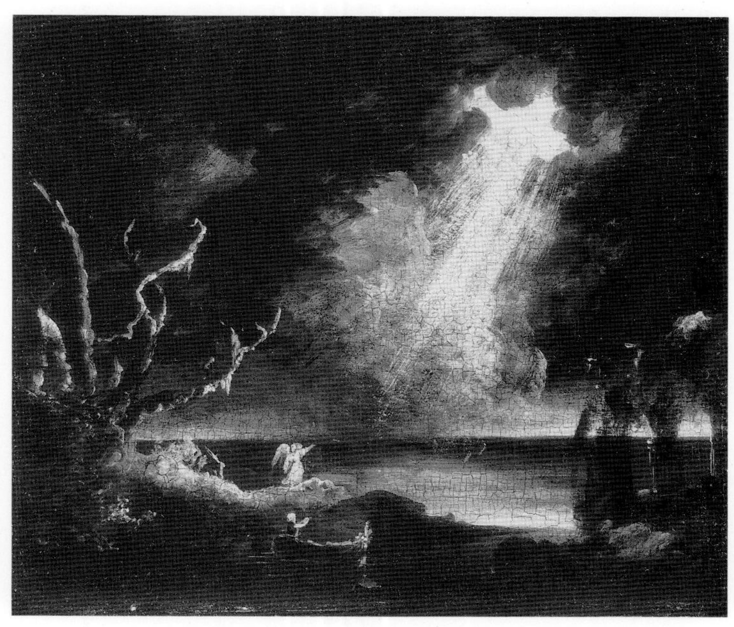

Study for *The Voyage of Life: Old Age*

c. 1837–39. Oil on wood panel,
12 x 13⅝″
Collection the Albany Institute of
History and Art, Albany, New York

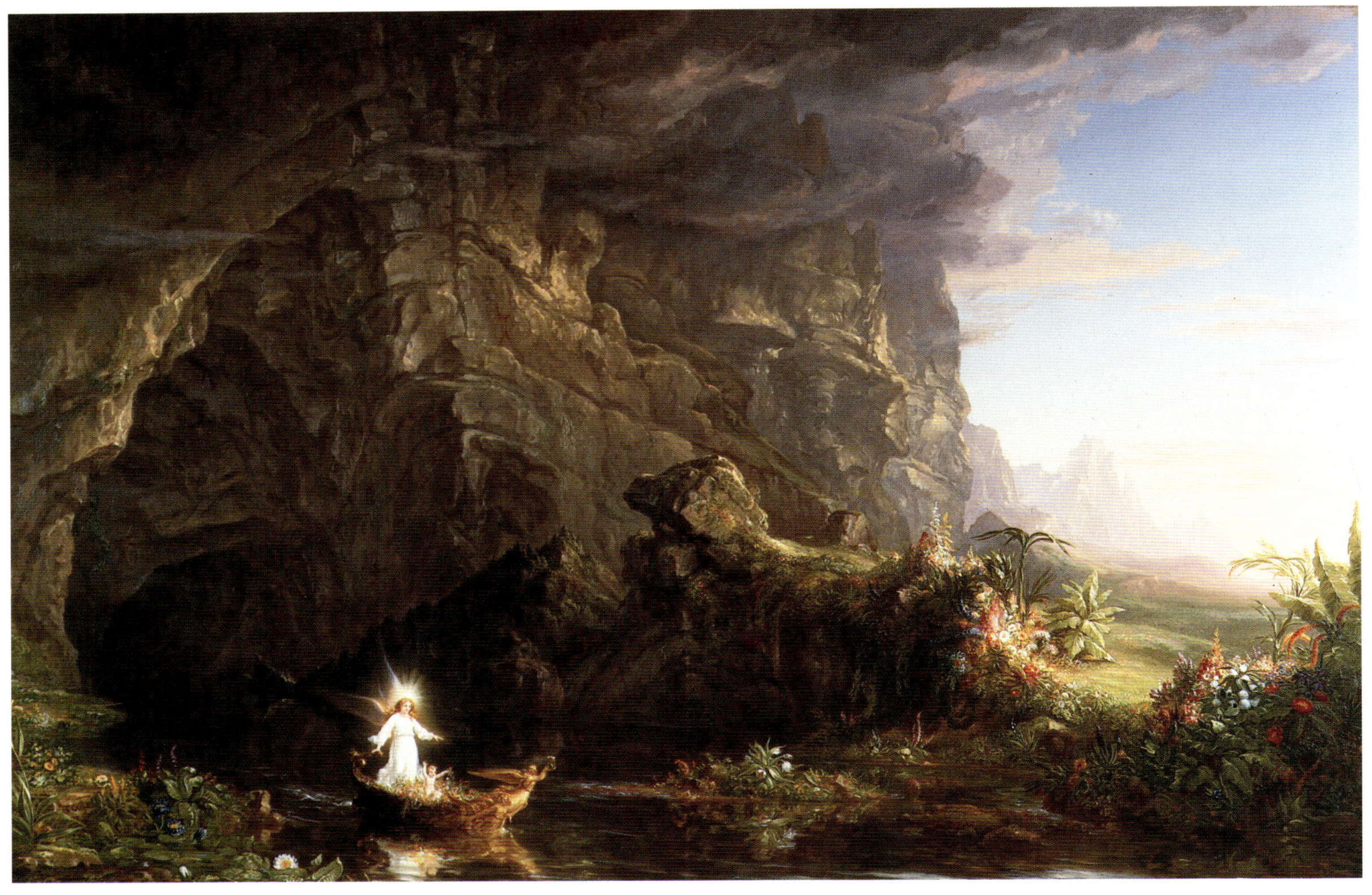

The Voyage of Life: Childhood

1839–40. Oil on canvas,
52 x 78″
The Munson-Williams-
Proctor Institute,
Utica, New York

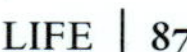

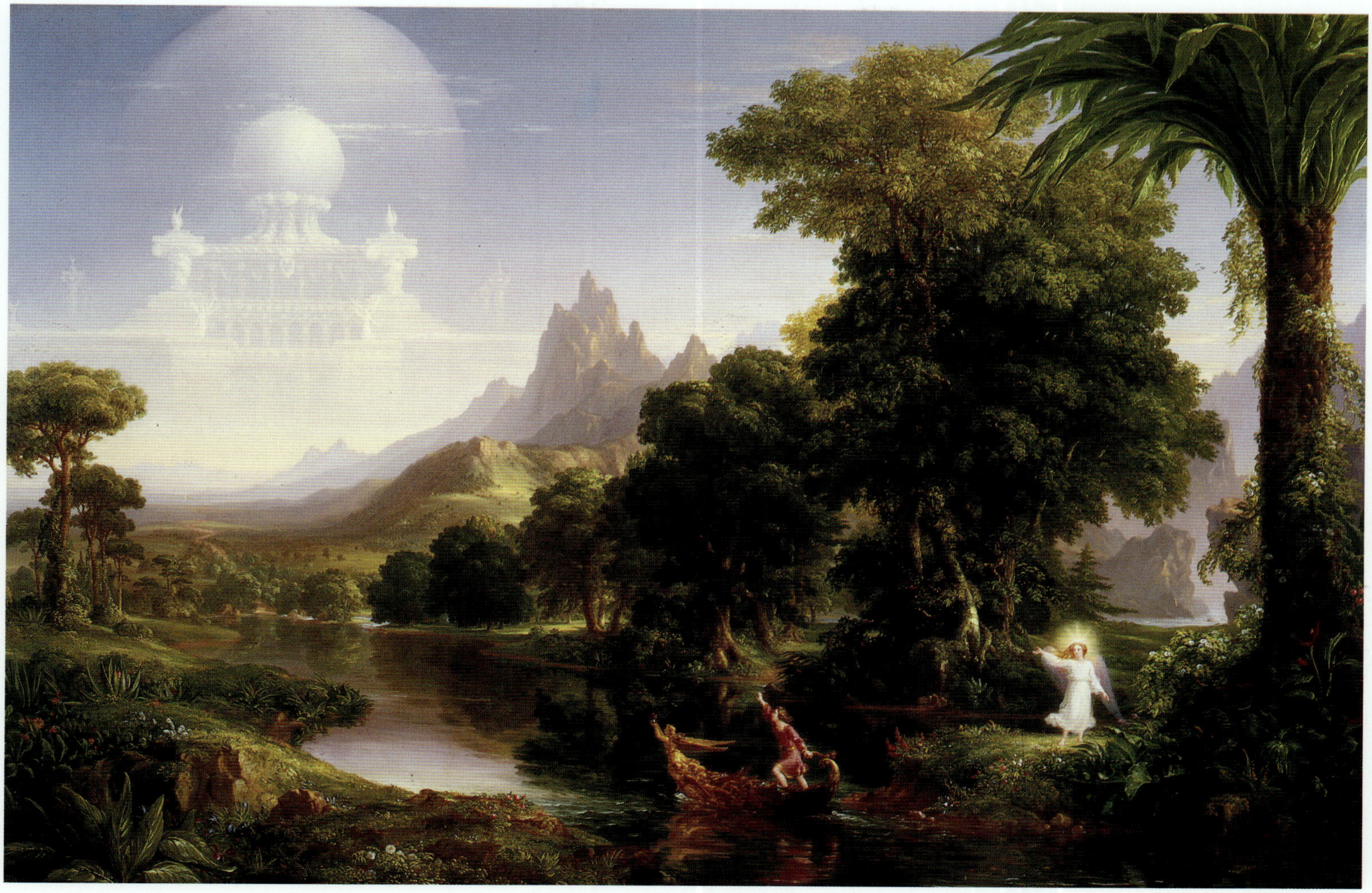

The Voyage of Life: Youth

1840. Oil on canvas,
52½ x 78½″
The Munson-Williams-
Proctor Institute,
Utica, New York

learned that Samuel Ward had died, and he noted sadly in his correspondence, "There would seem almost a fatality in these commissions. Mr. Reed died without seeing his series completed. Mr. Ward died soon after his was commenced." (Noble, 206) The series was not to be abandoned, however, and Cole was eager to pursue it. He was able to arrange to exhibit the series at the National Academy, where he finished the last two pictures in November 1840.

It is interesting to compare *The Voyage of Life* with *The Course of Empire.* The latter, more baroque and theatrical, was conceived as a panorama of extravagant proportions, one equal to the theory of the cycle of nations that inspired it. The solitary journey of the pilgrim in *The Voyage of Life,* however, is introspective and melancholy and probably representative of Cole's own feelings at this time in his life. Where *The Course of Empire* reflects the passage of time from early morning to evening, *The Voyage of Life* follows a time sequence corresponding to the seasons of the year. The first two pictures show the boat moving from left to right across the canvas; the last two reverse direction. Cole obviously recognized the necessity of displaying all four together on one wall. He devised an arrangement that would resolve the visual problem of runoff, which would have resulted if all four were composed in a similar direction.

Cole's description of the series is typical of the literary and religious inspiration that motivated him:

The Voyage of Life

> An Allegorical Series. The subject is comprised in Four Pictures. The first represents the period of Childhood; the second, Youth; the third, Manhood; the fourth, Old Age.
>
> 1. Childhood.—A stream is seen issuing from a deep cavern, in the side of a craggy and precipitous mountain, whose summit is hidden in clouds. From out the cave glides a Boat, whose golden prow and sides are sculptured into figures of the Hours. Steered by an Angelic Form, and laden with buds and flowers, it bears a laughing Infant, the Voyager, whose varied course the Artist has attempted to delineate. On either hand, the banks of the stream are clothed in luxuriant herbage and flowers. The rising sun bathes the mountains and flowery banks with rosy light.
>
> The dark cavern is emblematic of our earthly origin, and the mysterious Past. The Boat, composed of figures of the Hours, images the thought, that we

are borne on the hours down the Stream of Life. The Boat identifies the subject in each picture. The rosy light of the morning, the luxuriant flowers and plants, are emblems of the joyousness of early life. The close banks, and the limited scope of the scene, indicate the narrow experience of Childhood, and the nature of its pleasures and desires. The Egyptian Lotus, in the foreground of the picture, is symbolical of human Life. Joyousness and wonder are the characteristic emotions of childhood.

2. YOUTH.—The stream now pursues its course through a landscape of wider scope, and more diversified beauty. Trees of rich growth overshadow its banks, and verdant hills form the base of lofty mountains. The Infant of the former scene is become a Youth, on the verge of Manhood. He is now alone in the Boat, and takes the helm himself, and, in an attitude of confidence and eager expectation, gazes on a cloudy pile of Architecture, an air-built Castle, that rises dome above dome in the far-off blue sky. The Guardian Spirit stands upon the bank of the stream, and, with serious, yet benignant countenance, seems to be bidding the impetuous Voyager God speed. The beautiful stream flows for a distance, directly toward the aeriel palace; but at length makes a sudden turn, and is seen in glimpses beneath the trees, until it at last descends with rapid current into a rocky ravine, where the Voyager will be found in the next picture. Over the remote hills, which seem to intercept the stream, and turn in from its hitherto direct course, a path is dimly seen, tending directly toward that cloudy Fabric, which is the object and desire of the Voyager.

The scenery of the picture—its clear stream, its lofty trees, its towering mountains, its unbounded distance, and transparent atmosphere—figure forth the romantic beauty of youthful imaginings, when the mind elevates the Mean and Common into the Magnificent, before experience teaches what is the Real. The gorgeous cloud-built palace, whose glorious domes seem yet but half revealed to the eye, growing more and more lofty as we gaze, is emblematic of the daydreams of youth, its aspirations after glory and fame; and the dimly-seen path would intimate that Youth, in its impetuous career, is forgetful that it is embarked on the Stream of Life, and that its current sweeps along with resistless force, and increases in swiftness, as it descends toward the great ocean of Eternity.

3. MANHOOD.—Storm and cloud enshroud a rugged and dreary landscape. Bare, impending precipices rise in the lurid light. The swollen stream rushes furiously down a dark ravine, whirling and foaming in its wild career, and

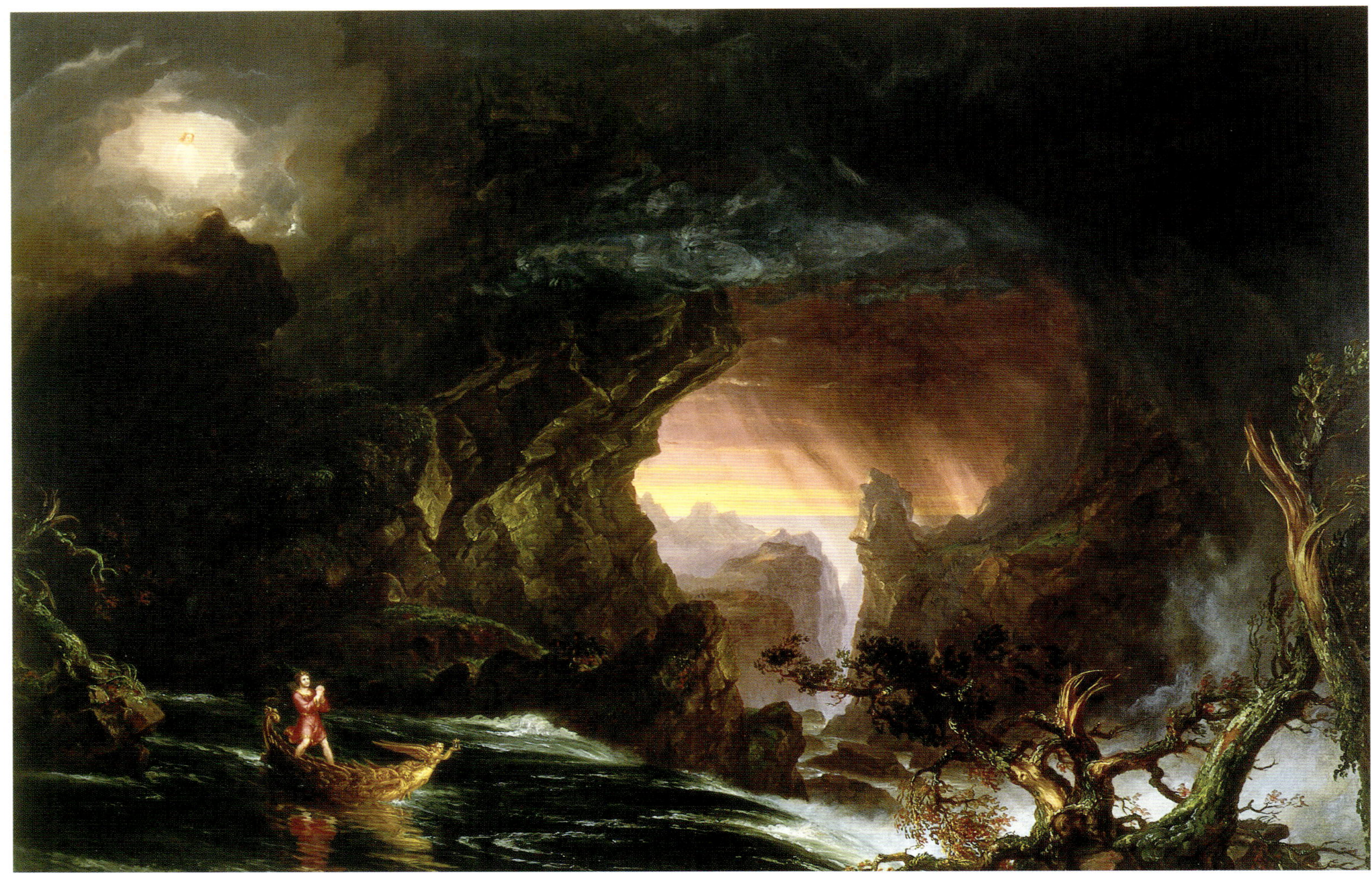

The Voyage of Life: Manhood

1840. Oil on canvas,
52 x 78″
The Munson-Williams-
Proctor Institute,
Utica, New York

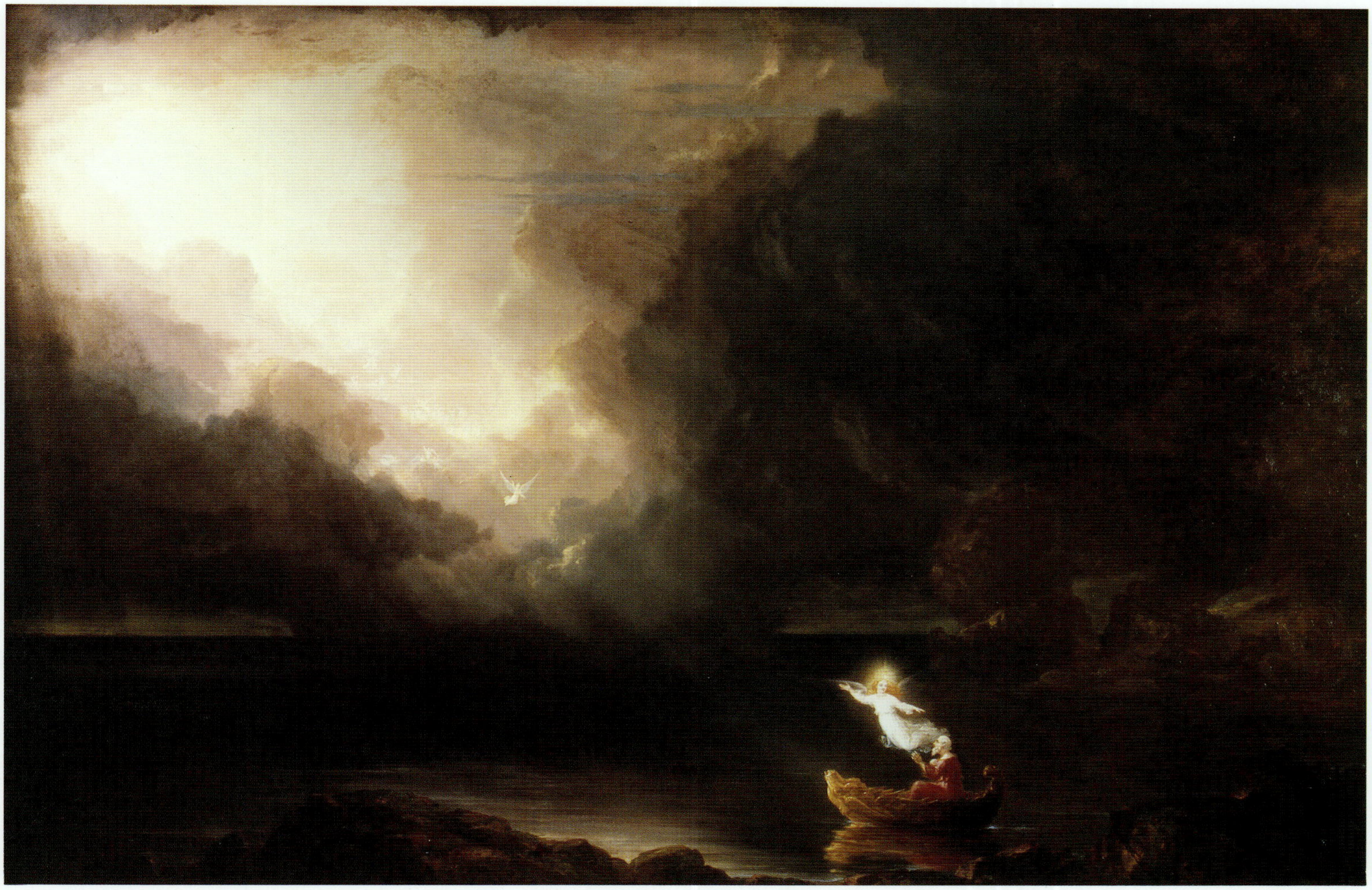

The Voyage of Life: Old Age

1840. Oil on canvas,
51¾ x 78¼″
The Munson-Williams-
Proctor Institute,
Utica, New York

speeding toward the Ocean, which is dimly seen through the mist and falling rain. The boat is there plunging amid the turbulent waters. The Voyager is now a man of middle age: the helm of the boat is gone, and he looks imploringly toward heaven, as if heaven's aid alone could save him from the perils that surround him. The Guardian Spirit calmly sits in the clouds, watching, with an air of solicitude, the affrighted Voyager: Demon forms are hovering in the air.

Trouble is characteristic of the period of Manhood. In childhood, there is no carking care: in youth, no despairing thought. It is only when experience has taught us the realities of the world, that we lift from our eyes the golden veil of early life; that we feel deep and abiding sorrow: and in the Picture, the gloomy, eclipse-like tone, the conflicting elements, the trees riven by tempest, are the allegory; and the Ocean, dimly seen, figures the end of life, which the Voyager is now approaching. The demon forms are Suicide, Intemperance and Murder; which are the temptations that beset men in their direct trouble. The upward and imploring look of the Voyager shows his dependence on a Superior Power; and *that* faith saves him from the destruction that seems inevitable.

4. OLD AGE.—Portentous clouds are brooding over a vast and midnight Ocean. A few barren rocks are seen through the gloom—the last shores of the world. These form the mouth of the river; and the Boat, shattered by storms, its figures of the Hours broken and drooping, is seen gliding over the deep waters. Directed by the Guardian Spirit, who thus far has accompanied him *unseen,* the Voyager, now an old man, looks upward to an opening in the clouds, from whence a glorious light bursts forth; and angels are seen descending the cloudy steps, as if to welcome him to the Haven of Immortal Life.

The stream of life has now reached the Ocean to which all life is tending. The world to Old Age is destitute of interest. There is no longer any green thing upon it. The broken and drooping figures of the Boat show that time is nearly ended. The chains of corporeal existence are falling away; and already the mind has glimpses of Immortal Life. The angelic Being, of whose presence, until now, the Voyager has been unconscious, is revealed to him; and, with a countenance beaming with joy, shows to his wondering gaze scenes such as the eye of mortal man has never beheld. (Noble, 214–16)

The Voyage of Life was well received by critics and the public, and Cole wanted to continue exhibiting the series in various showings. Indeed, he really wanted to buy the pictures back from the Ward family and began to entertain thoughts of duplicating the series if the Wards would not agree to sell.

His work and concern over *The Voyage of Life* was not his only activity at

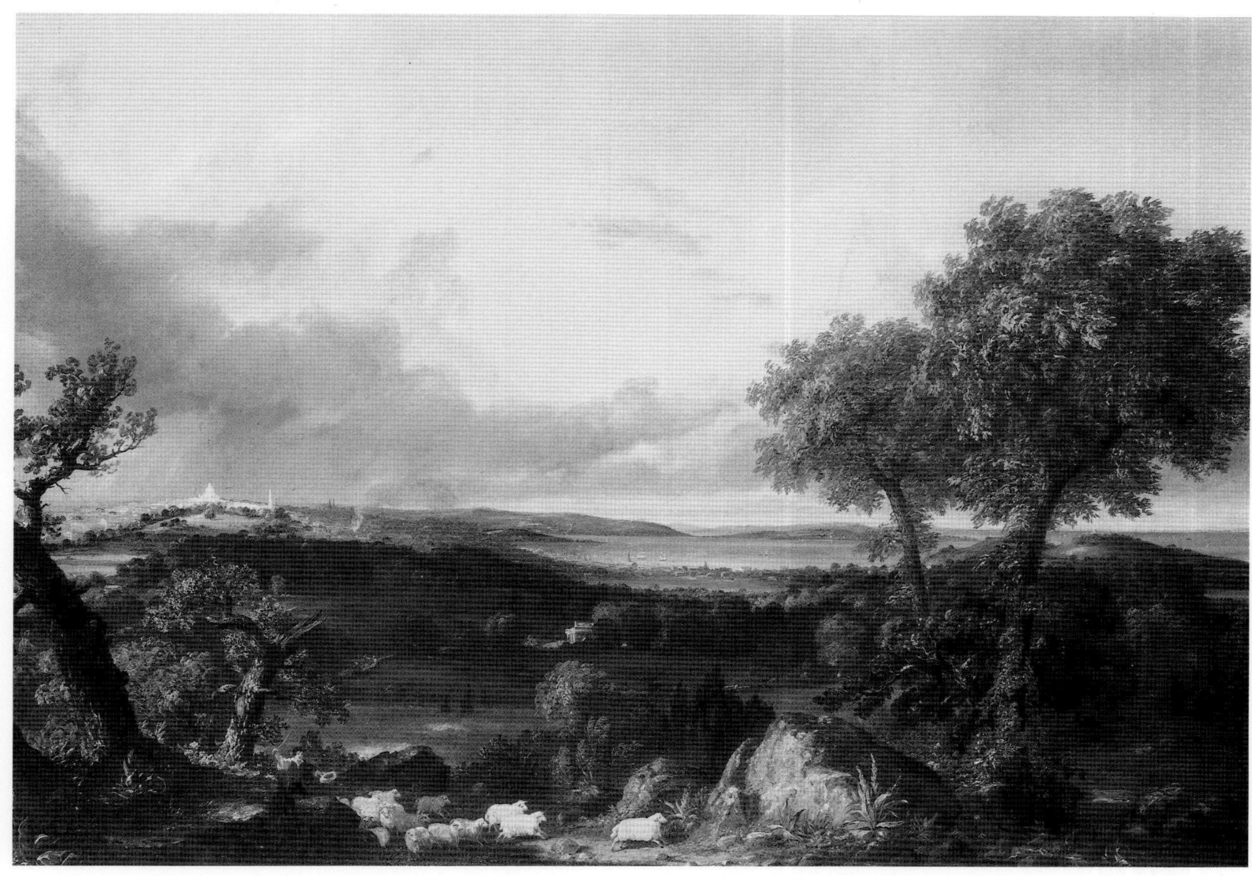

View of Boston

c. 1839. Oil on canvas,
34 x 47⅛″
Private collection

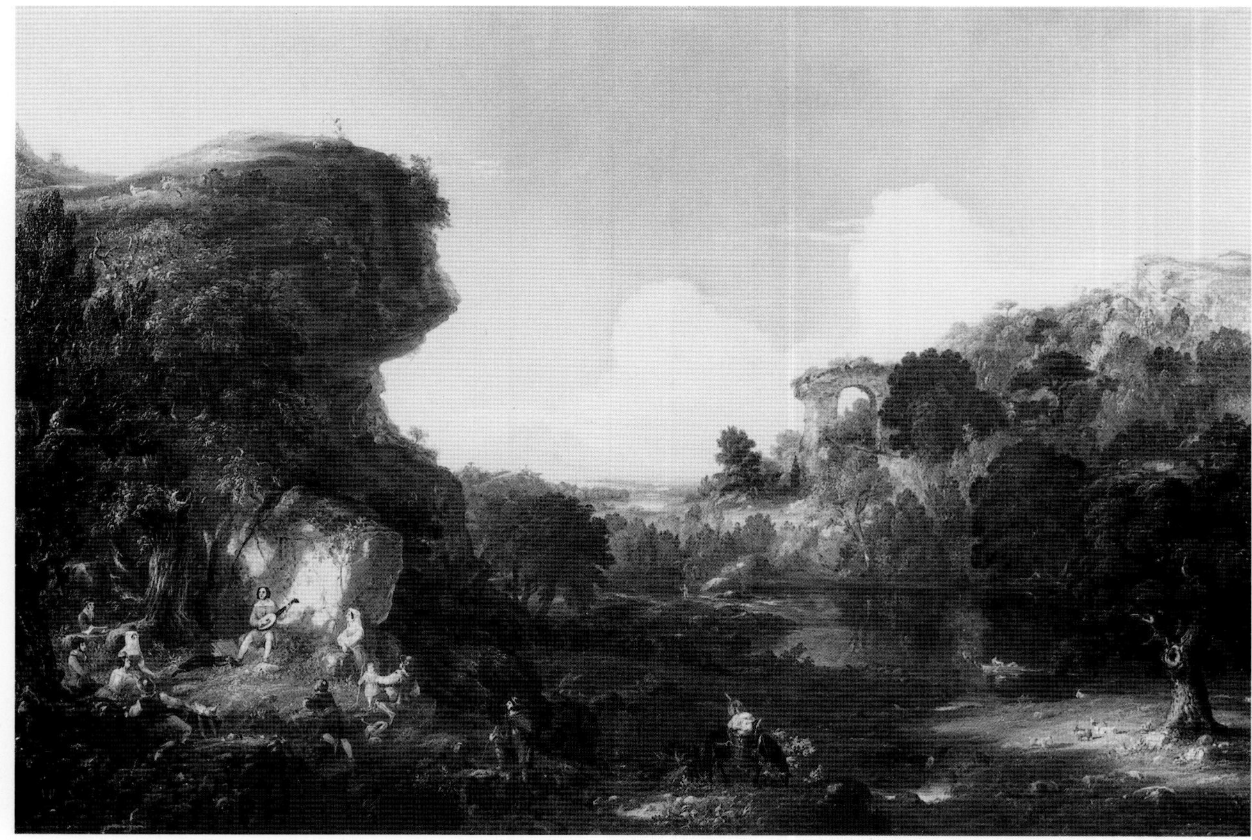

Italian Landscape

1839. Oil on canvas,
35 x 53″
Butler Institute of
American Art,
Youngstown, Ohio

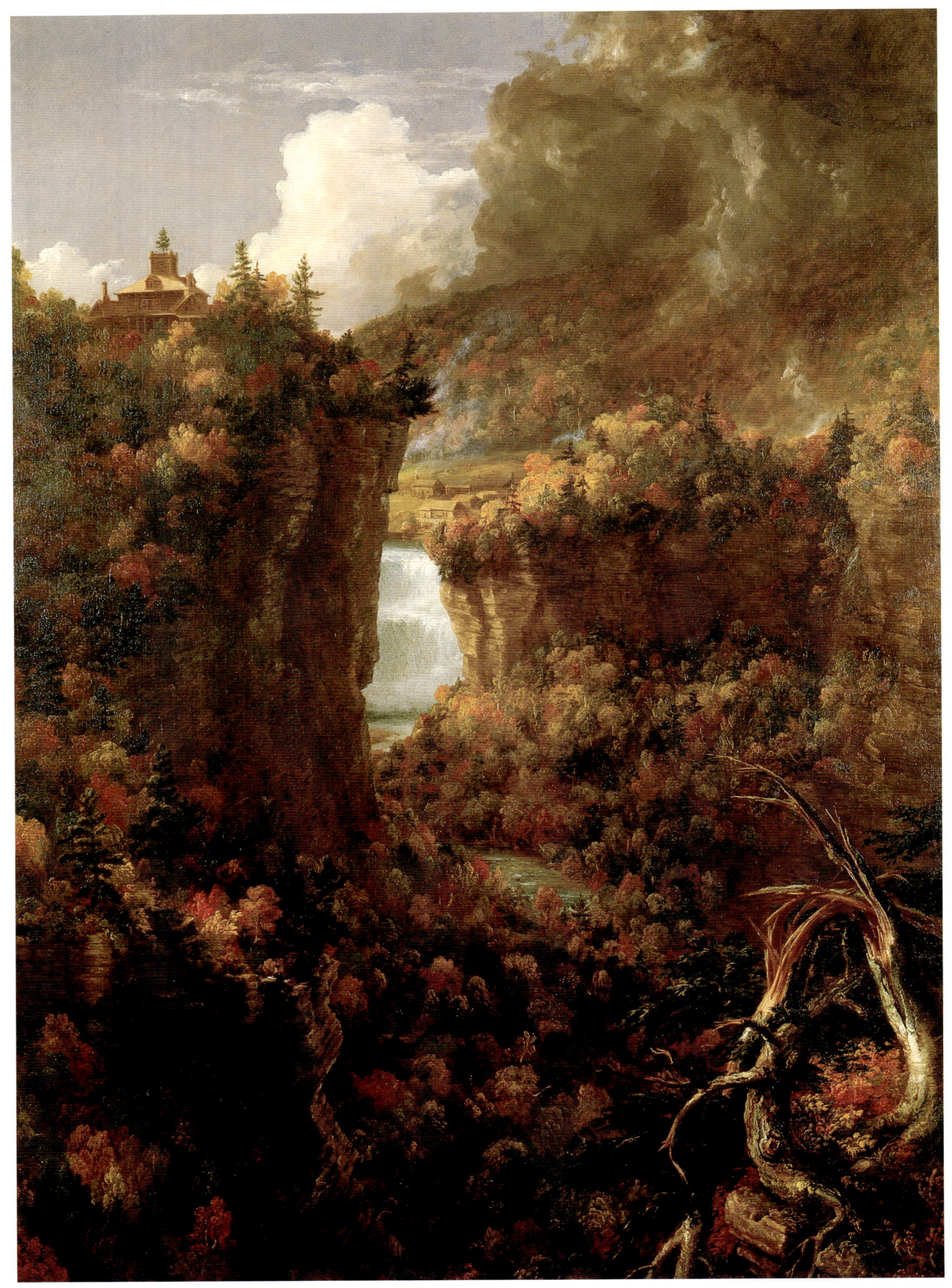

Portage Falls on the Genesee

1839. Oil on canvas, 84 x 60″
Collection, Historic Seward House, Auburn, New York

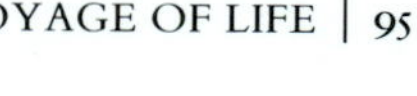

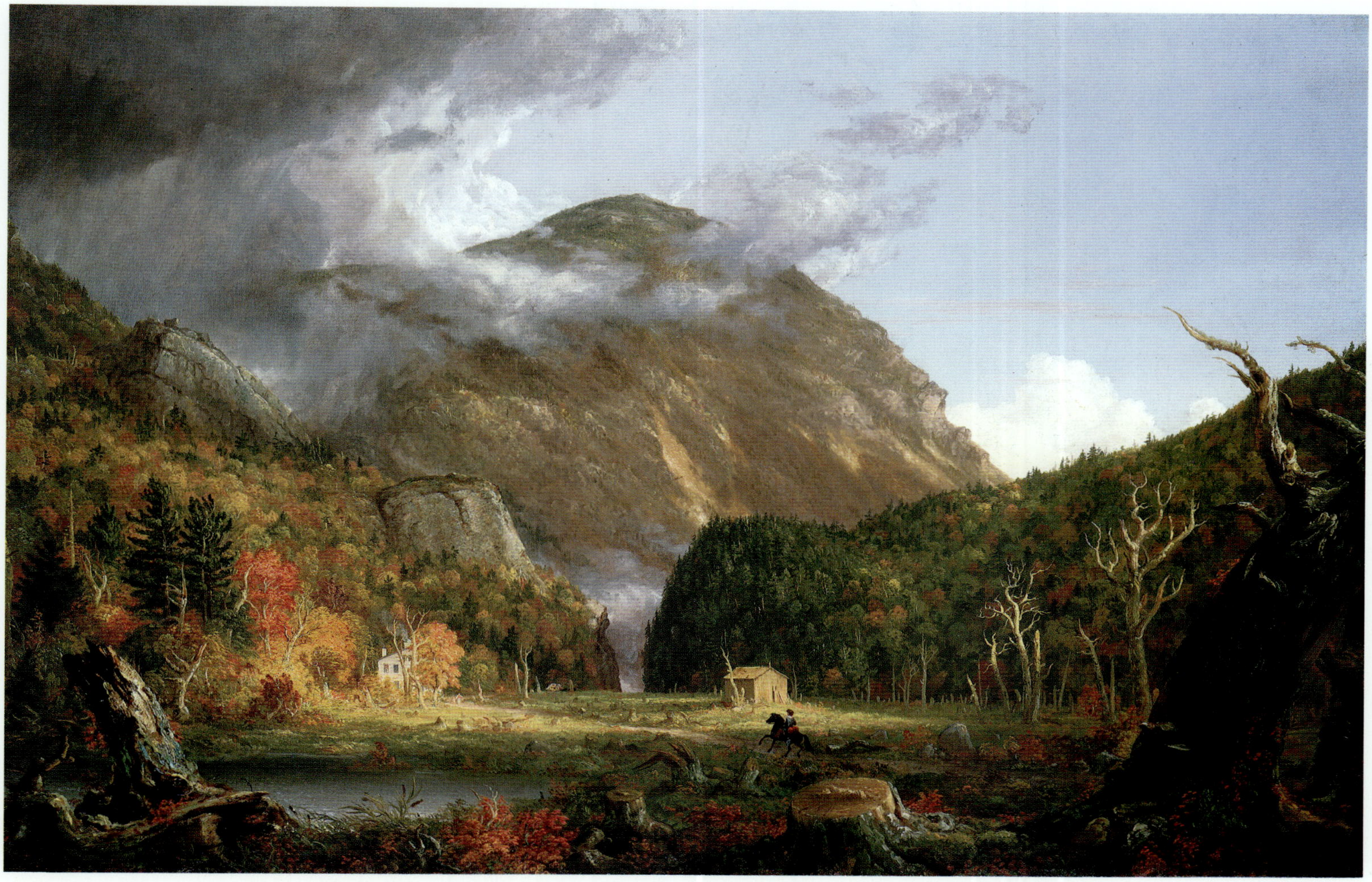

The Notch of the White Mountains (Crawford Notch)

1839. Oil on canvas,
40 x 61½″
National Gallery of Art,
Washington, D.C.,
Andrew W. Mellon Fund

this time, however. Consistent in his working process, he continued to develop other themes and subjects despite the dominance of one major commission. Cole showed another important and interesting work entitled *The Architect's Dream* in the spring exhibition of the National Academy. He had been commissioned to produce this fantasy by Ithiel Town, a prominent architect who worked primarily in and around New York and Hartford. Cole was obviously attracted to the theme, given his own earlier interest in architecture. He incorporated within a vast pictorial space an eclectic arrangement of forms representative of the historical evolution of architectural style, ending, as it were, with the Gothic. The picture is fascinating in its assembly of forms and in its compositional organization, which recalls the central picture in *The Course of Empire*: *The Consummation of Empire*. It did not suit the taste and imagination of Town, however, who requested that Cole paint another. This Cole refused to do, and the commission was withdrawn, but the painting is an interesting counterpoint, a witty interlude, perhaps, in the context of his work for the more somber *Voyage of Life*.

In his funeral oration for Thomas Cole, Bryant called *The Voyage of Life* "of simpler and less elaborate design than *The Course of Empire,* but more purely imaginative. The conception of the series is a perfect poem."

> The child, under the care of its guardian angel, in a boat heaped with buds and flowers, floating down a stream which issues from the shadowy cavern of the past, and flows between banks bright with flowers and the beams of the rising sun; the youth, with hope in his gesture and aspect, taking command of the helm, while his winged guardian watches him anxiously from the shore; the mature man, hurried onward by the perilous rapids and eddies of the river; the aged navigator, who has reached, in his frail and now idle bark, the mouth of the stream, and is just entering the great ocean which lies before him in mysterious shadow; set before us the different stages of human life under images of which every beholder admits the beauty and deep significance. The second of this series, with the rich luxuriance of its foreground, its pleasant declivities in the distance, and its gorgeous but shadowy structures in the piled clouds, is one of the most popular of Cole's compositions. (Noble, 217)

The series was engraved by Smillie, and as a result it achieved a wide audience and great popularity. But while the series was clearly literary in theme and conception, it also showed a return to the imaginary landscape that had formed the pictorial stage for Cole's earlier *Garden of Eden* and *Expulsion*. By the time he had

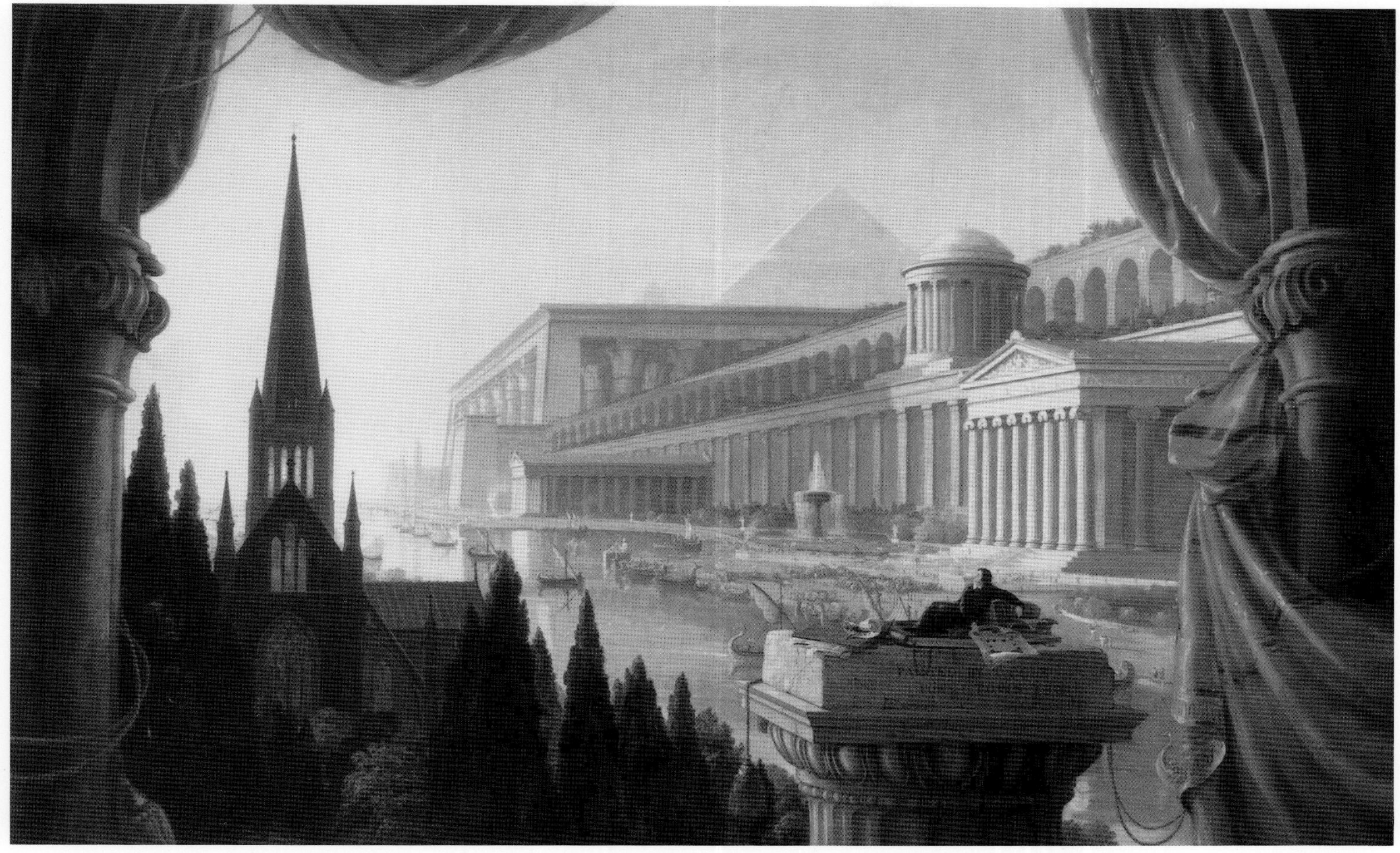

The Architect's Dream

1840. Oil on canvas,
53 x 84$\frac{1}{16}$″
The Toledo Museum of Art,
Toledo, Ohio,
Gift of Florence Scott Libbey

completed the commission, Cole seemed to need refreshment of spirit and new inspiration. He remarked in a letter of 1841:

> although American scenery was often so fine, we feel the want of associations such as cling to scenes in the old world. Simple nature is not quite sufficient. We want human interest, incident and action, to render the effect of landscape complete. (Noble, 219)

Cole lamented that he was not the painter he could have been "had there been a higher taste" and that he had, like so many others, been forced to adapt his art to a mercantile taste. His dark mood was abetted by poor health, and as a possible cure he determined to return to Europe where he could restore his spirit.

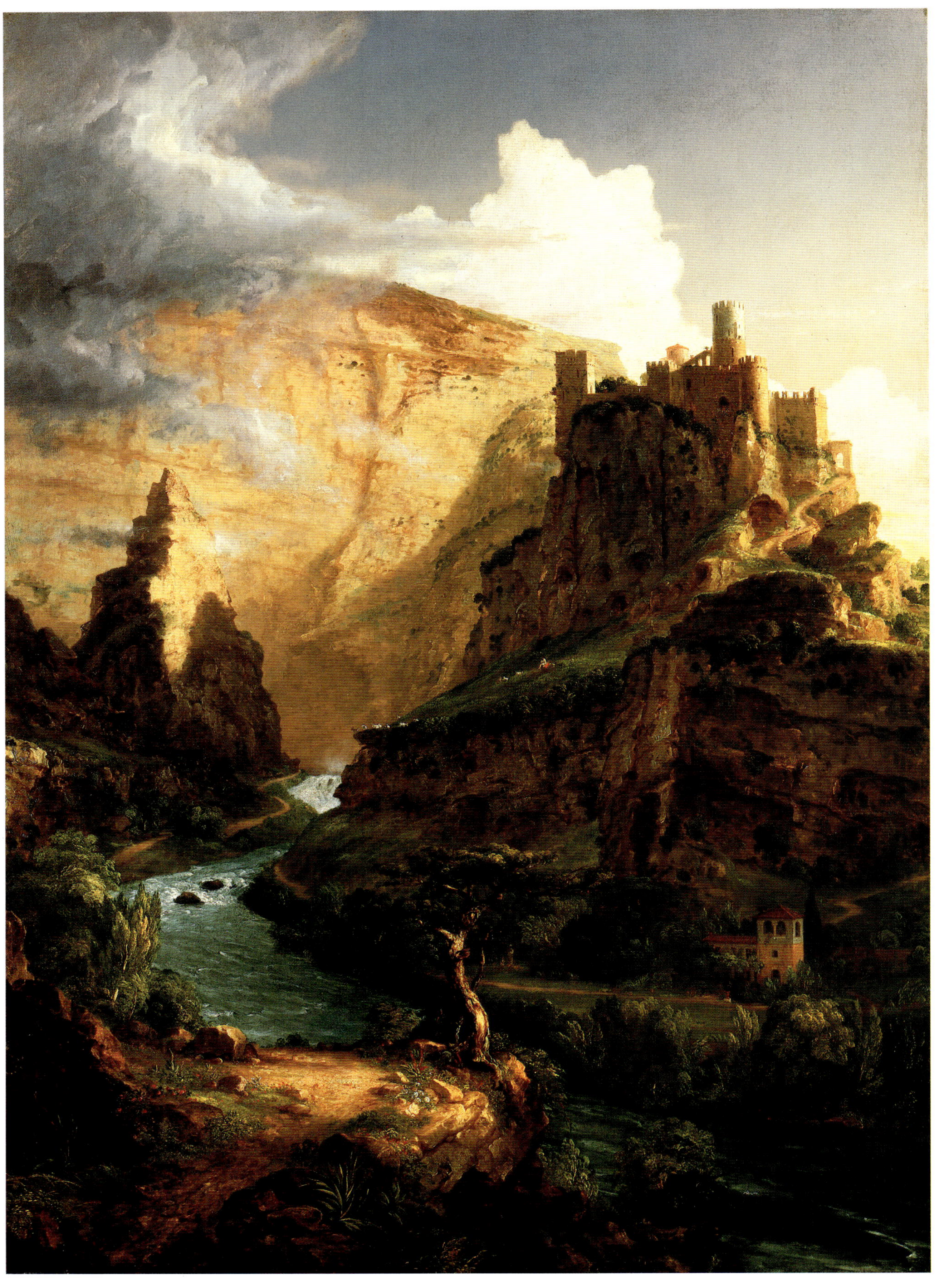

7. The Late Years

In August 1841 Cole sailed again for England, leaving his family in Catskill. Immediately upon arrival he visited the country, spending time at Kenilworth and Warwick castles and at Stratford. He was captivated both by the beauty of the countryside and the ruins, whose picturesque effects he described in great detail in his letters to his wife, which reveal something of his attitude toward these views and his own Romantic melancholy. "The ivy-clad towers, roofless halls, whose floors are covered with green turf and flowers, and cropped by flocks of sheep, and over which, through the dismantled windows and ragged loopholes, the sun casts his wandering rays, inspired me with a melancholy pleasure." (Noble, 225) His sketches from this tour formed the basis for later paintings of Kenilworth castle.

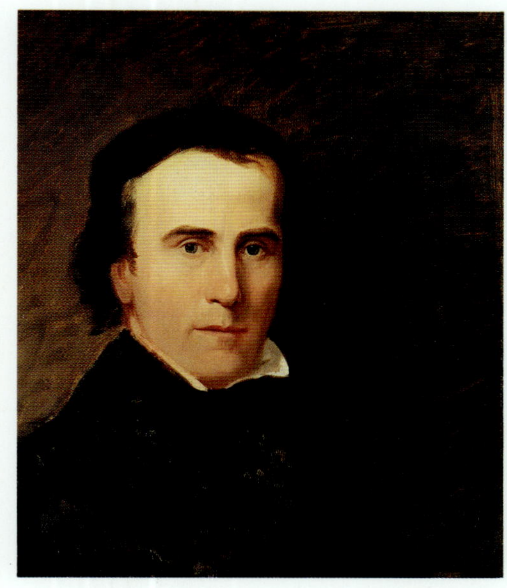

Self-Portrait

c. 1836. Oil on canvas, 22 x 18″
Courtesy The New-York Historical Society, New York City

Cole visited Paris in the fall, his spirits clearly buoyed by his change of scene and his ability to visit great princely collections of art. After visiting the Louvre he remarked, "I feel more an artist than I have done for years." (Noble, 226) He was enthusiastic about Correggio, Titian, and Claude, but he was captivated by Poussin, whom he considered uniquely great. The work of Claude and Poussin exerted a powerful influence on the artists of Cole's generation, both formally and spiritually. If John Martin's biblical landscapes represented the visual articulation of the sublime, Claude and Poussin represented the beautiful.

Leaving Paris, Cole visited the Alps and was moved by their size and majesty, describing his experience in rich prose.

> The snowy Alps, as they are seen afar off, are difficult to describe. They are too beautiful to be compared with anything of earth; they seem of an etherial tissue—like drapery composed of moon-beams, floating in the blue sky, and tossed by the breeze—silvery festoons suspended in the heavens. (Noble, 229)

It was here in the mountains that Cole's love of American nature seems to have reawakened, and he reasserted his feelings in a letter.

> You may fear, perhaps, that the wonderful scenery of Switzerland will destroy my feeling for our own: this will not be the case . . . Our scenery has its own peculiar charms, and . . . it will never lose its power. (Noble, 230)

OPPOSITE:
Valley of the Vaucluse

1841. Oil on canvas, 69 x 49⅛″
The Metropolitan Museum of Art, New York, Gift of William E. Dodge, 1903

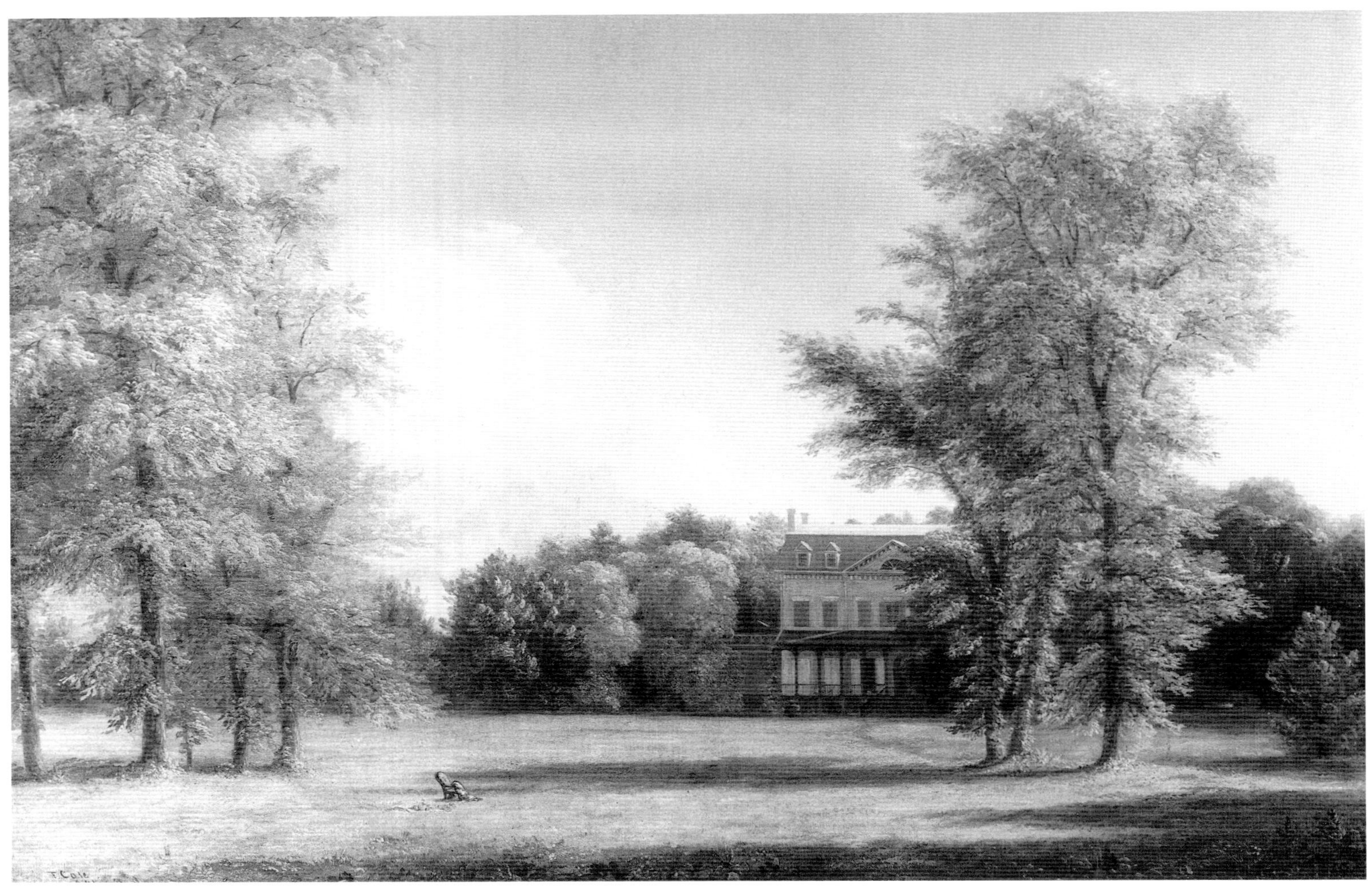

The Van Rensselaer Manor House

1841. Oil on canvas,
23½ x 35½"
Collection the Albany
Institute of History and Art,
Albany, New York,
Bequest of Katherine E. Turnbull

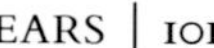

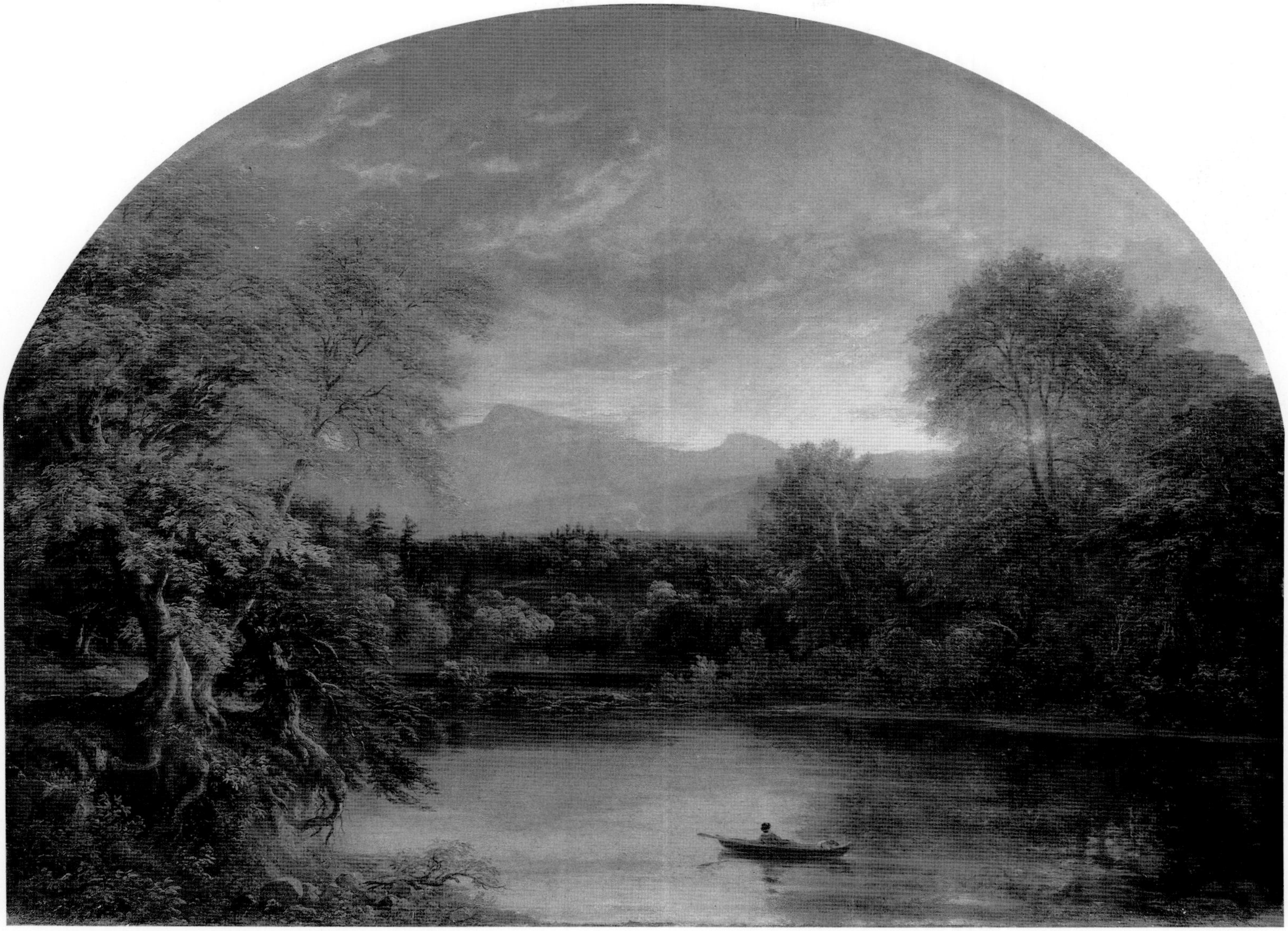

Sunset in the Catskills

1841. Oil on canvas,
22½ x 30″
Courtesy Museum of
Fine Arts, Boston,
Bequest of Mary Fuller Wilson

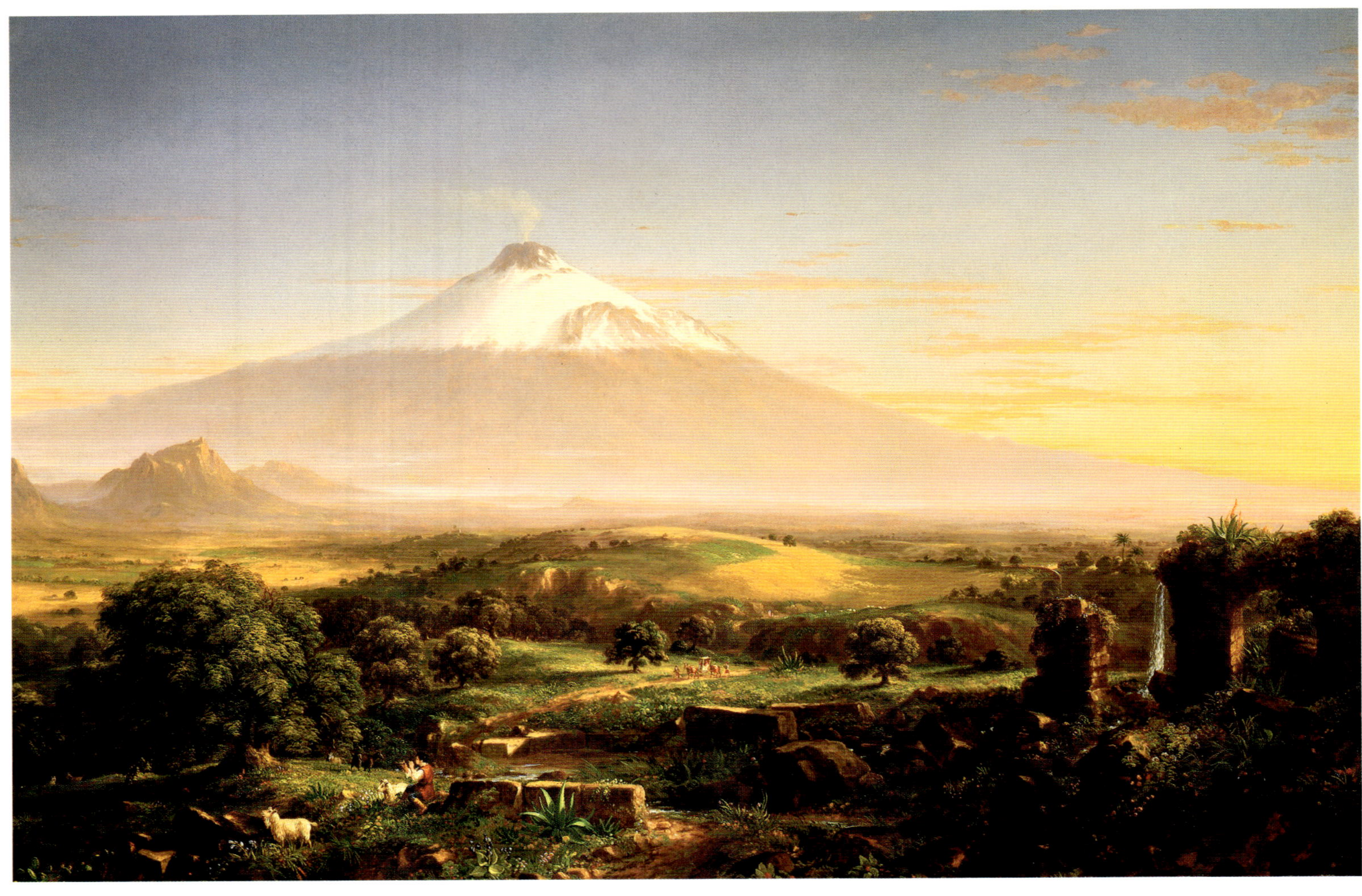

Mount Etna

1842. Oil on canvas,
32 x 48″
Collection IBM Corporation,
Armonk, New York

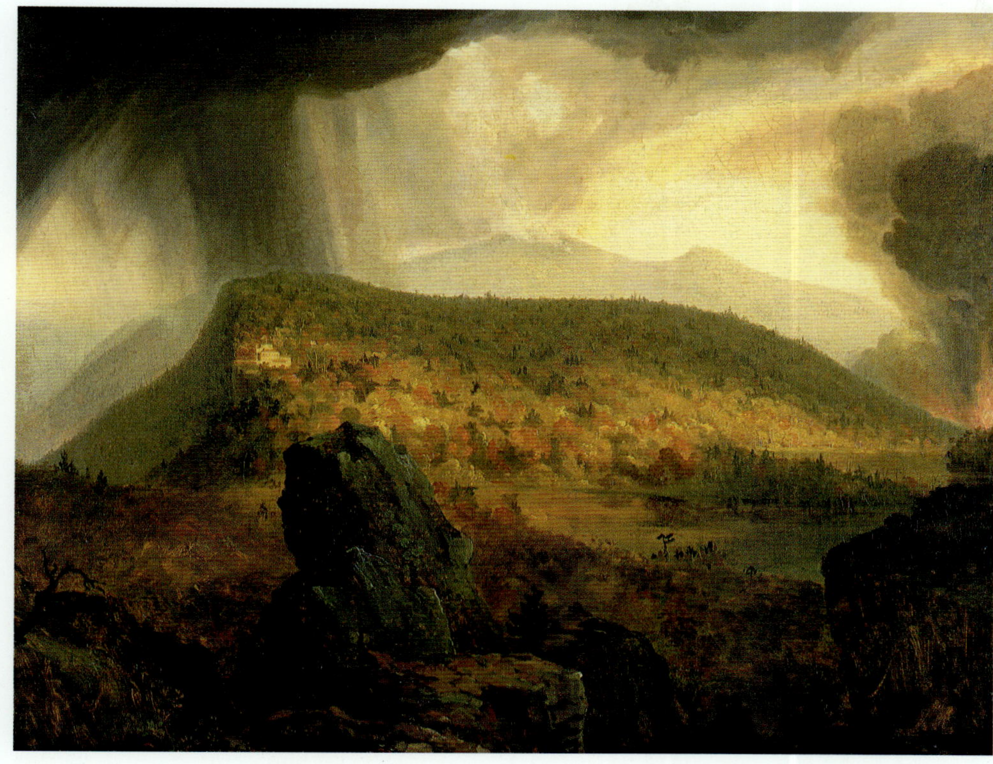

Catskill Mountain House

1843–44. Oil on canvas, 29 x 36″
Alexander Gallery, New York City

Cole later memorialized his experience of the Alps in a painting entitled *Valley of the Vaucluse,* which captures with scale and clarity the experience he described in viewing this impressive landscape.

Cole continued on to Rome, where he arrived in November and took a studio, working first upon his painting of Vaucluse. But his primary activity was the duplication of *The Voyage of Life,* which the American consul, Mr. Greene, and others strongly encouraged him to complete. By April Cole had finished the second series of *The Voyage of Life,* now at the National Gallery of Art, Washington. Cole appreciated the attention the works received in Rome, and particularly the flattering praise of Thorwaldson, the great sculptor, who visited his studio to view the pictures.

In April he went on a picturesque tour of the south and Sicily; the landscape and ruins took strong hold upon his imagination, and his experience ascending Mt. Etna to see the sunrise made a powerful impression on him. Cole, as always, sketched avidly, and his pictures of these scenes transcend the view, becoming eloquent and moving transcriptions of his experience of the landscape and the

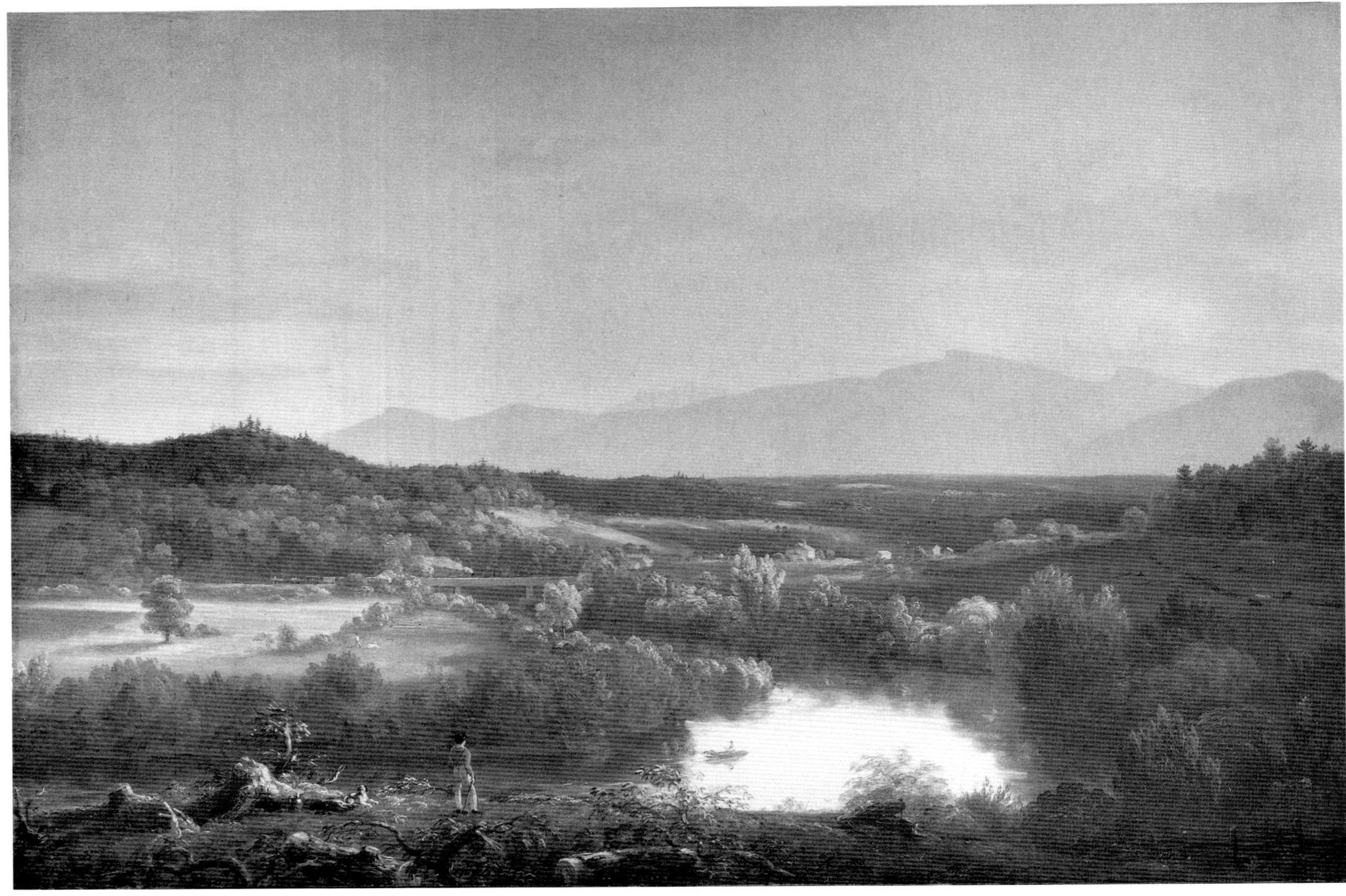

River in the Catskills

1843. Oil on canvas,
28¼ x 41¼″
Courtesy Museum of
Fine Arts, Boston,
Gift of Mrs. Maxim Karolik
for the Karolik Collection of
American Paintings, 1815–1865

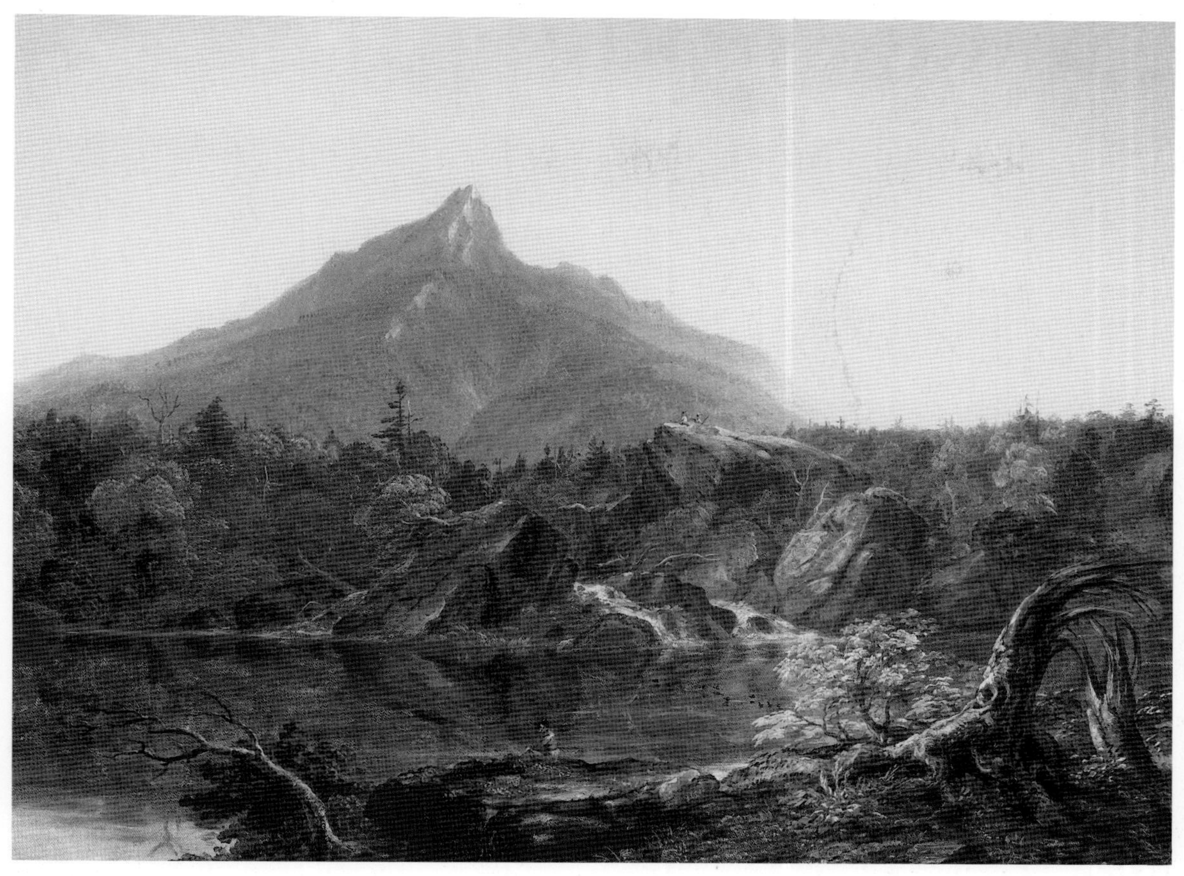

Corway Peak, New Hampshire

1844. Oil on canvas,
18 x 24″
Maier Museum of Art,
Randolph-Macon Woman's College,
Lynchburg, Virginia

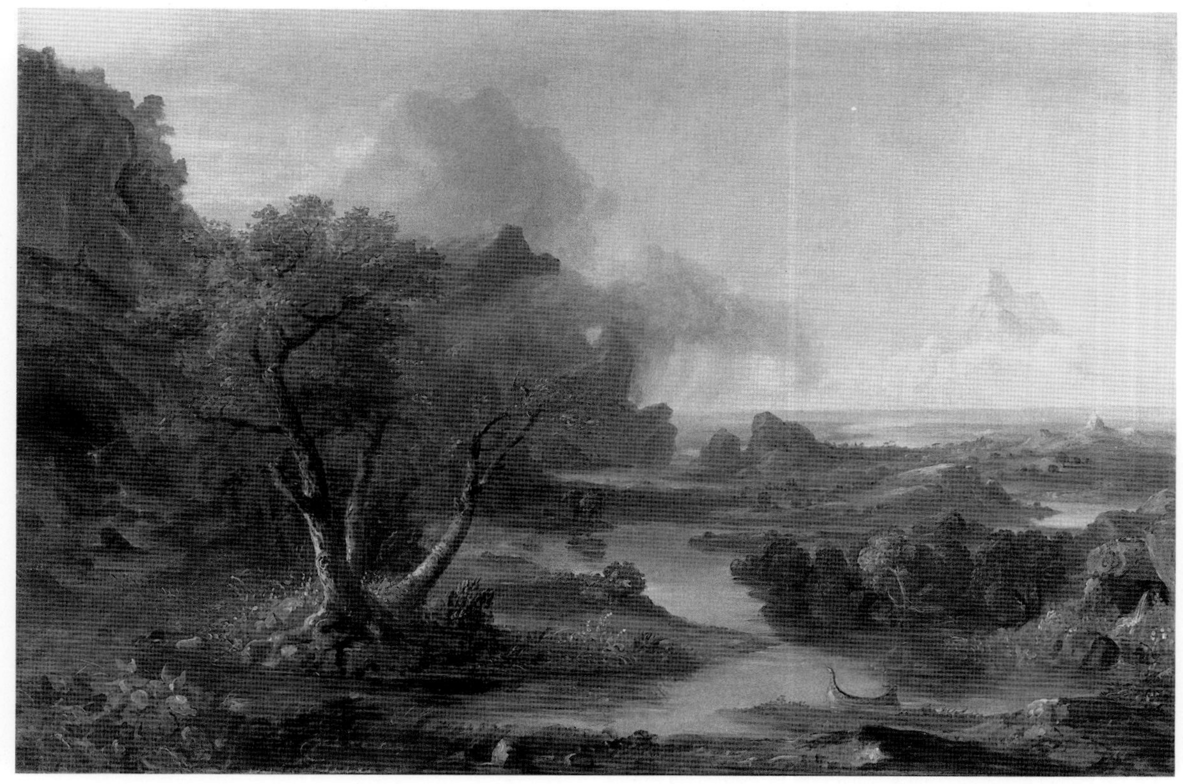

The Meeting of the Waters

c. 1847. Oil on canvas,
51 x 76″
Gift of Suzette Morton Davidson
to the Preston Morton Collection,
Santa Barbara Museum of Art,
Santa Barbara, California

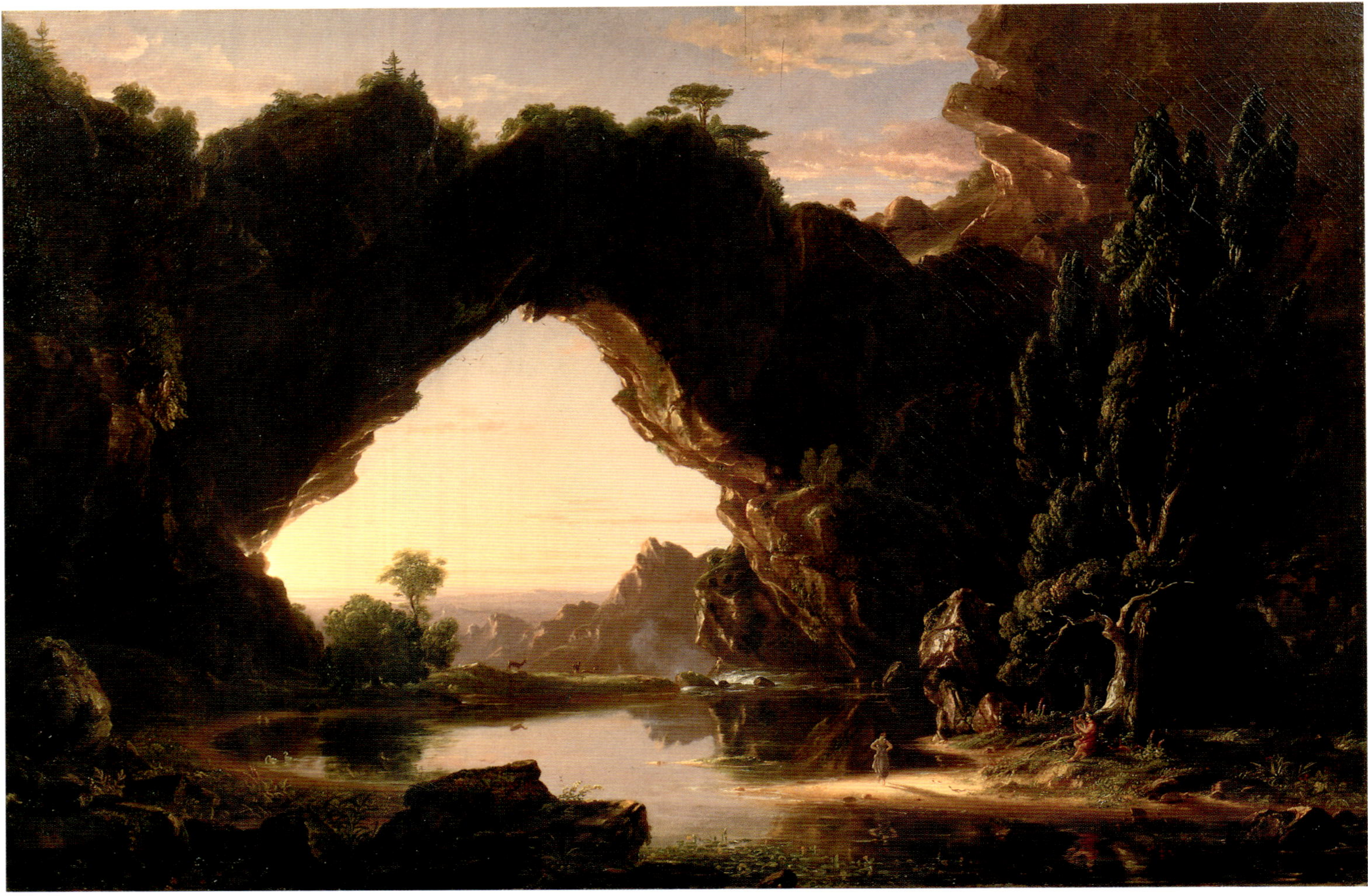

Evening in Arcady

1843. Oil on canvas,
32⅝ x 48⅜"
Wadsworth Atheneum,
Hartford, Connecticut,
Bequest of Mrs. Clara Hinton Gould

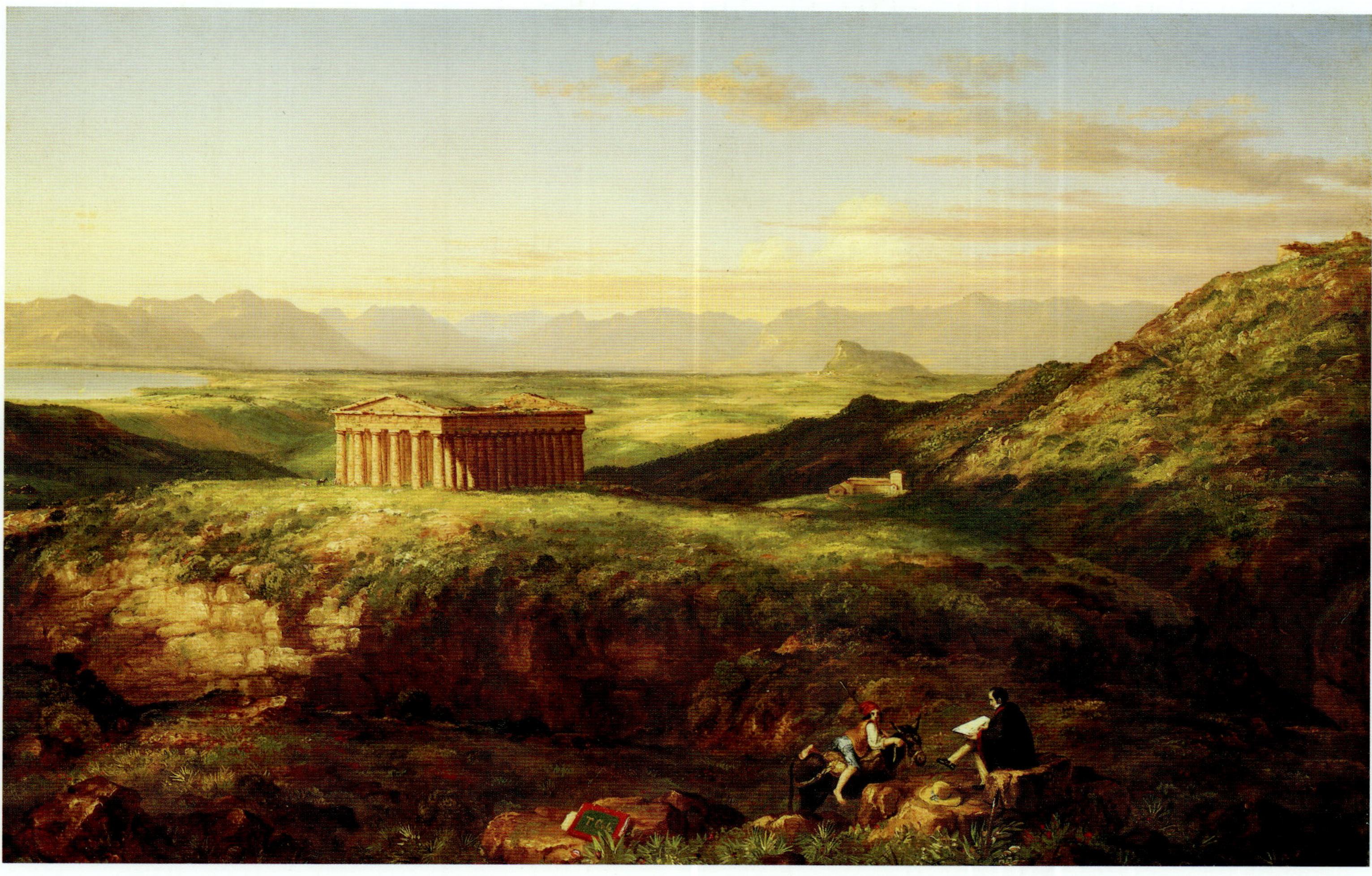

The Temple of Segesta with the Artist Sketching

c. 1843. Oil on canvas, 19½ x 30″
Courtesy Museum of Fine Arts, Boston, Gift of Mrs. Maxim Karolik for the Karolik Collection of American Paintings, 1815–1865

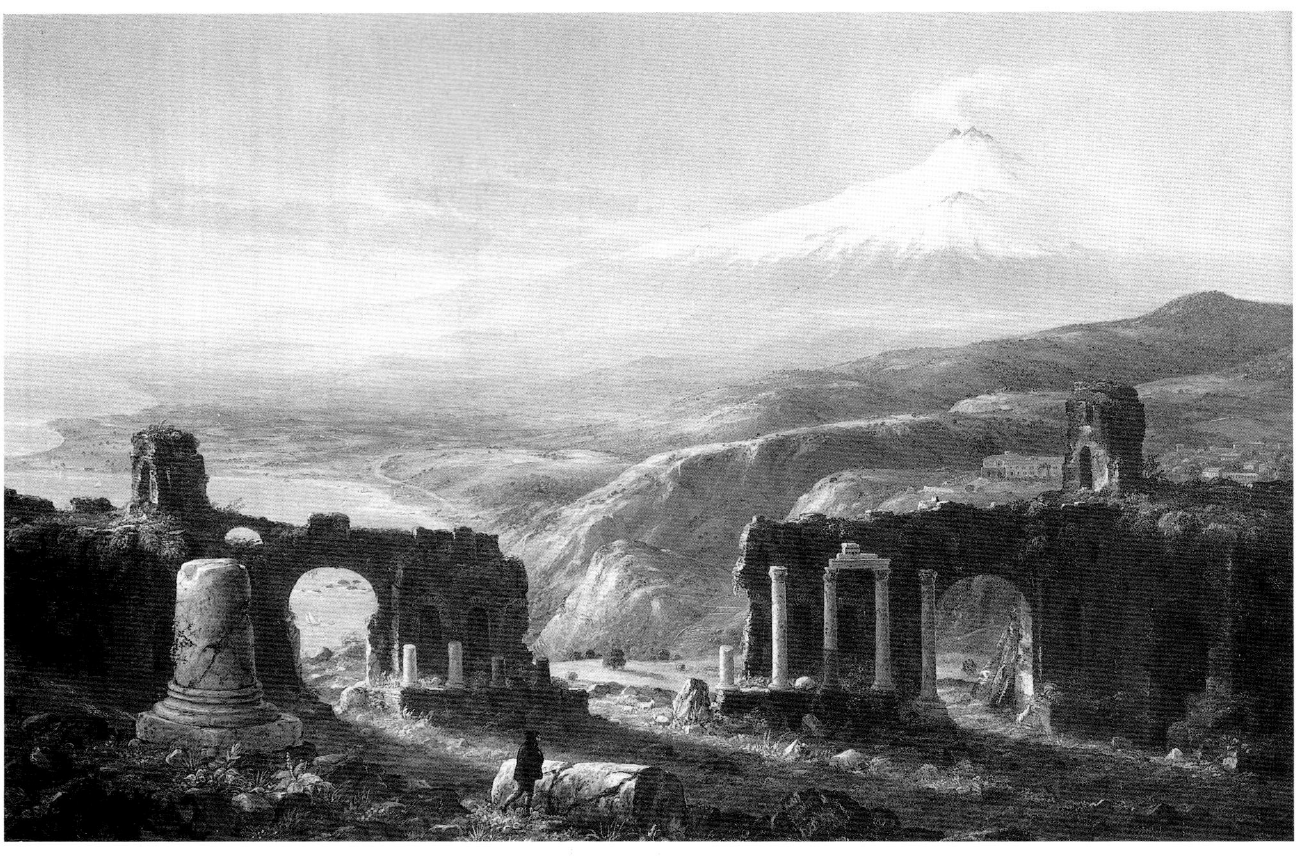

Prospect of Mount Etna
1844. Oil on canvas, 32½ x 48″
Lyman Allyn Art Museum, New London, Connecticut

light of Italy—his Italian landscapes resonate with color and mood. When he returned to America in the summer of 1842 he was able to view his beloved Adirondacks with renewed pleasure.

At this moment in his life Cole's mood began to become more introspective, and religious themes, always important to him, began to fascinate him more and more. In his mind and imagination nature and God literally became one. "Art, in its true sense, is, in fact, man's lowly imitation of the creative power of the Almighty." (Noble, 251) Cole had always believed that the landscape of America and its vast wilderness territory were reflections of the biblical Garden and that nature reflected the evidence of the Almighty. His interest in the late works tended to reflect these feelings even though he produced many Italian views, obviously for money and on commission, and more straightforward and conventional religious themes.

In 1842 he joined the Anglican church, received baptism, and attended com-

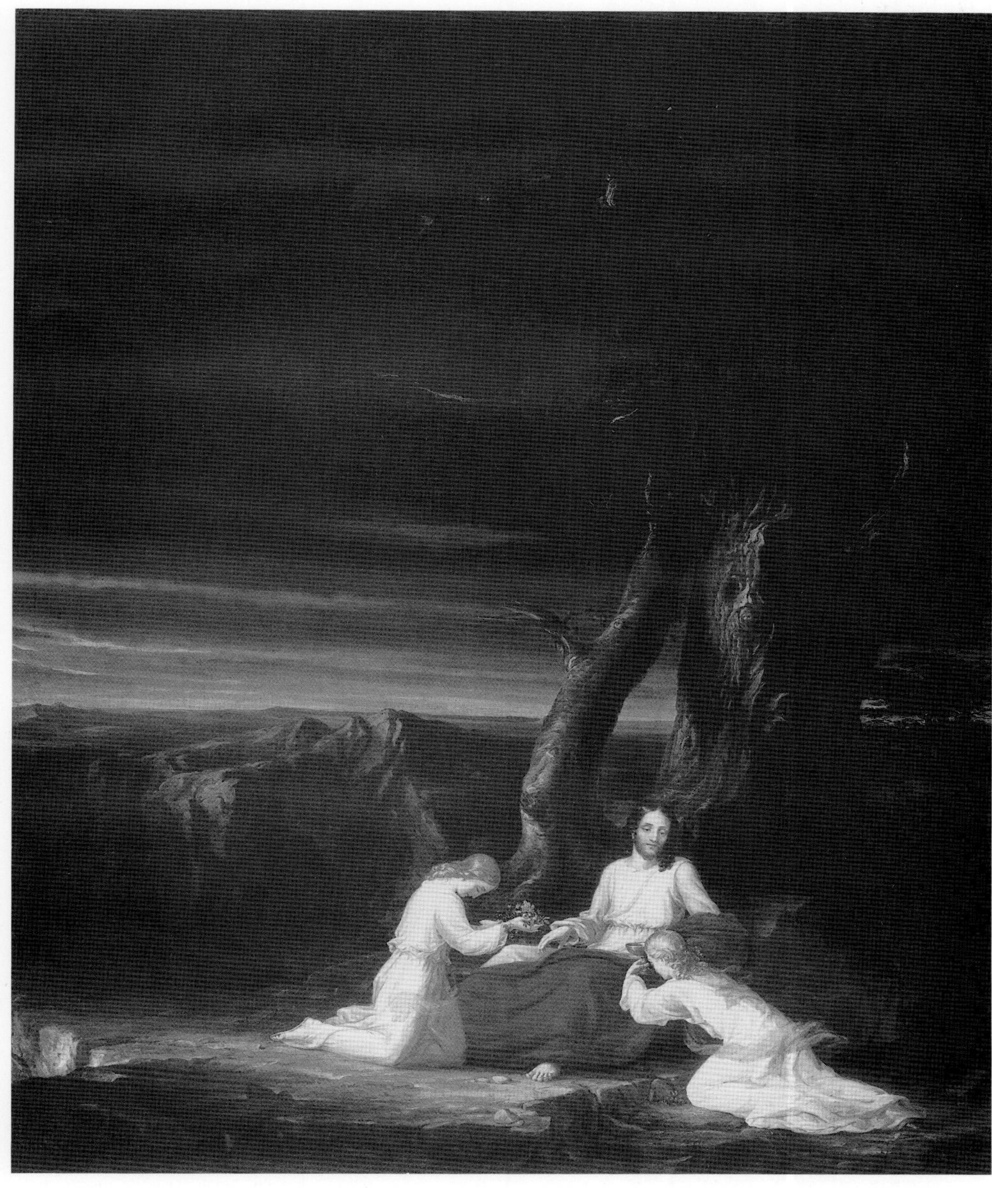

Angels Ministering to Christ in the Wilderness

1843. Oil on canvas, 72⅜ x 57⅜"
Worcester Art Museum, Worcester, Massachusetts

munion, influenced and assisted by his pastor and biographer, Louis Legrand Noble. Nature worship and its more subjective equivalent, Transcendentalism, had long been attacked by the orthodox religious establishment, and for Noble to have brought Cole, the most eloquent visual spokesman of his generation for the union of God with wild nature, was indeed a triumph for the church. This conversion might explain Cole's turn to more explicitly religious themes.

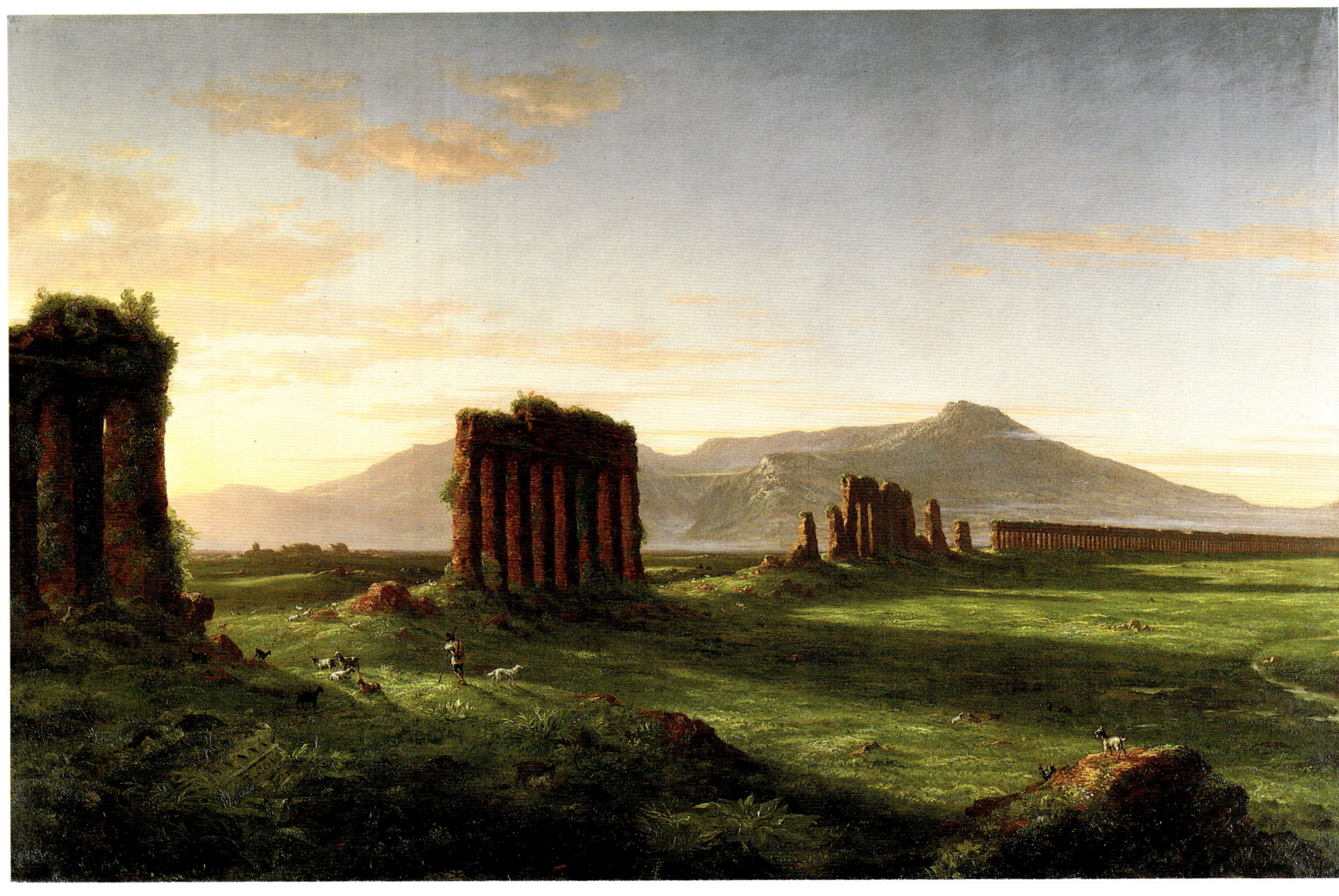

Roman Campagna

1843. Oil on canvas,
32½ x 48″
Wadsworth Atheneum,
Hartford, Connecticut,
Bequest of Mrs. Clara Hinton Gould

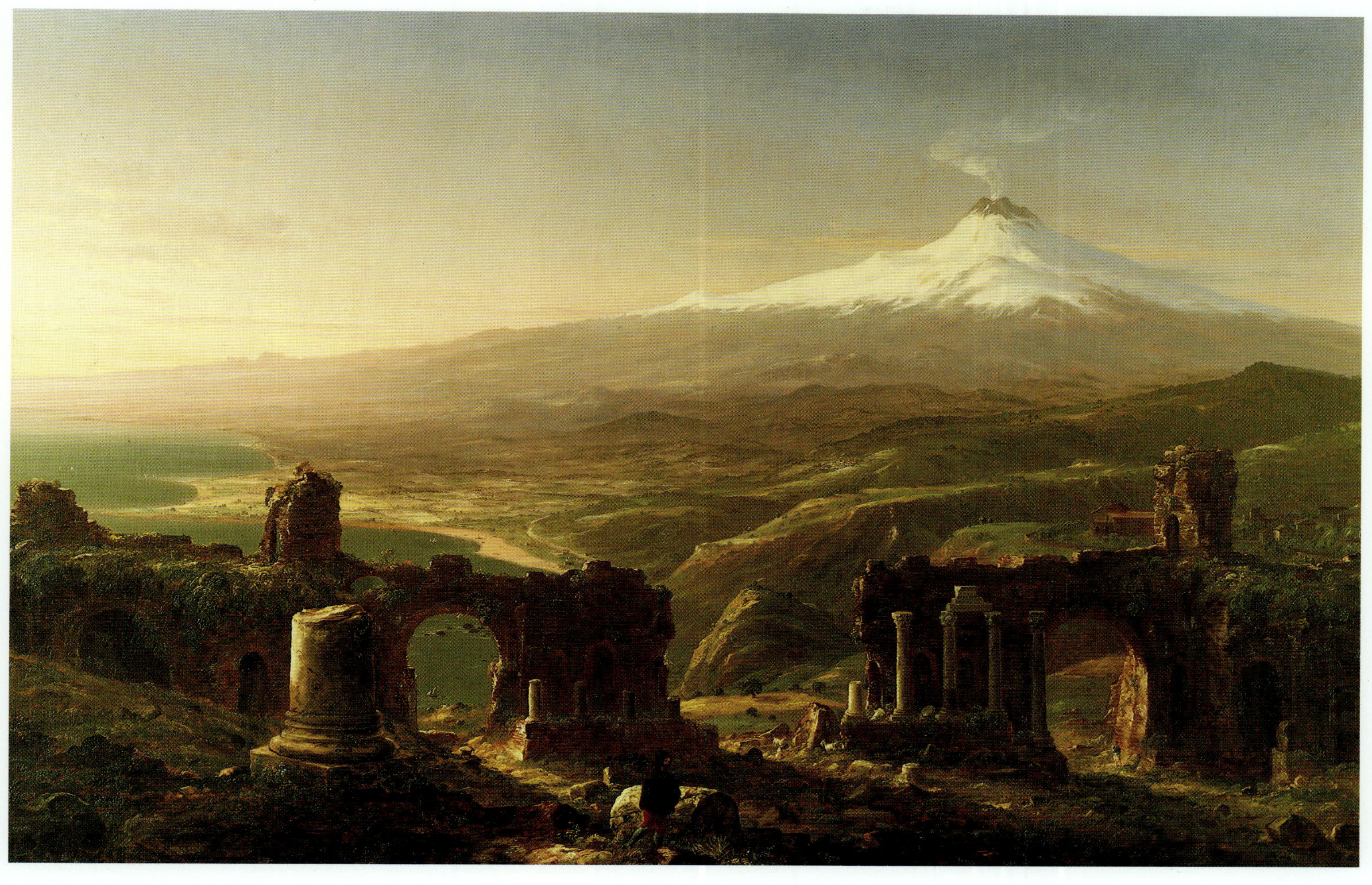

Mount Etna from Taormina

1843. Oil on canvas,
$78\frac{5}{8}$ x $120\frac{5}{8}$″
Wadsworth Atheneum,
Hartford

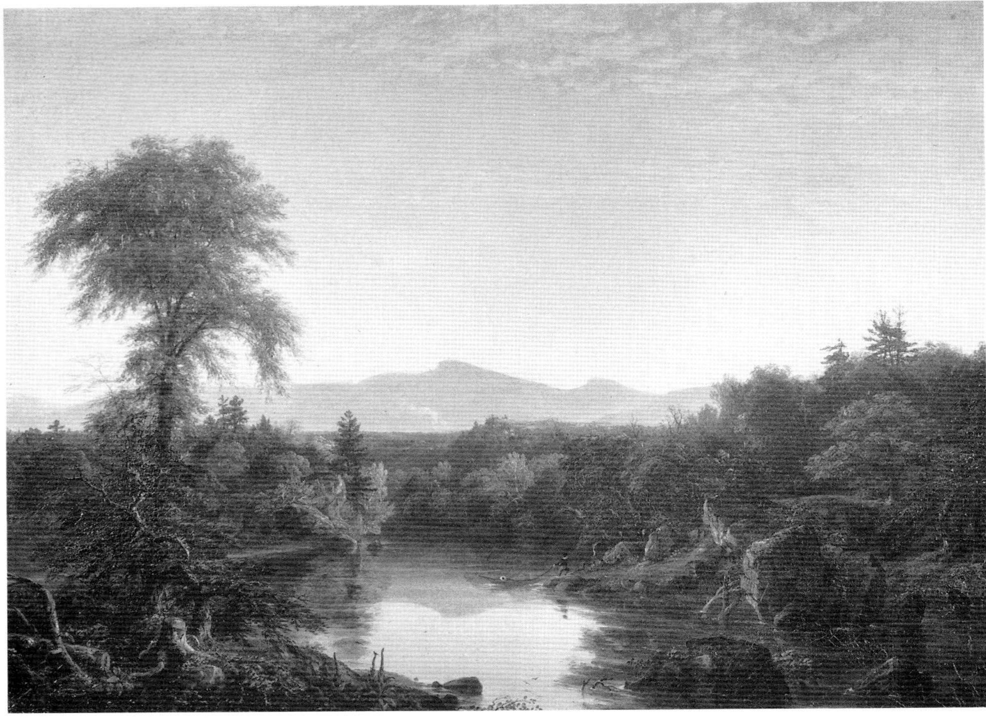

Catskill Creek

1845. Oil on canvas, 26½ x 36″
Courtesy The New-York Historical Society, New York City

He exhibited *Mount Etna from Taormina,* one of four versions painted, at the Academy in 1842, and he lectured on the subject of Sicilian scenery and antiquities at the Lyceum. In his letters and writings he began to speculate about old age and the hereafter.

His painting of this time focused almost exclusively on views drawn from his recent trip. He painted *Roman Campagna, Mount Etna, Kenilworth Castle*, and others, but religious painting was foremost on his mind. He was preoccupied with painting *Angels Ministering to Christ in the Wilderness*, a sacred picture that, as Cole described it, he had "painted . . . in a serious spirit, and I hope its effect will be religious." (Noble, 261) The dark and barren landscape was of a kind favored by the artist for religious compositions and looked back to the kind of landscape favored by John Martin in his illustrations for *Paradise Lost*. Cole afterward cut down the size of the picture to reduce the emphasis of the landscape in favor of the figural composition.

The Italian landscape figured prominently in his commissions now, and in 1843 he painted another large canvas titled *Mount Etna from Taormina,* a luminous picture that shows Cole's preferred view from a high vantage point looking

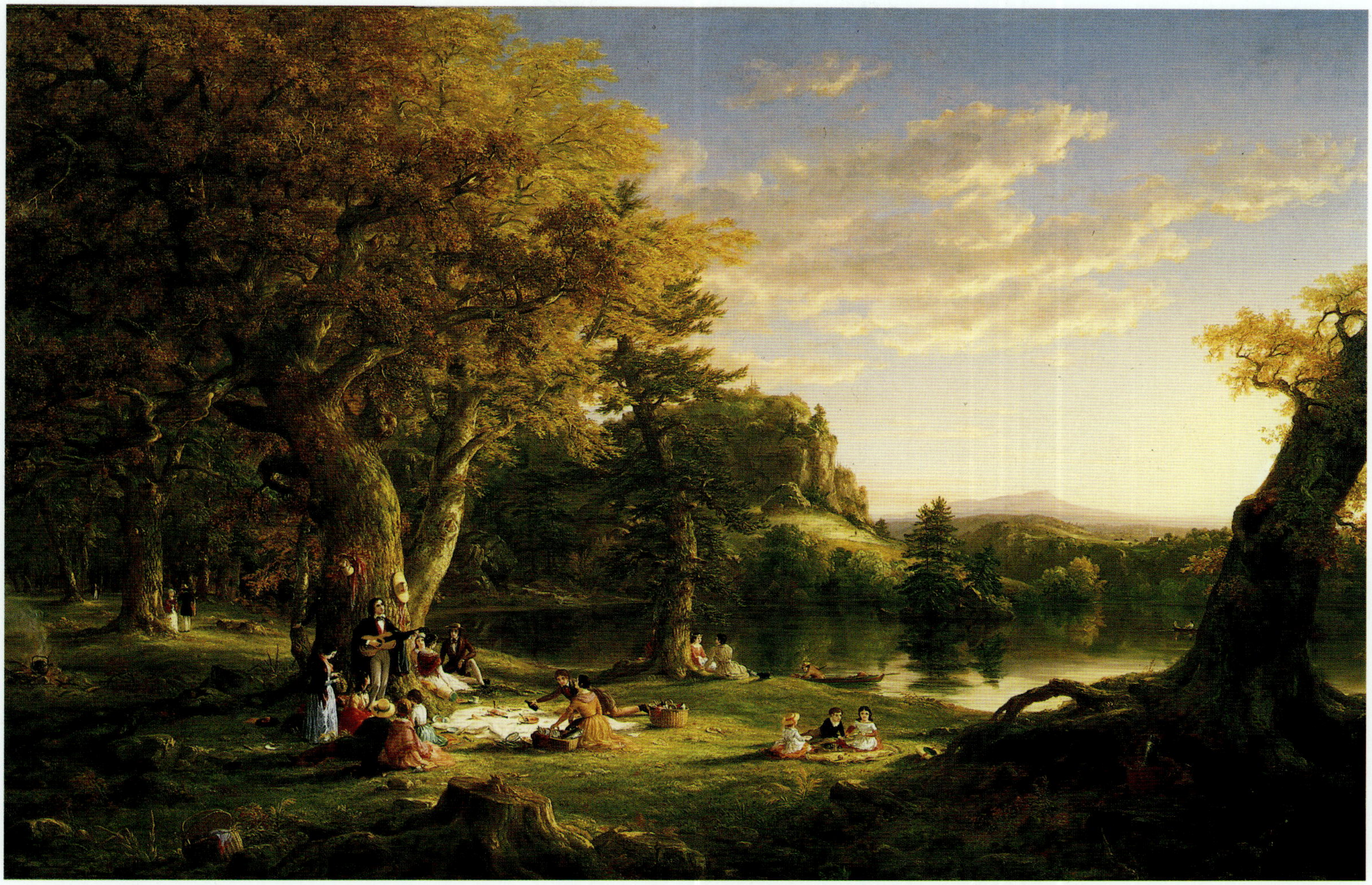

The Pic-Nic

1846. Oil on canvas,
$44\frac{7}{8}$ x $71\frac{7}{8}$"
The Brooklyn Museum.
A. Augustus Healy Fund

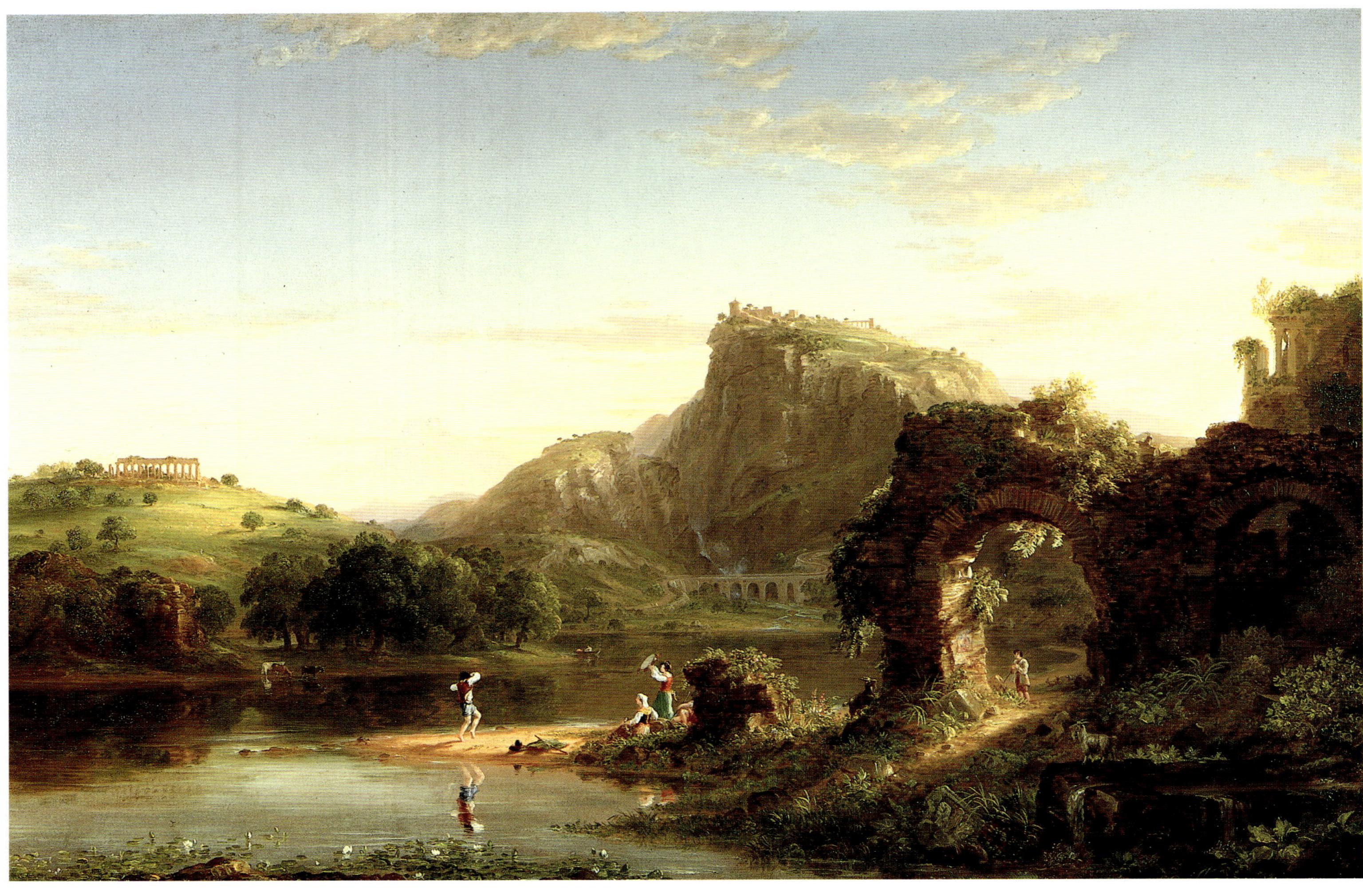

L'Allegro

1845. Oil on canvas,
21 1/16 x 48"
The Los Angeles County
Museum of Art,
Gift of the Art Museum Council and
the Michael J. Connell Foundation

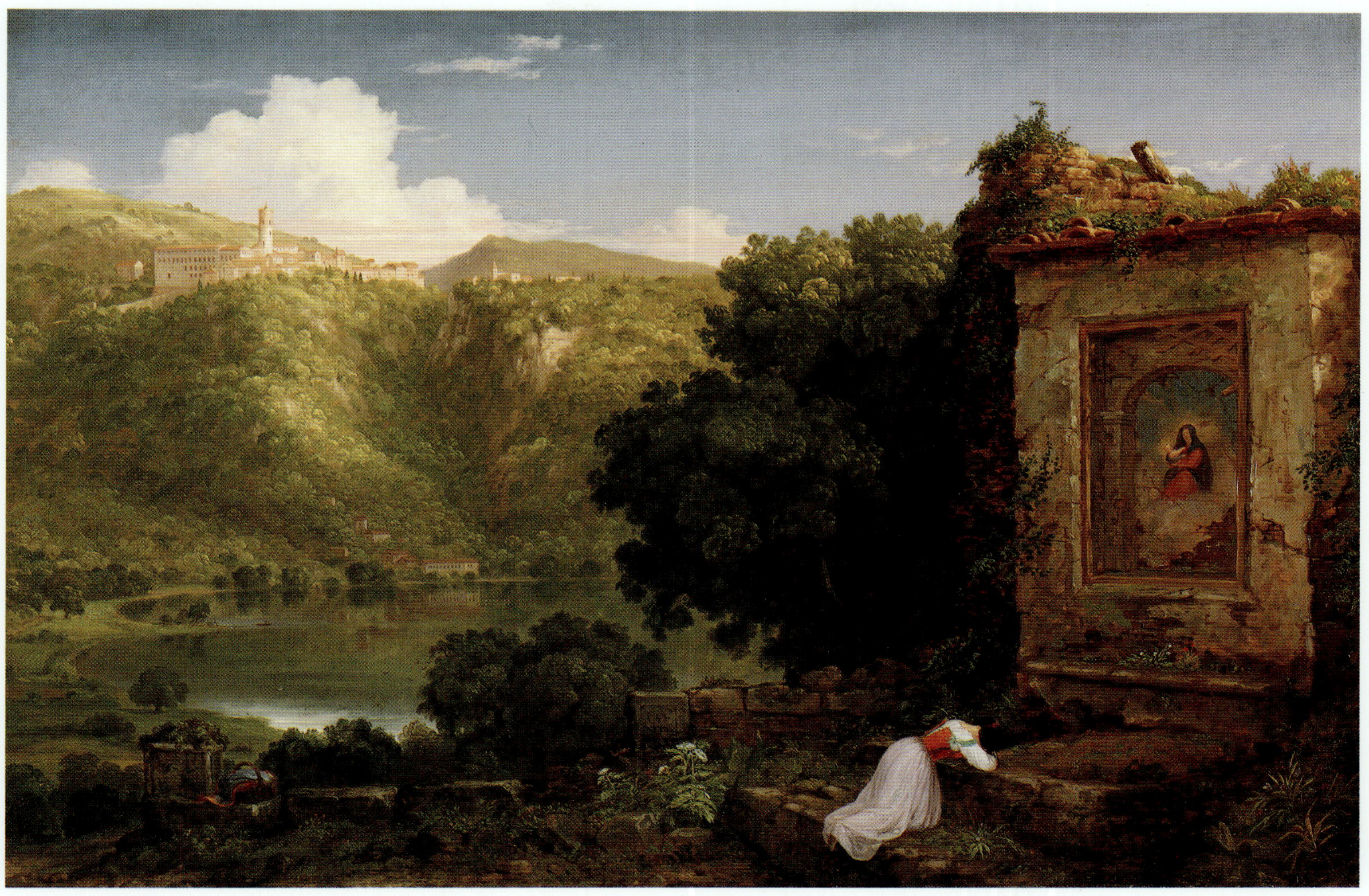

Il Penseroso

1845. Oil on canvas,
32¼ x 48″
The Los Angeles County
Museum of Art,
Trustees Fund, Corporate Donors
and General Acquisition Fund

down into space to emphasize the landscape. In 1845 he turned his attention to a pair of pictures after Milton's similarly titled companion poems, *L'Allegro* and *Il Penseroso*. Cole had long been interested in this subject, which made its way onto the list of paintings earlier in his career. The two pictures were commissioned by Charles M. Parker, whom Cole had met in Rome, and Cole was permitted to select the subject. The pictures have only recently been reunited; they are beautifully wrought masterpieces of Cole's later years, when thin, luminous veils of light emanated from his canvases, and they reflect the mood of Milton's poems.

> Some time walking not unseen
> By Hedgerow Elms, on Hillocks green,
> Right against the Eastern gate,
> Where the great Sun begins his state,
> Rob'd in flames, and Amber light,
> The clouds in thousand Liveries dight;
> While the Plowman near at hand,
> Whistles o'er the Furrow'd Land,
> And the Milkmaid singeth blithe,
> And the Mower whets his scythe,. . .
> L'Allegro (ll. 57–66)
> But, O sad Virgin, that thy power
> Might raise *Musaeus* from his bower,
> Or bid the soul of *Orpheus* sing
> Such notes as, warbled to the string,
> Drew Iron tears down *Pluto's* cheek,
> And made Hell grant what Love did seek.
> Il Penseroso (11. 103–108)

He wanted to paint another large panoramic cycle now and described an idea of painting "Sowing and Reaping" in correspondence with Daniel Wadsworth, but apparently he never began work on this proposal. He did paint *The Old Mill at Sunset* at this time, a lovely, poetic canvas that Noble described as a "rich and tender melody. If the expression may be allowed, it is a picture song." (Noble, 268) In the 1840s sunset imagery began to become popular, and his use of this theme could be interpreted as a metaphorical reference to the dwindling of the American frontier and the recession of wild nature. This is a thoroughly

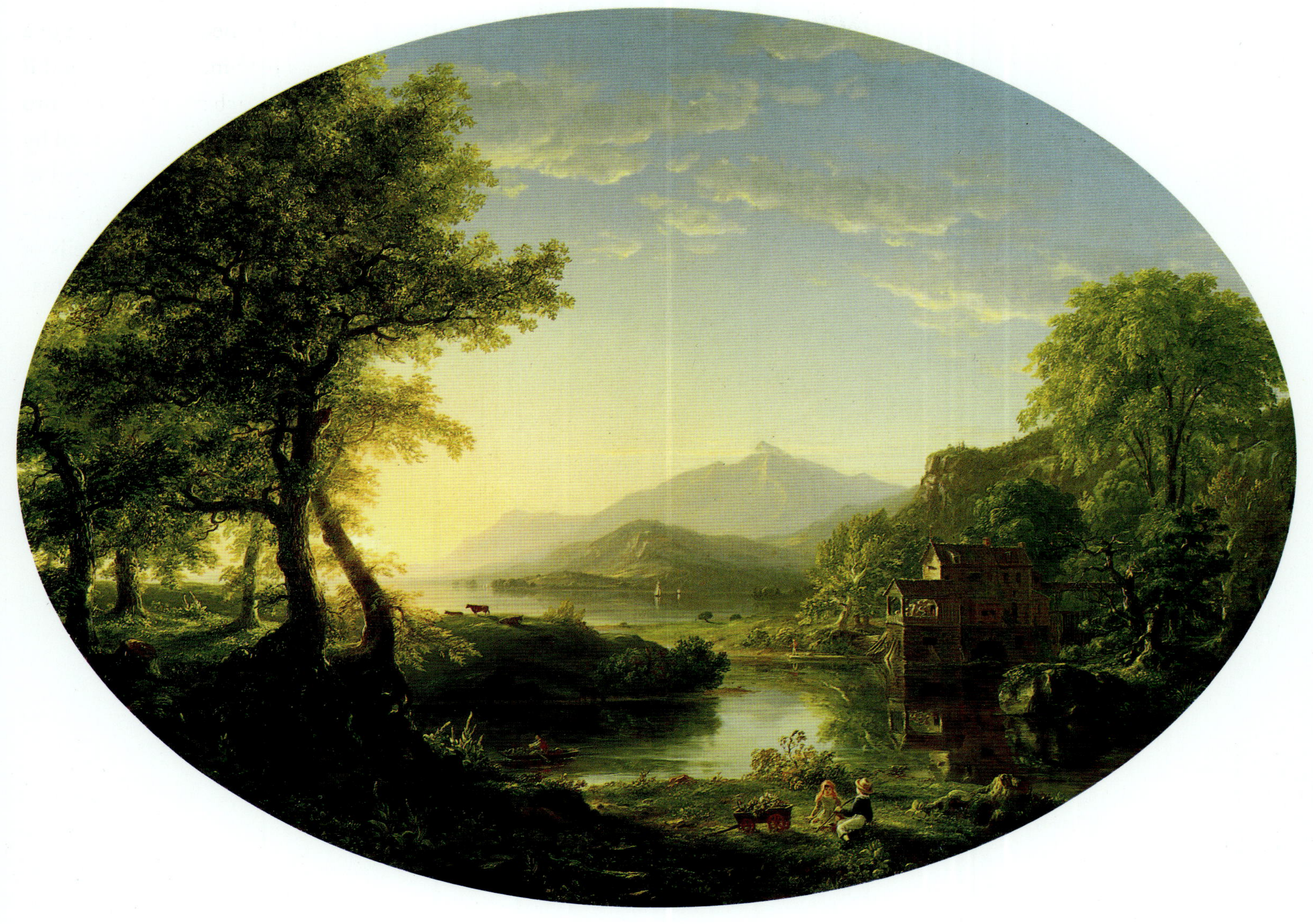

The Old Mill at Sunset

1845. Oil on canvas,
26⅛ x 36″
Alexander Gallery, New York

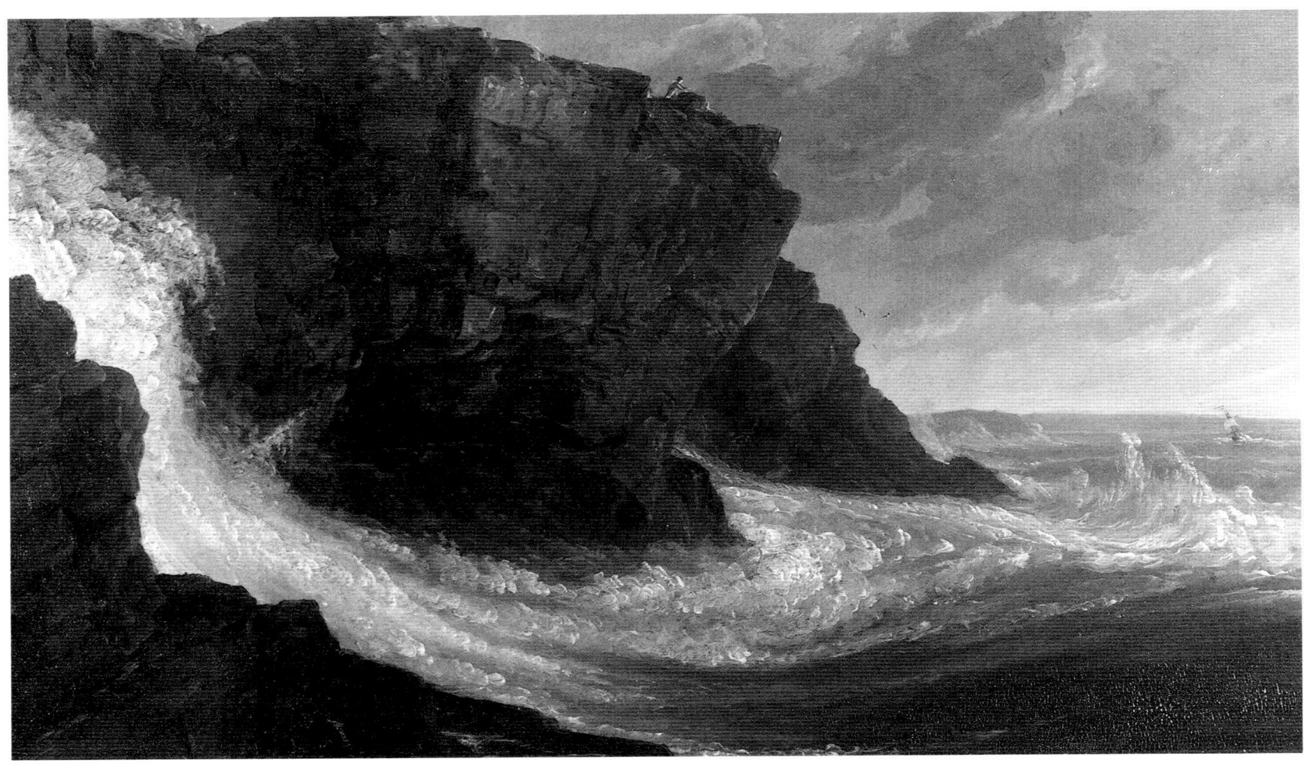

Frenchman's Bay, Mount Desert Island, Maine

1845. Oil on wood panel, 14 x 23″
Collection the Albany Institute of History and Art, Albany, New York

domesticated theme of a kind he found interesting and to which he would return in *The Pic-Nic*. This picture, completed in 1846, shows the complete domination of man over the landscape. This kind of scene would become more and more popular as the century progressed and affirms the domestication of nature, which was fast becoming only a backdrop for a Sunday afternoon social gathering.

In 1844 Cole visited Maine and painted on Mount Desert Island. He was impressed with the sublimity of the sea and the majesty of the landscape. *Frenchman's Bay* reflects his response to the rugged coast, which he described in his letters: "The whole coast along here is iron-bound—threatening crags, and dark caverns in which the sea thunders. The view of Frenchman's bay and islands is truly fine." (Noble, 270)

His experience of Maine might have stimulated a renewed interest in purely American scenes, and he now executed several of his finest landscapes, among them *Mountain Ford,* a painting that attempts to evoke the concept of the sublime

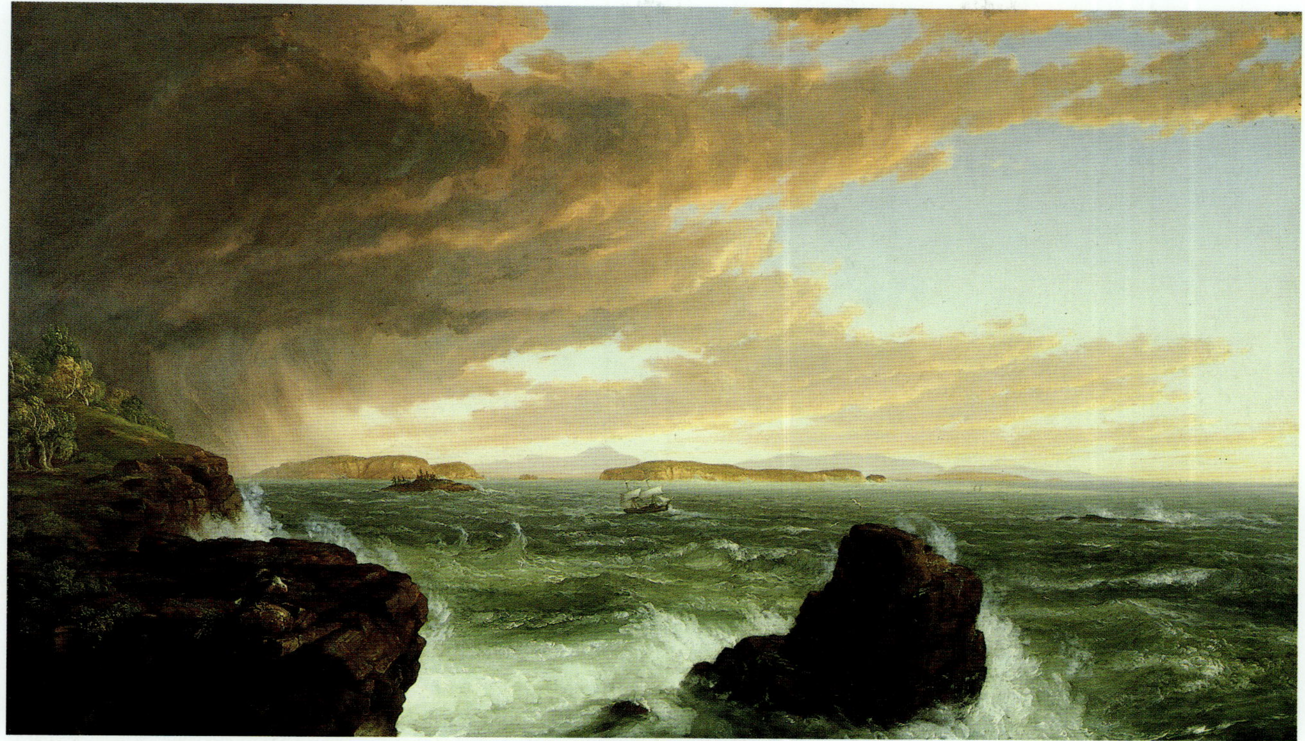

View Across Frenchman's Bay from Mount Desert Island, After a Squall

1845. Oil on canvas, 38½ x 62″
Cincinnati Art Museum, Cincinnati, Ohio, Gift of Alice Scarborough

as the horse rears back in anticipation and fear of danger in the wild landscape beyond. *Home in the Woods* and *The Hunter's Return* are also compositions on an American theme produced at this time, and they reveal the change in Cole's attitude toward nature and, perhaps, the change in the real circumstances of America as civilization overtook "wild nature." In these pictures, awe has disappeared, and man is at ease in nature and is depicted as having domesticated her. But Cole's mind was set on painting an elevated religious theme. Finally in 1846 he began work on what was to be a great religious series on the subject of "the Cross and the World." It was not a commission but a theme he wished to paint personally, tired as he was of painting to avoid "pecuniary difficulties." His writings of this period are filled with religious vocabulary and melancholy, although he continued to find pleasure and solace in his trips into the wilderness. In early 1847 he noted that he had just about completed *The Pilgrim of the Cross* and had commenced work on the second picture, *The Pilgrim of the World*. This series was never to be finished, however, as Cole became ill and died soon thereafter.

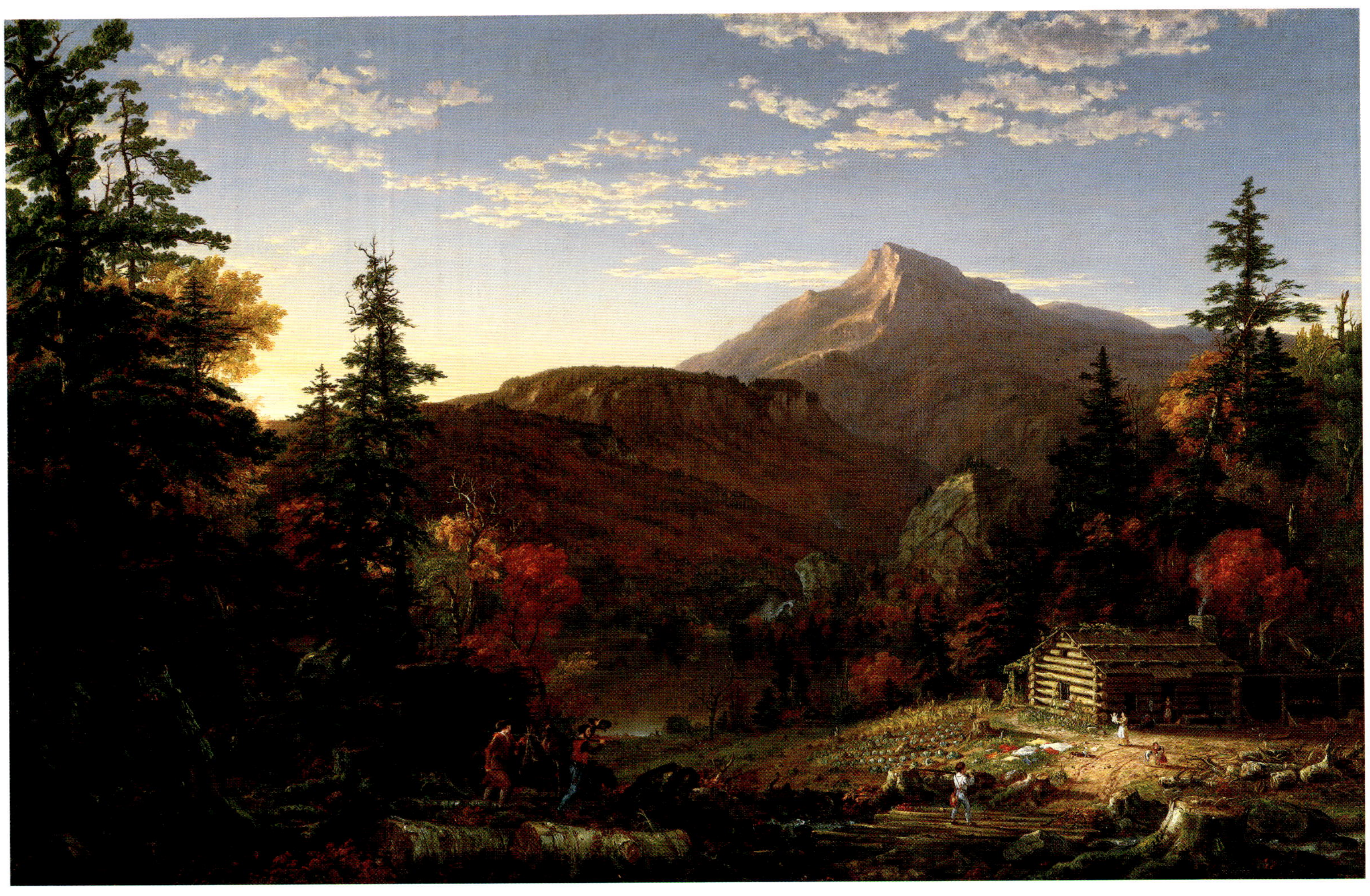

The Hunter's Return

1845. Oil on canvas,
$40\frac{1}{8}$ x $60\frac{1}{2}$″
Amon Carter Museum,
Fort Worth

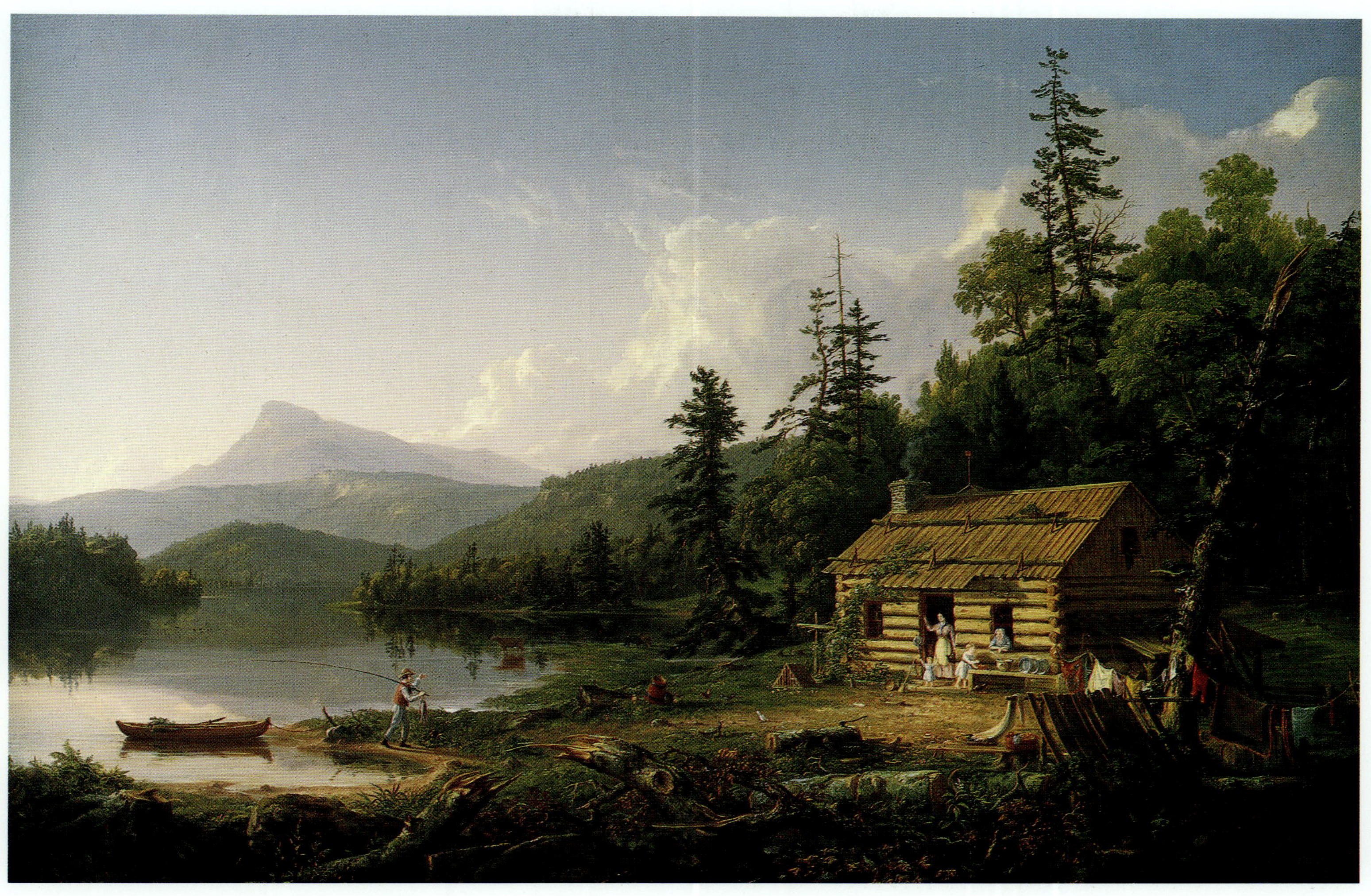

Home in the Woods

1847. Oil on canvas,
44 x 66″
Reynolda House,
Museum of American Art,
Winston-Salem, North Carolina

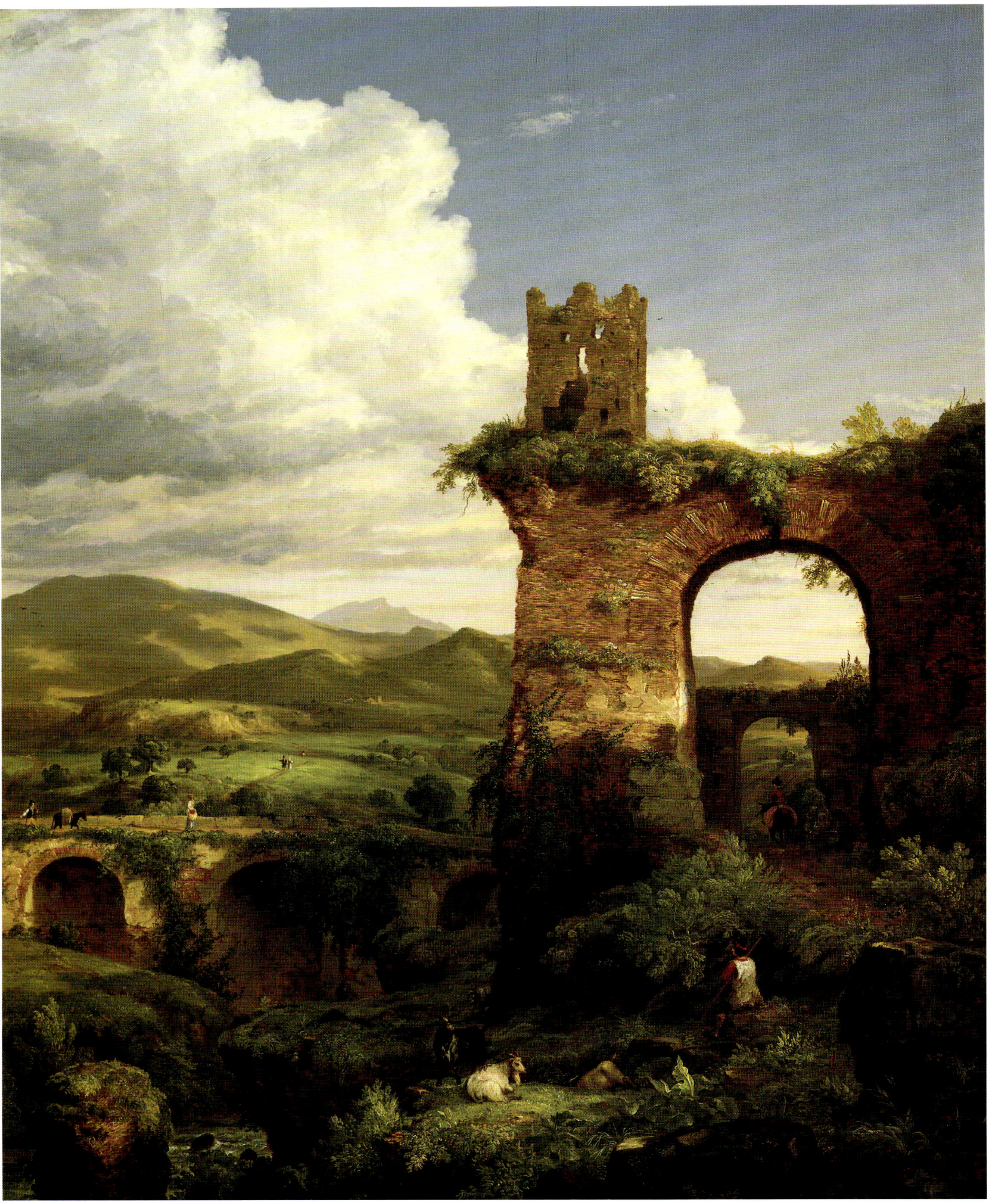

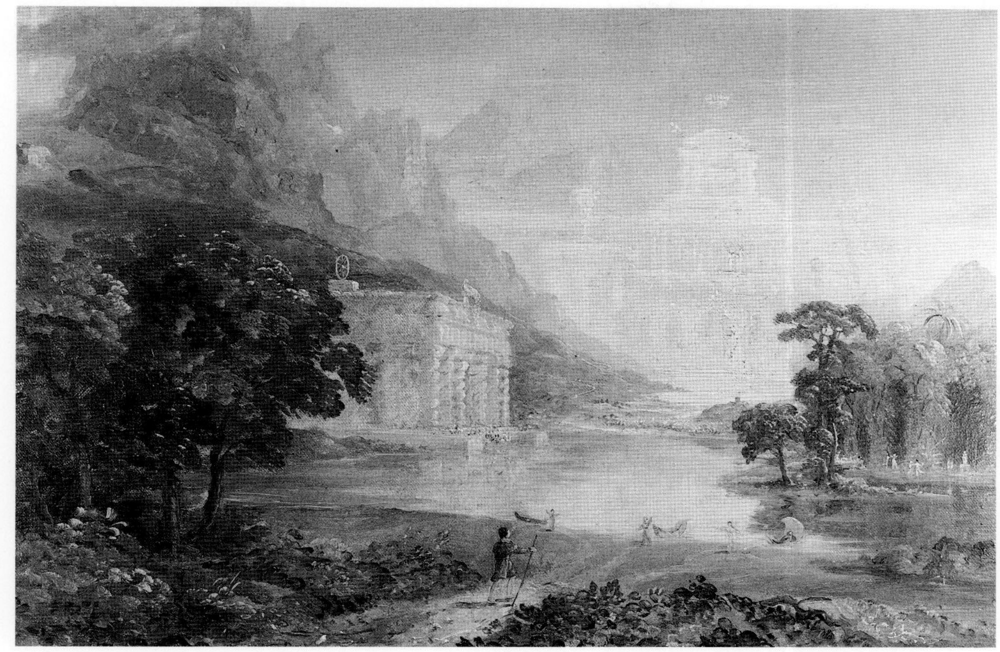

Study for
The Cross and the World:
The Pilgrim of the World on His Journey

c. 1846–47. Oil on canvas,
12 x 18″
Collection the Albany
Institute of History and Art,
Albany, New York

By mid-century Thomas Cole had achieved a position as the foremost American landscape painter, and his work embodied the Romantic imagination of his period. Cole in many ways defined the Romantic era, and in his heroic ambition he identified closely with the new country he adopted in youth and embraced in his art. While his work derived from the English landscape tradition and owed a debt to John Martin, J. M. W. Turner, and Richard Wilson, Cole's primary formal influences were Claude, Poussin, and the tradition of pastoral landscape their work represented. Salvator Rosa was an important source for the more forceful and energetic brushwork that appeared in the tradition of the picturesque. But the English Romantic poets Wordsworth and Byron were equally important to the development of a landscape tradition in America, and they were central to the development of Cole's attitude toward the landscape, as was Milton.

Cole assimilated the theories of the sublime and the beautiful, Alison's theory of associationism and in the creative ferment of his imagination gave new definition to the picturesque; in his art he celebrated the natural landscape as had no other artist of his day. He gave identity to America by elevating its landscape to the level of history painting, and indeed, he created a new and prophetic

OPPOSITE:
Arch of Nero

1846. Oil on canvas,
60 x 48″
Collection the Newark Museum
Newark, New Jersey,
Purchase 1957,
Sophronia Anderson Bequest Fund

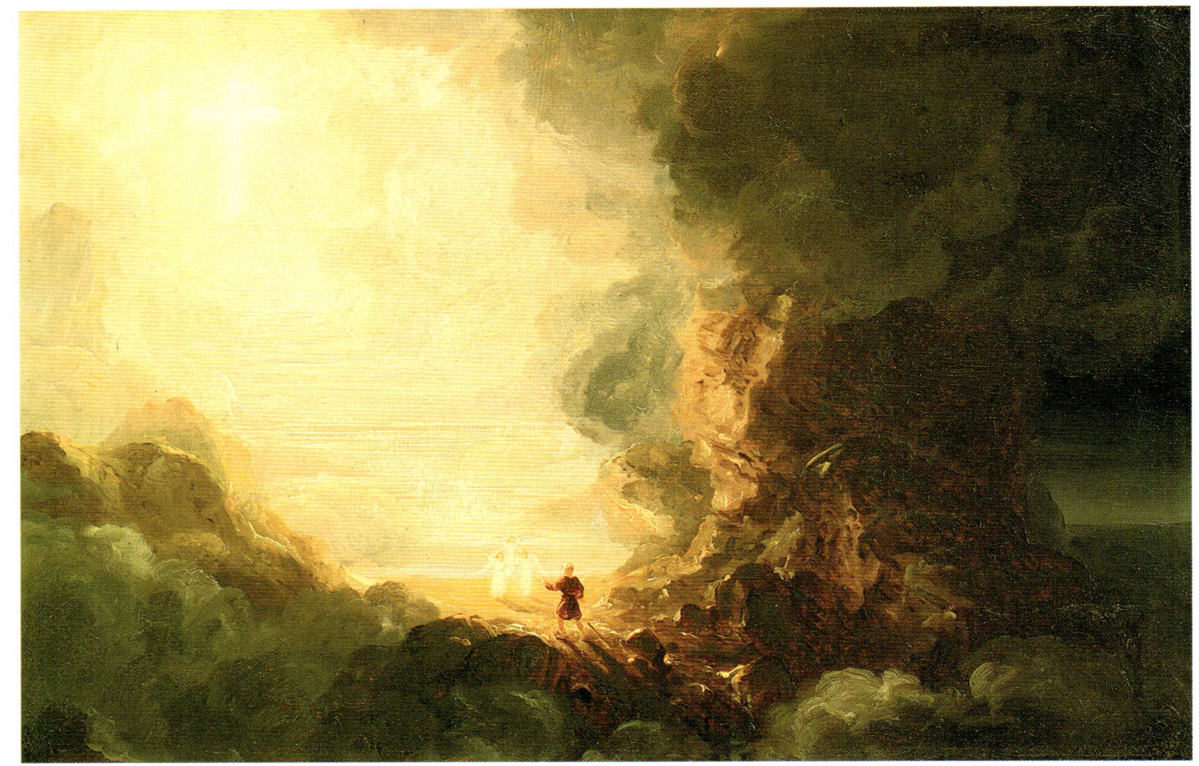

Study for
The Cross and the World: The Pilgrim of the Cross at the End of His Journey

c. 1846–48. Oil on canvas, 12 x 18″
National Museum of American Art, Smithsonian Institution, Washington, D.C., Museum Purchase

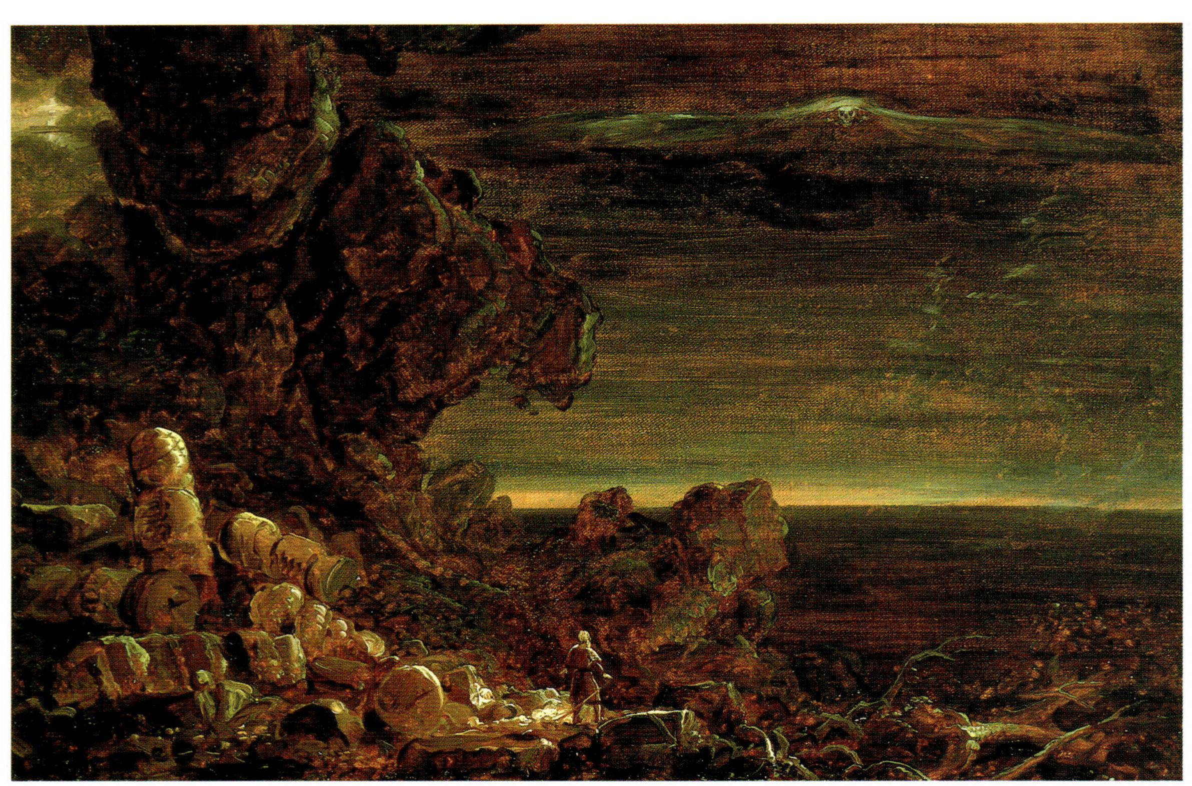

The Pilgrim of the World at the End of His Journey

c. 1846–48. Oil on canvas, 12 x 18″
National Museum of American Art, Smithsonian Institution, Washington, D.C., Museum Purchase

Unfinished Landscape (The Cross at Sunset)

c. 1847. Oil on canvas,
32 x 48½″
Thyssen-Bornemisza Collection,
Lugano, Switzerland

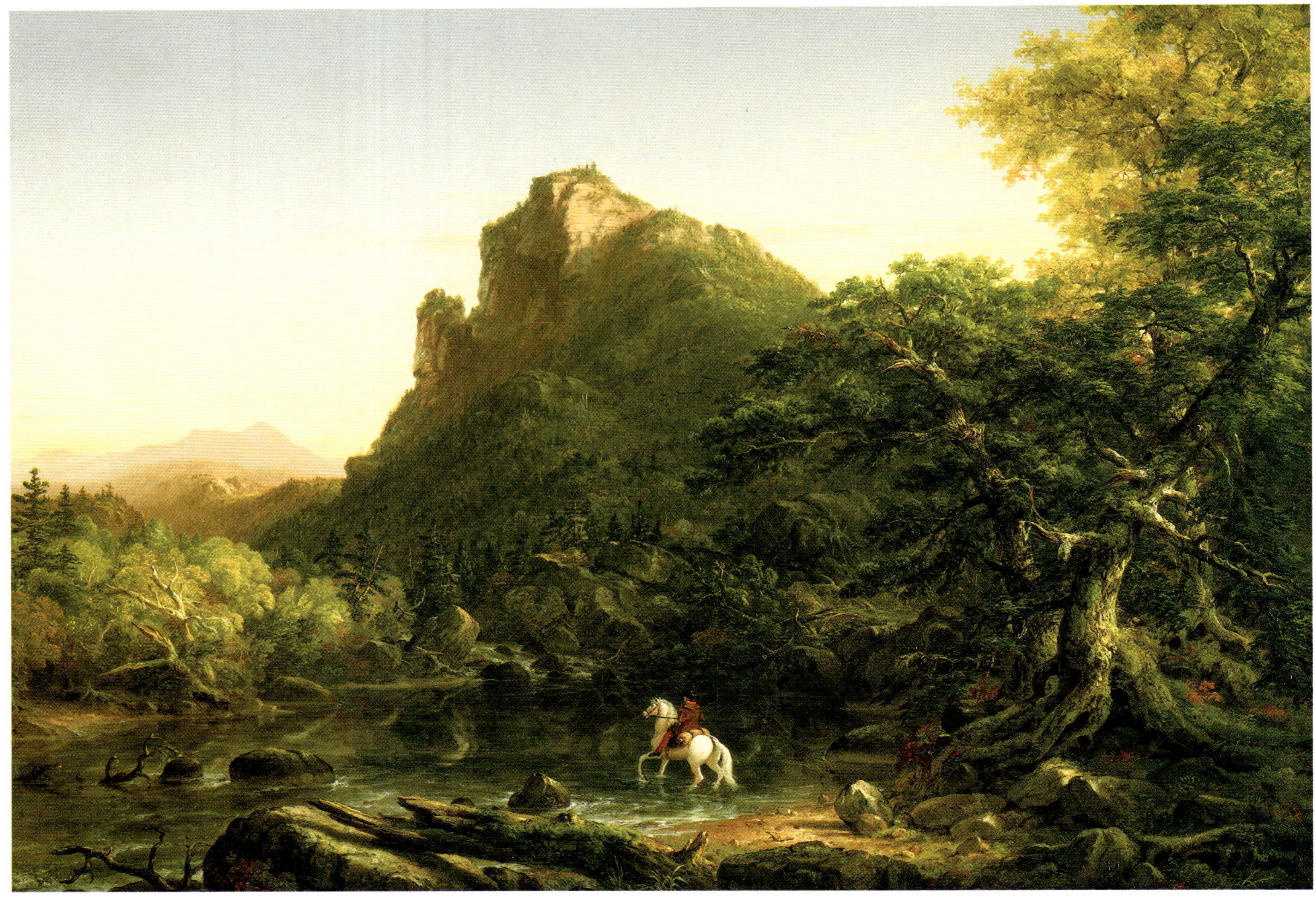

The Mountain Ford

1846. Oil on canvas,
28¼ x 40$\frac{1}{16}$"
The Metropolitan Museum of Art,
New York,
Bequest of Maria DeWitt Jesup, 1915

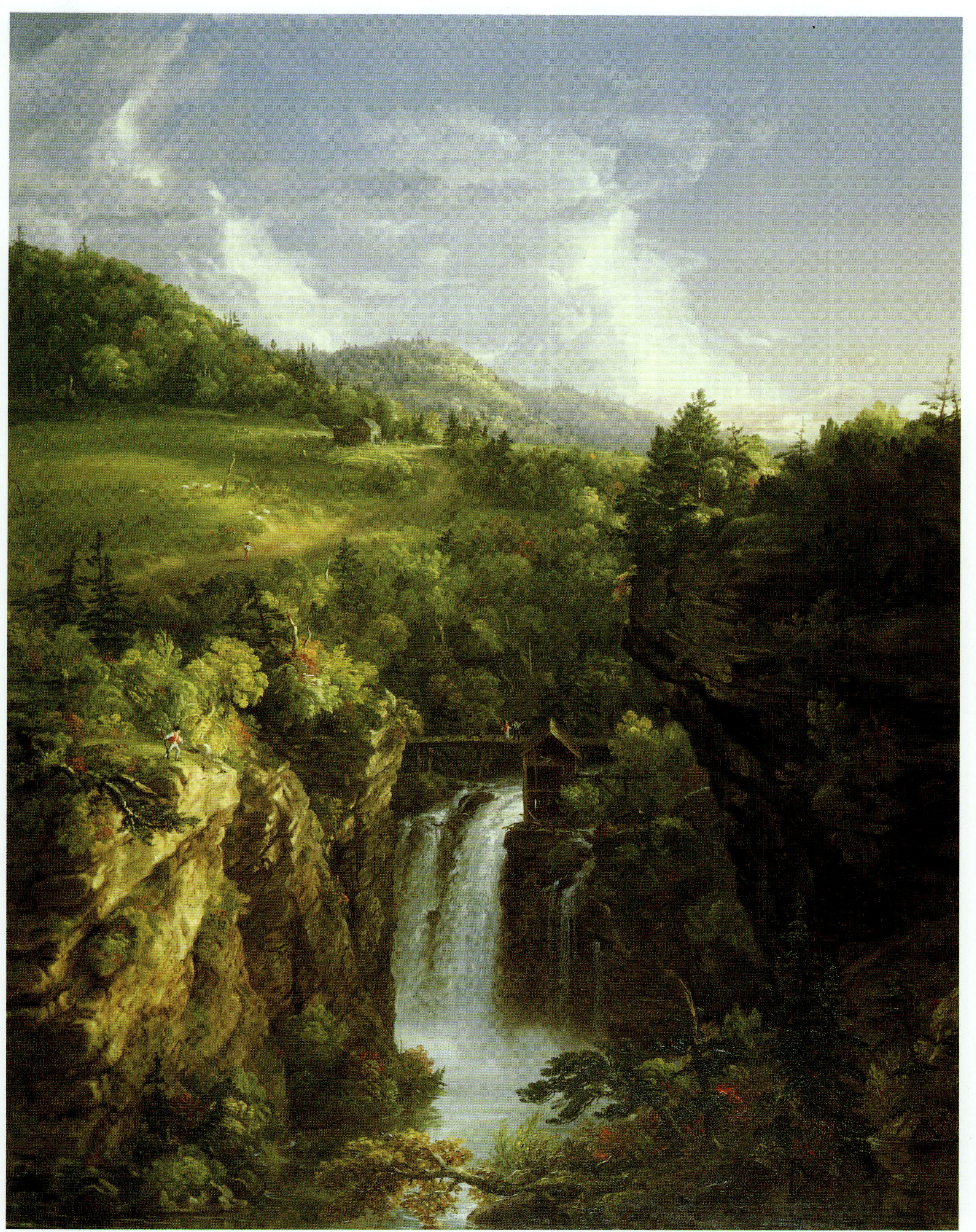

Genesee Scenery

1847. Oil on canvas, 51 x 39½″
Museum of Art, Rhode Island School of Design, Providence, Jesse Metcalf Fund

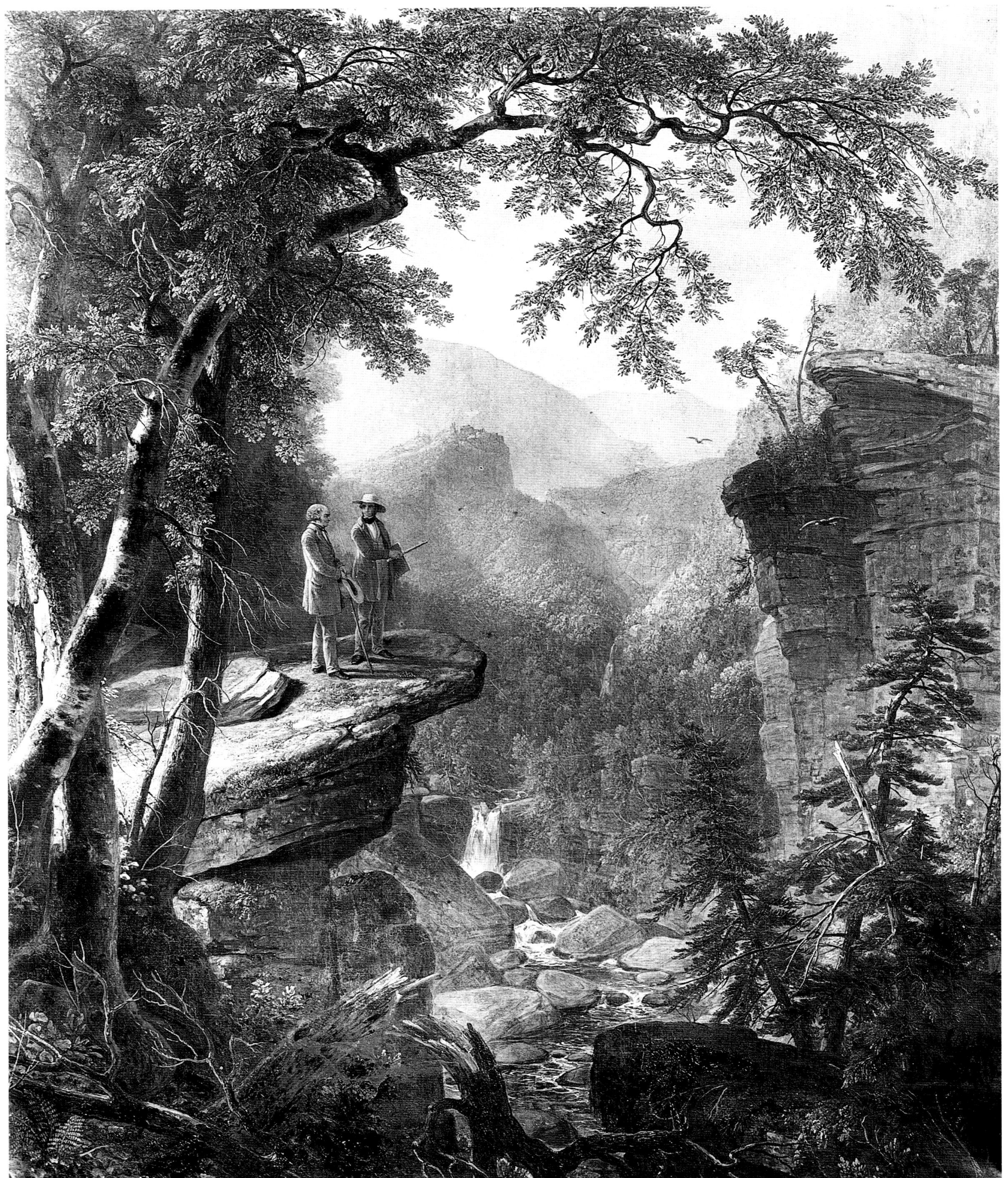

history of the New World. He interpreted nature as a divine manifestation of America's unique moral and spiritual position in history. Cole was truly a pilgrim on a religious quest to interpret the world of nineteenth-century America. He appropriately deserves, as Noble had hoped, "a place among the Spencers and Miltons of Poetic art." (Noble, 311) In his funeral oration for Thomas Cole, William Cullen Bryant, his great friend, gave him the highest compliment possible when he said, "The paintings of Cole are of that nature that it hardly transcends the proper use of language to call them acts of religion."

Cole's art also had an important influence on other artists of his and the following generation. Cole's union of art and literature was carried to perhaps its logical conclusion in the magnificent landscapes of his pupil Frederic Edwin Church. Church learned a great deal from Cole, and his own ambitions were predicated on the lofty goals Cole established in his own art. Church's early style and sense of composition took their inspiration from Cole, whose sunset pictures in the last years of his life, such as *The Old Mill at Sunset* and *Home in the Woods,* provided models for Church's own works. Church would, of course, surpass Cole in the pyrotechnics of his art, carrying the sunset to an apocalyptic conclusion in such paintings as *Twilight in the Wilderness* of 1860, but his vision was an extension of his master's. No more eloquent testament to the relationship of the two artists exists than Church's melancholy *To the Memory of Cole* of 1848.

Cole's picturesque scenes, his sense of light and composition provided a model and an inspiration for a host of other artists, notably Jasper Francis Cropsey. He also served as inspiration to such Luminist artists as John Frederick Kensett and Robert Swain Gifford. Cole was, in fact, the father of Romantic landscape in America and his legacy was as enduring as his own love of wild nature and the feeling it aroused in him, compelling him to paint some of the most beautiful landscapes of his day.

OPPOSITE:
Asher B. Durand
Kindred Spirits

1849. Oil on canvas,
46 x 36"
New York Public Library,
Astor, Lenox, and Tilden Foundations

Appendix: Cole's List

In a sketchbook inscribed "Thomas Cole, N York, 1827," which is now among the Cole papers at the New York State Library at Albany, is the artist's running list of possible subjects for pictures. Howard S. Merritt extracted the list from the sketchbook, annotated and numbered it, and it was included in *Annual II: Studies on Thomas Cole, an American Romanticist,* published by the Baltimore Museum of Art in 1967. The list, with Merritt's numbering and notations (in italics) and current updating of the locations of several pictures, is reprinted here with permission of the publisher.

1. Preaching in the woods as is seen in the Western country
2. Camp Meeting at night—a fire light & moonlight
   A sketch for a Camp Meeting scene is in the same sketchbook.
3. Elijah in the Wilderness—Standing at the mouth of the cave
   Painted in England late in 1829 or early in 1830 and exhibited at The British Institution in 1830. Dimensions to the outside of the frame were 58" by 75", as listed in Algernon Graves, The British Institution 1806–1867, *London, 1908, p. 109. Several studies for the subject are in this same sketchbook. A painting attributed to Cole, measuring 59½" by 69", and with "Elijah" appearing in old writing on paper on the stretcher, was with Mortimer Brandt, New York City, in 1967. It is a wild, John Martin-like composition, showing a prostrate figure on a surf-beaten rocky coast, a waterspout and storm effect, with sunlight shafting through at left center. Although the dimensions correspond closely enough to the painting Cole exhibited, the composition bears no relationship to the sketchbook studies nor, indeed, to the biblical text. It is more likely that this is a subject such as the* Translation of Elijah, *listed No. 4 below.*
   Cole returned to the subject, Elijah at the Mouth of the Cave, *in a work painted in 1844–45 and exhibited at the National Academy of Design in 1845. Before 1855 it became the property of G. K. Shoenberger of Cincinnati who also, according to the western correspondent of* The Crayon, *I (1855) p. 92, owned the duplicate series of* The Voyage of Life *that Cole painted in Italy in 1841–42. This version of the series has recently been rediscovered; it was published by Edward H. Dwight and Richard J. Boyle in* Art in America, *LV (1967) pp. 60–63.*
   On 15 June 1858 Elijah at the Mouth of the Cave *was sold by G. Harding to Cole's widow. Worthington Whittredge, writing to Theodore Cole on 25 February 1863, sought to arrange its purchase for N. W. Scarborough of Cincinnati. The outcome of these negotiations and the present location of this later version are unknown.*
4. The translation of Elijah
5. Children of Israel in the Wilderness
6. Hagar in the Wilderness
   Studies for this work are in the sketchbook. It was painted in the spring of 1829 and taken by Cole to England. According to Noble, 1964 edition, p. 79, Cole painted another picture over it. We learn from the London correspondent of the New York Mirror, *writing in the issue for 12 March 1831, that Cole had used some unstable colors in the work and painted over it the* Solitary Lake in New Hampshire, *now hanging in Olana, the former home of his pupil Frederic Church. A painting of* Hagar and Ishmael, *attributed to Cole, was with the Vose Galleries of Boston in 1944 and is illustrated in* Art Digest, *18, 1 July 1944, p. 7.*
7. Scene from Rip van Winkle—playing at bowls
   Drawing for this subject owned by the Albany Institute of History and Art
8. Chaos—a tumultuous assembly of wild shadowy forms which the imagination must make out
9. Garden of Eden
   High mountains the highest with a cloud—middle distance lake [*illegible*] Promontories with woods—cliffs—nearer Plains with [*remainder of description too faint to read clearly*]
   Painted in 1827–28 and exhibited at the National Academy of Design in 1828. Purchased by Charles Wilkes in 1829 and again exhibited at the Academy. Present location unknown. Drawing for this subject is in The Detroit Institute of Arts (No. 39.357).
10. A picture the principle of which must be vast height and depth—
11. Bridge of Fear
    Three drawings of this natural bridge-like formation are in The Detroit Institute of Arts (Nos. 39.219, 39.220, 39.367). The last of these was evidently the basis for Evening in Arcadia, *No. 99 of this list.*
12. Deer hunt. For Mr. [*illegible*]
13. Landing of Columbus—
14. The world as seen at the distance of 6 or 7 hundred miles—one side lighted by the sun—in a vast void with a few stars shining—
    A small sketch accompanies this description.
15. Expulsion of Adam and Eve from the Garden of Eden—with stupendous mountain masses. After sunset, the sun lighting the ridges in the Garden—
    Painted in 1828 and exhibited that year at the National Academy of Design. It was sold to Dr. David Hosack just prior to Cole's departure for England in 1829. Now in the M. and M. Karolik Collection, Museum of Fine Arts, Boston.
16. Happy Valley—Rasselas
17. First morning after the creation
    First evening—
18. The Expulsion from the Garden—moon & firelight
    This is the painting referred to in no. 15, in the M. and M. Karolick Collection, Museum of Fine Arts, Boston.
19. The delivery of the law from Mt. Sinai
    Painted, probably in 1828, and now in the collection of the Shelburne Museum, Shelburne, Vermont. A drawing for the subject is in this same sketchbook.
    This painting has been reattributed by Ellwood C. Parry III as the work

of Henry Cheever Pratt. See "When a Cole is Not a Cole: Henry Cheever Pratt's Moses on the Mount," American Art Journal 4 *(1971): 123–40.*

20. Flight into Egypt
21. Shipwreck of St. Paul
22. Romeo and Juliet—moonlight
23. Mutability [*crossed out by Cole*] Ruins or the Effects [*"Works" written above Effects and then crossed out*] of Time. In the distance vast mountains, ruins of pyramids & temples—near a rocky coast with parts of the wreck of a ship. Near a broken cistern—a fountain flowing partly into it—a broken column—broken tablet—dead trees—broken vases, a human skull—a broken sword. The distant ruins should partly be standing in the sea as though the waters had encroached—a bridge over the dry bed of a river—the stream flowing at some little distance. It must be a sunset—aquaduct broken with the water pouring out of the end—
    In a sketchbook of 1828 at The Detroit Institute of Arts is a similar description with a tentative drawing of the subject. It is clearly an early thought concerning the painting that was to become the last in The Course of Empire *series and indicates an occupation with this theme from as early as 1828.*
24. Philip the freedman and the old soldier performing the funeral rites of Pompey on the Egyptian shore—after or just at sunset—the wreck of the fishing boat and the fire raised on some masses of rock, with the two human figures standing by in the foreground. In the distance pyramids, buildings of different kinds—mountains—some distant figures—
    Cole's subject here is derived from Plutarch's Life of Pompey.
25. Byron's Darkness—volcano light
26. Last Judgement—
27. Scene from the Course of Time—Book I, page 24—"Upon a little mount that gently rose, he sat clothed in white robes, &c."
28. A wild river with men fording—
29. Chocorua Peak in a snowstorm
30. Travelers encamping
31. Emigrants
32. Preaching in the [*fields?*]
33. A sunrise in the Garden of Eden
    A sunset in the Garden of Eden
34. Indian battle
35. First rainbow after the deluge
36. The crucifixion
    An oil sketch of a Calvary, *measuring 9 x 11⅛ inches, was in 1966 at Schweitzer Gallery, New York. Illustrated in* Connoisseur, *162 (June 1966) p. CXI.*
37. Dante's Gate of Hell with the inscription—a cave
38. The Cross appearing in the Heavens to Constantine the Great—
39. Rocks and trees heaped confusedly together as having been carried by the floods from the mountains
40. A picture in which nothing shall be but bare rocks and clouds—rocks piled on rocks
    Perhaps this subject was suggested by the seventh stanza of Book II of James Beattie's "The Minstrel."
41. Mountains on the moon
    Drawing of this subject in The Detroit Institute of Arts (No. 39.358).
42. World after the Deluge
    Either late in 1828 or early in 1829, Cole painted what he called a Deluge scene. The picture was purchased by Dr. David Hosack just prior to Cole's departure for England in June, 1829. It was exhibited at the National Academy of Design in 1829, listed as The Subsiding of the Waters of the Deluge. *Exhibited again at the Academy in 1831. In a review of the latter exhibition in the* New York Mirror, *7 May 1831, it is described as follows: "The vast flood, gradually subsiding, leaves the peaked mountain tops visible; and the drenched world, as it again meets the light, has an air of deep solemnity and solitude extremely impressive. The effect is increased by the skull in the foreground. . . ." Now in the collection of the National Museum of American Art, Smithsonian Institution, Washington, D.C. 1983.*
43. Picture for Mr. W. H. Elliot of Boston to be painted in Europe
    In a letter to Cole dated 18 December 1833, Francis Alexander wrote from Boston that the Evening View *done for W. H. Elliot is now owned by Mr. Preston. In another letter from Boston of 22 May 1843, Henry C. Pratt wrote to Cole that the landscape he had "painted here" for Wm. H. Elliot had been sold at auction that same day for $110. Cole evidently painted at least one landscape for Elliot, but whether or not in Europe is not clear.*
44. Emigrants for one of the first [*illegible*]
45. [*illegible*] Lake
46. The story of the regicides Goffe, Whalley & Dixwell afford in my opinion fine subjects both for poetry & painting. A poem in which Goffe, on the solitary rock near New Haven, should be made to give vent to his feelings as an exile—his thoughts springing from the past & looking forward to the future—the first part might be Morning the second Noon the third Evening the fourth Night
47. Lear's madness in the storm
48. "As when the goatherd from a rocky point
    Sees rolling o'er the deep, and wafted on
    By western gales a cloud that, as it comes
    In distant prospect viewed pitch black appears,
    And brings worst weather, lightning, storm & rain,
    He shuddering, drives his flock into a cave—"
    Cowper's trans Iliad Book 4
49. Solitude
50. Abraham and Isaac

51. Narcissus—a tranquil scene

52. Adam and Eve finding the body of Abel
Cole painted a Dead Abel *in late 1831—early 1832 in Florence, intended as a study for this subject which, however, was never carried out. The study is now in the Albany Institute of History and Art.*

53. The entombment of Christ
Small pencil sketch for this composition is in this same sketchbook.

54. "And David lifted up his eyes, and saw the Angel of the Lord standing between the earth & heaven, having a drawn sword in his hand stretched out over Jerusalem. Then David & the elders of Israel who were clothed in sackcloth, fell upon their faces." I Chronicles 21 Chapter 16 verse

55. Visions

56. Abraham and his son Isaac descending from the mountain—

57. The meeting of Isaac and Rebekah—"And Isaac went out to meditate in the field at eventime: and he lifted up his eyes, and saw, and, behold, the camels were coming. And Rebekah lifted up her eyes, and when she saw Isaac, she lighted off the camel." Genesis Chap. 24

58. "And when Esau heard the words of his father, he cried out with an exceedingly great and bitter cry, and said to his father, 'Bless me, even me also, O my father'." Genesis Chap. 27

59. Indians fording a rapid river—

60. The curtains of Death—

61. Several passages in Beattie's Minstrel
These passages are written out on pages of the sketchbook apart from the running list.

62. (Historical) Almachius a Christian separating the gladiators in the Flavian Amphitheater—see note to C Harold 4th canto

63. Views of the sources of the rivers of the U S America—or of England—would do well for series of engravings—
In a letter to Thomas S. Cummings on 7 September 1838, Cole wrote, ". . . it is my intention to make an excursion, a short one (that is, in time) up the N [orth] River to L [ake] George to take several sketches for Heath's Picturesque Annual. By the by I must tell you that I am employed to furnish 30 views for an annual (Heath's Picturesque) — which is to be entirely devoted to scenery on the Hudson—Irving will probably write the work. . . ." *Unfortunately, neither this series nor the series of river sources ever materialized. The reason is not known; perhaps the field was pre-empted by N. P. Willis'* American Scenery. *Several of the plates for this, engraved after W. H. Bartlett's drawings, were made in 1838 and 1839, though the complete work was not published until 1840.*

64. L'Allegro & Il Penseroso—see Milton
Both pictures are now in the collection of the Los Angeles County Museum of Art.

65. A view of Boston & harbour &c &c from Mr. Forbes'—Milton Hill—To be painted upon my return for Mr. Bates—30 Portland Place London—Nov. 6, 1830—Price to be 50 pounds.
From the correspondence between Cole and Joshua Bates, we learn that Cole, possibly in 1836, painted a view of Boston from Roxbury to satisfy this commission. Then realizing this was not the view Bates wanted, he went again to Boston (1837?) but was disappointed with the view from Mr. Forbes' house. As he wrote to Bates, "I have found the view from Milton Hill one that is incompatible in a picture—the view is too wide for the field of a picture and a part of it would certainly be unsatisfactory—& that the view towards Boston—it is monotonous & contains not a drop of water to be seen—and of Boston only the State House dome and a steeple two & those from a distance over [8?] miles. . . ." Meanwhile Francis Alexander, in a letter to Cole from Boston on 25 August 1837, told him he had found just the right view for him—from Mr. Sargent's house in Dorchester. The painting finally sent to Bates was done, as Cole wrote, from a sketch made from near this house. Bates acknowledged the receipt of the painting in a letter from London of 17 October 1839, expressing great satisfaction with it. Present whereabouts unknown. A View of Boston *attributed to Cole, measuring 34" by 47½", was sold for $560 as No. 329 in the sale of the effects of Montague Flagg at the Anderson Galleries, New York City, April 11–14, 1923. Private collection, 1986.*

66. A scene from Byron's Manfred
Painted in 1833 and exhibited that year at the National Academy of Design. Also shown in the Cole memorial exhibition at The American Art Union in 1848, whose catalogue lists its measurements as 50" by 38" and its owner as Mrs. J. J. Chapman.
From the passage below which was quoted in the N.A.D. catalogue, it appears certain that this is the painting illustrated as fig. 29 in Wolfgang Born, American Landscape Painting, *New Haven, 1948. At the time of publication the work belonged to Mrs. L. T. Gager of Washington, D.C. Now in the collection of the Yale University Art Gallery.*

Manfred—Scene 2—A lower Valley in the Alps—a Cataract
Enter Manfred—
It is not noon—the sunbeam's rays still arch
The torrent with the many hues of heaven,
And roll the sheeted silver's waving column
O'er the crags headlong perpendicular,
And fling its lines of foaming light along,
And to and fro, like the pale courser's tail,
The giant steed to be bestrode by death,
As told in the Apocalypse. No eyes
But mine now drink this sight of loveliness;
I should be sole in this sweet solitude,
And with the spirit of the place divide
The homage of these waters.—I will call her—

(Manfred takes some of the water into the palm of his hand, and flings it in the air, muttering the adjuration. After a pause, the witch of the Alps rises beneath the arch of the sunbeam of the torrent.)

67. Italian Subjects—Cicero's Villa Mola di Gaeta, Nemi with
68. the Madonna, English Burying ground—
69. *The* View of Lake Nemi *was painted, perhaps in 1843, and exhibited at the National Academy of Design in 1846. It was then owned by Charles Parker. Present location unknown.* View of the Protestant Burying Ground, Rome *was exhibited at the Academy in 1834. It now hangs in Olana, the former home of Frederic Church. There is no evidence that a picture of Cicero's Villa was ever painted.*

70. The Vale of Tempe—described by Aelian—History of Greece by Gillies
For the descriptive text of this Eden-like landscape see John Gillies, History of Ancient Greece, *Philadelphia, 1829, pp. 114–115.*

71. Battle of Thermopylae—The Point of time might be the death of Leonidas—the fighting for his body—or the contest behind the Phocian wall after the appearance of Hydarmes—Xerxes witnessing the scene from rising ground—He or Leonidas should be in the foreground. There was a terrible storm during part of the battle.

72. The miracle of Delphi—from Gillies History of Greece—"The Delphians having learned, by the unhappy fate of Abe, that their religious employment could not afford protection, either to their property or to their persons, consulted the oracle, 'Whether they should hide their treasures under ground, or transport them to some neighboring country?'. The Pythia replied 'That the arms of Apollo were sufficient for the defense of his shrine'. The Delphians, therefore, confined their attention to the means necessary for their personal safety. The women and children were transported by sea to Achia; the men climbed to the craggy tops of mount Cirphis, or descended to the deep caverns of Parnassus. Only sixty persons, the immediate ministers of Apollo, kept possession of the sacred city . . . scarcely had the Persians reached the temple of Minerva the Provident, situated at a little distance from town, when the air thickened into an unusual darkness. A violent storm arose; the thunder and lightning were terrible. At length the tempest burst on Mount Parnassus, and separated from its sides two immense rocks, which rolling down with increased violence, overwhelmed the nearest ranks of the Persians . . . . A universal panic seized them; at first they remained motionless, in silent amazement; they afterwards fled with disordered steps and wild despair."

73. A series of pictures illustrating the stages and mutation of—being an illustration of man and progress of mankind from barbarism—to civilization and destruction—the 1st pictures—savage state—religion idolatry—occupation the chase—amusements wild dances and songs 2nd state—Religion—Philosophy—occupation agriculture—amusements music & dancing & poetry 3rd state—luxurious. Religion—ceremonious. Occupation—commerce. Amusements—amphitheatrical 4th state—vicious or state of destruction.
This is an early description of the series that was to be developed into The Course of Empire. *The definitive description of Cole's intentions about this series is given in [a] letter of 29 January 1832 to Robert Gilmor. The description above evidently is a later one than that which appears on a separate page of this same sketchbook. . . . Though neither of these entries is dated, it appears likely that the earlier one dates from 1828–29 while No. 73 is 1831–32.*

74. The migration of the settlers from Massachusetts to Connecticut—through the wilderness—see Trumbull's history of Connecticut—history of the U.S.—

75. View from Groton, Connecticut—which was the residence of Sassacus Chief of the Pequods—

76. Major Halket finding the bones of his father & brother in the forest. From Galt's life of West—

77. Elijah after resuscitating the widow's son bringing him to her—

78. The hunter's return. A log hut in the forest—several figures. Two men carrying a deer on a pole—a child running to meet them & a woman standing in the door of the cabin with a child in her arms—a dog—my wild scene—
Painted in 1845 and exhibited at the memorial exhibition at The American Art Union in 1848, when the picture was in the collection of G. W. Austen. Tuckerman considered this one of the best of Cole's American scenes and describes it in Book of the Artists, *New York, 1867, p. 231. The description accords with Cole's. Present whereabouts unknown. Now in the collection of the Amon Carter Museum, Fort Worth, Texas.*

79. Salvator Rosa on the point of being thrown from the precipice by the bandits—saved by the main bandit's wife in his absence—
This purported episode is described in Lady Sidney Morgan, The Life and Times of Salvator Rosa, *London, 1824.*

80. The vale of Joy
The Vale of Gloom

81. Morning, Noon, Evening, Night—a series

82. Last Indian—dead hemlock

83. Allegory of Human Life—a series. 1st—the source of a river—issuing from a cave & a child in a boat—with a guardian Angel steering—2nd—The child become a youth is seen in the boat—the river has increased & the scene become extensive & grand—the guardian just stepping out of the boat & pointing forward—leaving the youth to his own reason for guide.
4 [*sic*] The river tumbles over rocks—a stormy scene—the boat dashes among troubled waters—the man struggling to save himself & bark—guardian still seen at a distance watching.
5 [*sic*] View of a dark ocean—the boat with an old man just entering on it. Chaos and darkness spread before—but through an opening in the clouds a glorious city seen—and seen approaching the old man the guardian who points to the city—Words or verses might be inscribed on rocks or elsewhere explanatory—on the mouth of the cave. In the second scene in the distance might be a palace—castles—in distance—visions—
This is probably Cole's first description of what was to become his famous series, The Voyage of Life, *painted for Samuel Ward and completed in*

1840. The contract between Cole and Ward stipulated that the series was to be in the style of The Course of Empire. *The series is now in the collection of the Munson-Williams-Proctor Institute, Utica, New York. Concerning the second version of* The Voyage of Life, *see comments to No. 3. The subject is listed again in No. 85 and elaborated upon in No. 91.*

84. The ages
85. The Voyage of Life in four pictures—
86. The Poet's Pilgrimage
87. The hero
88. Seasons—each picture represents the same scene—
89. L'Allegro. An ancient oak standing on a grassy knoll under whose shadow shall be peasants dancing—piping—children playing. Milkmaid—mower—woods, fields, cottage with smoke rising. A mansion, a church among the trees—the prospect looking from on high over a lower country—farms, village & seaport. Before sunset in summer, light clouds flying, breeze seen in trees—a cascade—goats & sheep & birds. Children chasing a butterfly in the foreground—Penseroso. Twilight—a gothic ruin—the last gleam of sunset seen through the delapidated arches & windows—overgrown with ivy—a still pond—deep & gloomy woods—a single figure—owl & bats—

These two paintings were executed for Charles M. Parker, whom Cole had met on his second stay in Rome in 1842. Parker and his wife commissioned two paintings, the subjects to be at Cole's discretion, which were shown in The American Art Union memorial exhibition in 1848. Possibly these were the same paintings owned by Parker and shown at the National Academy of Design in 1846, with titles of Italian Sunset *and* View of Lago di Nemi, near Rome *(see. No. 68). Now in the collection of the Los Angeles County Museum of Art.*

90. The Past & The Present—this might be American scenery—a scene in its primeval wildness—with Indians—the same under the hand of civilization—but a better illustration would perhaps be a Temple or city of ancient Greece or Italy in its glory—sacrifices & processions. The same in a state of ruins. Perhaps Paestum would do—the American might be past, present & future—

Commissioned by P. G. Stuyvesant, who left the choice of subject and size to Cole. The paintings were completed in the fall of 1838; they are now owned by Amherst College. Like The Departure *and* The Return, *No. 92, the projected American setting for these works was given up in favor of a medieval one in the vein of Sir Walter Scott.*

91. Plan of a series of pictures called "Human Life—An Allegory." The first picture shall be a view of a streamlet issuing from a dark cave & pursuing its course between banks adorned with flowers & graceful trees which quiver in the morning breezes. The scene shall not be extensive but beautiful & gay. Over the mouth of the cave shall be an inscription in the rock—"Life issues from the womb of dark oblivion" or something to that effect. Then might be added—"And angels guide & watch it through the vale of Earth." Or "From dark oblivious gulf the stream of Life proceeds. Angels protect & guide the human voyager when first his bark is launched." A boat of fantastic form is floating down the stream, a guardian Angel steering it & a glad child plucks delightedly the flowers that stoop into the boat from the luxuriant banks.
The second picture—the streamlet has become a river—the scene expanded—lofty mountains rise in the distance while the intermediate region is diversified with woods & verdant lawns & wild romantic hills—lastly of such as the magician's wand create—crown the kingly steeps & palaces of beauty peep from the shady groves. The boat is gliding down the stream but the child is now a youth verging on manhood—he steers the boat with looks of exultation & hope. The guardian has left the boat & standing on the shore points onward with a grave & anxious look. On a rock by the side of the stream is this inscription, "When boyhood's season is past, reason must guide while guardian spirits watch."—
The third picture—The scene is dark & tempestuous. The rapid river foams over broken rocks—the boat is whirled along—and the voyager now in the prime of manhood grasps with fear the helm & casts toward heaven an imploring look—from behind some rocks the guardian Angel still attendant watches the imperiled boat with looks of fear & anxiety.—In this gloomy landscape may be seen dark dismal looking buildings—crumbling ruins overgrown with dank vegetation—Inscription on a rock says "the prime of life is trouble & unrest & pain. But the Guardian Spirit still is near though hidden to human eye."
The fourth picture—A dark ocean spreads at the mouth of the river—and the boat shattered & worn floats onward with an old man sitting alone unheedful of the helm—before him black clouds stoop down & mingle with the sea & all is gloom—the Guardian Angel treading on the sea advances toward the boat & points above the clouds where may be seen a glorious prospect—A city dazzling with golden light—an inscription on a neighboring rock reads thus—"Pass on ye voyagers of Life's wild stream. Before you open mysterious gates of the great Heaven of the Soul."

92. Morning & Evening—or The Departure & The Return—2 pictures. A youth taking leave of his family at the door of a cottage—morning—a picturesque cottage—an ancient oak overshadowing it—an extensive view of mountains, woods, cultivated fields, and a distant view of the ocean. The youth full of joyous hopes—points toward the distant sea—while his sister clings to him weeping and his parents lift their hands as imploring the benedictions of prayer—

2nd picture—the youth returns a man & the family meets him again before the door of the cottage. The mother is enfolded by him in his arms while the father appears to be thanking heaven for the happy return of his son. All must appear older—the youth manly & noble and more richly dressed than on his departure—the old man infirm—the sister grown to womanhood and a youth who may be discovered in the first picture seems to take a particular interest in her—other appropriate objects may be introduced to make the scene still more rich & interesting—This scene must be at sunset—the same location preserved in both pictures though different views and different seasons—many rural objects may be introduced—shepherds with their flocks—peasants with their [*illegible*] &c. There may be a seaport in view—a ship lying at anchor. Morning may be an American scene—Evening an Italian one. The morning all freshness, newness—youthful vigour—the Evening—Decay and Ruin. The morning may be a wild scene with a hunter's cabin.

The Departure *and* The Return *were painted, but completely changed in mood and setting, for W. P. van Rennselaer in 1837. They are now in the Corcoran Gallery, Washington D.C. Indication of the change appears on a separate note among Cole's papers:*

In the painting of Departure & Return there may be two stories. At the same time that the youth is starting from the cottage—issuing from the castle may be seen a cavalcade & amidst it a youth on a white horse—crossing a bridge—perhaps going to hunt or war. In the Return—may be seen a procession on the bridge advancing toward a castle—a body on a bier—and the white horse led behind. This part of the picture may be quite subordinate to the other—

In 1841 Cole painted another work called The Return. *H. C. Pratt, writing to Cole from Boston on 2 December 1843, said that a painting thus entitled was sold at auction among Flandin's pictures the previous week; the price was $230 and Charles Eldridge the purchaser. Jonathan Mason in a letter to Cole from Boston on 19 February 1844 refers to it as a large picture showing a baronial castle. This is surely the painting,* The Return from the Tournament, *given to the Corcoran Gallery in 1958 by Josephine C. Dillingham. Illustrated in* The Corcoran Gallery of Art Bulletin, *No. 3, (June 1959) p. 8.*

93. Two pastoral landscapes. A morning & evening—
94. The Golden Age—The Age of Iron &c from Hesiod & Ovid
95. Grandeur & Decay
96. The opening scene in Ivanhoe
97. The Sun Dial—a series
98. Scene from the Odyssey. When Ulysses approaches the Cyclopean coast and sees the cyclops cave—Book 19th, line 211 to 224—fine subject—

    A pencil sketch entitled Ulysses & companions arriving in the bay near Polyphemus' Cave *is in The Detroit Institute of Arts, No. 39.353.*
99. Evening in Arcadia & Morning—

    Evening in Arcadia *was painted in 1843 for Miss Hicks, and is now in the Wadsworth Atheneum, Hartford.*
100. The soldier of his country—for Mr. Stuyvesant [*later crossed out*]

    Two pictures—

    First a cottage in a rich pastoral country—at the door is seen a young soldier receiving from the hands of his mother or sister a banner—while his father with uplifted hands commends him to Heaven (or he may be receiving his father's sword—girding it on) while his mother implores the blessing of Heaven—around are assembled peasants rudely armed with agricultural implements scythes, axes &c—on a high hill is a beacon tower the fire burning in it—in the distance may be seen a village in flames & the sea & a number of ships as of an invading army—or pirates—in the middle ground may be seen peasants driving cattle into the interior—women & children flying as from pursuit—Morning.

    Second—The Young Soldier returns crowned with success—the family meets him at the door of the cottage—his mother embraces him—his followers are at a little distance as though he had rushed before them to embrace his family—the beacon light has ceased to burn—and peace & tranquility again comes over the scene—Sunset.
101. Cimabue the painter discovering Giotto as a shepherd boy drawing—see Vasari
102. A child discovered by its mother gathering flowers by a stream in a wood—
103. Repose. Figure sleeping in a wood—dog—horizontal
104. Young shepherd playing on a pipe in a shady wood by a stream—a girl watching him unperceived—
105. Scene in Spenser's Fairy Queen—the approach of the Knight and Una to the cave in Errour's wood—
106. Scene of Una & the lion—
107. "A large lyre hung in the opening of the rock & gave its melancholy music to the wind. But no human being was to be seen."
108. The meeting of two knights in a wood—see Costumes
109. Cross in the wilderness—Mrs. Heman's poem

    Painted in 1845 and shown at the National Academy of Design that year and loaned by G. W. Austen to The American Art Union memorial exhibition in 1848. Present whereabouts unknown. A painting thus entitled and attributed to Cole was sold for $100 as No. 286 in the sale of property of W. J. Cooke, D. Driscoll, et al. at the Metropolitan Art and Auction Galleries, New York City, March 8–10, 1923. Now in the collection of the Louvre, Paris.
110. Four seasons—series. Spring with children playing in a beautiful scene—flowers and blossoming trees—winter—old people sitting in a room by the fire reading—a view of a wintry landscape through a large Gothic window
111. Two scenes from a story of Mrs. Sedgwick's, related in a

letter from certain Baths in Germany—1. The parting of lovers—the youth having taken leave of a girl is journeying on—the girl is sitting beneath a tree her fan on her lap clasping a little dog that is striving to follow her love—2. The girl seen reclining among the ruins of a castle at sunset—the little dog recognizing the lover who is approaching unobserved—

112. Death and funeral of Charles the [*1st?*]
113. Moses ascending Mount Pisgah
114. The Greeks under Zenophon—first beholding the sea
115. "As o'er the lake in evening's glow
The temple threw its lengthening shade
Upon the marble steps below,
There sat a fair Corinthian maid
Gracefully o'er a volume bending,
While by her side a youthful sage?
Held back her ringlets, lest, descending,
They should [*illegible*] all the page."
Perhaps for Mr. Carey's picture
116. Four paintings in the Louvre by young Patel pleased me—Spring, Summer, Autumn & Winter. The Summer pleased me most—there was in the middle ground a ruin in the midst of a grain field in which the reapers were at work. The field extended to the foreground & in the distant sky there was a rainbow—all executed with great delicacy of handling & pleasing though not very true color—the picture suggested a plan for a series—1 the reaping of grain as the present 2 the ruin as the past 3 the rainbow in sky as the future.
117. Elijah and [*Gehaziel?*]
118. Daniel Boone looking from the eminence over the vast forest & seeing the Ohio for the first time—
119. The meeting of the waters. The confluence of two rivers, one a rapid & broken stream the other placid & flowing gently—in the foreground two lovers—sitting on a flowery bank—

Now in the Preston Morton Collection of American Art, Santa Barbara Museum of Art, Santa Barbara, California.

120. There is a tree in West Chester county under which Washington is said to have stood paring an apple—
121. A lake in the midst of the mountains—an American scene of the most beautiful character.
122. A sea coast scene. A dog on the beach by a dead body after a storm—

The following are descriptions given on separate pages of the sketchbook outside of the regular sequence:

[I] Heaven. In the extreme distance and high in the picture—the Throne. A mass of dazzling light*—around it should rise (but not above) pinnacles of crystal Ruby Topaz and other transparent stones—below these involving their bases should be rolling gorgeous clouds and through an opening in them should be seen the river of life descending perhaps in a cataract as if from the foot of the throne—this river then wends its way through the lower region midst groves and meadows on either side of this deep vale should rise graceful and lofty mountains—principally clothed with forests and with shrubs—then from mountain to mountain should be thrown mighty archways perhaps of cloud—perhaps of marble and ornamented with sculpture and vast pictures. Through these arches should be seen beautiful vallies reaching to infinity—each a different character—one a smooth and level [*illegible*] with a peaceful lake—another more broken with waterfalls and rocks. The spectator may be supposed to be about the middle region and around and below him graceful trees, groves & rivulets—splendid plants & flowers. This forms the foreground. There may be two points of sight in this picture—the one looking upwards toward the throne the other into the extensive valley far below—Multitudes of figures may be seen variously engaged—some playing on harps—some in attitude of adoration—some [*meeting?*] poets & painters, &c. Upon the arches may be seats like in an amphitheater with myriads of figures—or hanging gardens may be suspended on them. The clouds beneath the pinnacles may be of 3 strata each different in its character—heaped pile on pile—the river may descend in numerous cataracts [*illegible*] perspectively. The arches above may be three or four together and above that part towers of cloud arise to a vast height. Perhaps three arches if immense will be sufficient. The picture might be painted with the throne supposed to be above & behind the spectator—known to be there by the intense rays diverging from the top of the picture. There might be far below altars & amphitheater of alabaster—clouds mountains there might be in many stages sinking one below another as they retire in the distance—thus by their rising perspectively and sinking geometrically an immense distance could be gained.

*This is the source of light for the whole picture—above and around it must be seen the colours of the rainbow—first yellow then red to blue with proper gradations.

[II] Two miles on this side of the fort, the road
Crosses a deep ravine; 'tis rough and narrow,
And winds with short turns down the precipice;
And in its depth there is a mighty rock,
Which has, from unimaginable years,
Sustained itself with terror and with toil
Over a gulf, and with the agony
With which it clings seems slowly coming down;

Even as a wretched soul hour after hour,
Clings to the mass of life; yet clinging, leans;
And leaning, makes more dark the dread abyss
In which it fears to fall: beneath this crag
Huge as despair, as if in weariness,
The melancholy mountain yawns . . . below,
You hear but see not an impetuous torrent
Raging among the caverns, and a bridge
Crosses the chasm; and high above there grow,
With intersecting trunks, from crag to crag,
Cedars, and yews, and pines; whose tangled hair
Is matted in one solid roof of shade
By the dark ivy's twine. At noonday here
'Tis twilight, and at sunset blackest night.
Shelley, "The Cenci"

[III] Lo! where the stripling, wrapt in wonder, roves
Beneath the precipice o'erhung with pine;
And sees, on high, amidst th'encircling groves,
From cliff to cliff the foaming torrents shine
Book I, Stanza XIX

And oft he trac'd the uplands, to survey,
When o'er the sky advanc'd the kindling dawn,
The crimson cloud, blue main, and mountain gray,
Book I, Stanza XX

And oft the craggy cliff he loved to climb,
When all in mist the world below was lost.
What dreadful pleasure! there to stand sublime,
Like shipwrek'd mariner on desert coast,
And view th'enormous waste of vapour, tost
In billows, lengthening to th'horizon round,
Now scoop'd in gulfs, with mountains now emboss'd!
And hear the voice of mirth and song rebound,
Flocks, herds, and waterfalls, along the hoar profound!
Book I, Stanza XXI

Oft when the winter storm had ceas'd to rave,
He roam'd the snowy waste at even, to view
The cloud stupendous, from th'Atlantic wave
High-towering, sail along th'horizon blue:
Where, midst the changeful scenery, ever new,
Fancy a thousand wondrous forms descries,
More wildly great than ever pencil drew,
Rocks, torrents, gulfs, and shapes of giant size,
And glittering cliffs on cliffs, and fiery ramparts rise.
Book I, Stanza LIII

Thither he hied, enamour'd of the scene.
For rocks on rocks pil'd, as by magic spell,
Here scorch'd with lightning, there with ivy green,
Fenc'd from the north and east this savage dell.
Southward a mountain rose with easy swell,
Whose long long groves eternal murmur made:
And toward the western sun a streamlet fell,
Where, through the cliffs, the eye, remote, survey'd
Blue hills, and glittering waves, and skies in gold array'd.
Book II, Stanza VII

Along this narrow valley you might see
The wild deer sporting on the meadow ground,
And, here and there, a solitary tree,
Or mossy stone, or rock with woodbine crown'd.
Oft did the cliffs reverberate the sound
Of parted fragments tumbling from on high;
And from the summit of that craggy mound
The perching eagle oft was heard to cry,
Or on resounding wings, to shoot athwart the sky.
Book II, Stanza VIII
Beattie, "The Minstrel" [See No. 61.]

Chronology

1801 Born 1 February at Bolton-le-Moor, Lancashire, England. Father a woolen manufacturer.

c. 1815 Enters a print works as an engraver of simple designs for calico. Later works with an engraver in Liverpool.

1818 Sails with family to America, arriving on 3 July in Philadelphia. Works for a while as a wood engraver. Family moves to Steubenville, Ohio in the fall.

1819 Winter trip to St. Eustatius, West Indies. Returns in May to Ohio.

1820–23 Works for his father in Steubenville designing patterns for wallpaper and continues his wood engraving. Develops strong interest in nature. Begins to paint portraits and undertakes a walking tour as a portrait painter to St. Clairsville, Zanesville, and Chillicothe. Family moves to Pittsburgh while Cole remains in Ohio painting theater sets.

1823 Moves to Philadelphia to develop his art; "the winter of my discontent," he calls it. Studies at the Pennsylvania Academy of Fine Arts and paints small landscapes and ornamented Japan ware. Writes prose and poetry.

1825 Moves to New York in the spring and takes a studio in his father's house. Sells three landscapes to George Bruen for $21. Begins sketching trips up the Hudson and on return paints *A View of Fort Putnam, Lake with Dead Trees,* and *The Falls of the Kaaterskill,* sold for $25 each to John Trumbull, William Dunlap, and Asher B. Durand.

1826 Elected a founding member of the National Academy of Design and exhibits in the spring exhibition. Visits Catskill, New York and the Adirondacks, resulting in important picturesque compositions.

1827 Spends summer at Catskill and sketches in the White Mountains.

1828 Exhibits *The Garden of Eden* and *The Expulsion from the Garden* at the National Academy. His first attempts at "a higher style of art." Visits White Mountains, continues important correspondence with Robert Gilmor, of Baltimore.

1829 Makes plans to travel to Europe. Visits Niagara Falls, sails for London on 1 June.

June *1829*–*May 1831* In England, visits important artists such as J. M. W. Turner, and he paints. Exhibits landscapes at the Royal Academy, the British Institution, and the Gallery of British Artists. Engraves views for J. H. Hintony, *History and Topography of the United States,* II, 1832.

1831 Visits Paris. Disappointed in French landscape school.

1831–32 Visits Florence, Naples, Volterra; loves this "land of poetry and beauty." Produces several landscapes and begins work on *The Angel Appearing to the Shepherds.* Continues correspondence with Robert Gilmor. In Rome he works in a studio "which tradition has consecrated as the studio of Claude." Returns to New York in November 1832.

1833 Introduced to Lumon Reed, merchant-collector who commissions an Italian landscape, which leads to the commission for *The Course of Empire.*

1835 Lecture on "American Scenery" at the New York Lyceum on 9 May. Visits Schroon Lake, Adirondacks. Continues work on *The Course of Empire.*

1836 Luman Reed dies on 7 June. Completes and exhibits *The Course of Empire.* In November marries Maria Bartow of Catskill and resides there permanently.

1837 Paints *The Departure* and *The Return* for William P. Van Rensselaer.

1838 Paints *The Dream of Arcadia, Schroon Mountain, The Past*, and *The Present.* Enters design contest for the Ohio State Capitol.

1839 Samuel Ward commissions *The Voyage of Life* but dies in November just after Cole commences work.

1840 Continues work on *The Voyage of Life.* Paints *The Architect's Dream,* which is rejected by Ithiel Town, the commissioner. Exhibits *The Voyage of Life* in the fall.

1841–42 Visits Europe again, spending time in London, Paris, and Rome. Paints second set of *The Voyage of Life* in Rome. Visits Sicily in 1842. Returns to United States in July 1842. Joins Anglican Church.

1843 Exhibits second set of *The Voyage of Life* in Boston and New York.

1844 Visits Mt. Desert Island, Maine with his first pupil, Frederic E. Church.

1845 Paints *L'Allegro* and *Il Penseroso* for Charles Parker.

1846 Takes second pupil, Benjamin McConkey. Begins planning what would be his last series, *The Cross and the World.*

1847 Visits Niagara Falls. Exhibits *Prometheus.*

1848 Dies 8 February after a brief illness.

Selected Bibliography

Thomas Cole's papers and journals are in the Manuscripts and History Division of the New York State Library, Albany. His notebooks and sketchbooks from 1827 to 1847 are in The Detroit Institute of Arts, as are some letters, poems, catalogues, clippings, and miscellaneous papers, and the Estate of Thomas Cole, Print Collections. There are miscellaneous clippings and articles in The New York Public Library. A sketchbook and some drawings are in the Art Museum, Princeton University and at the Museum of Fine Arts, Boston.

American Paradise: The World of the Hudson River School. Exhibition catalogue, The Metropolitan Museum of Art. Introduction by John K. Howat. New York: 1988.

Annual II: Studies on Thomas Cole, an American Romanticist. Baltimore Museum of Art. Baltimore: 1967.

Cole, Thomas. "Essay on American Scenery." *The American Monthly Magazine,* I, New Series (January 1836). Reprinted in John W. McCoubrey's *American Art 1700–1760,* H. W. Janson, ed. New Jersey: 1965, pp. 98–110.

Hussey, Christopher. *The Picturesque, Studies in a Point of View.* Handon, Conn.: 1967.

Jarves, James Jackson. *The Art Idea.* Benjamin Rowland, ed. Cambridge, Mass.: 1960.

McCoubrey, John W. *American Art 1700–1760.* H. W. Janson, ed. New Jersey: 1965.

Merritt, Howard S. *Thomas Cole.* Exhibition catalogue, Memorial Art Gallery of the University of Rochester. New York: 1969.

Noble, Louis Legrand. *The Life and Works of Thomas Cole.* Elliot S. Vesell, ed. Cambridge, Mass.: 1964 (first published 1853).

Novak, Barbara. *American Painting of the Nineteenth Century.* New York: 1969.

______. *Nature and Culture.* New York: 1980.

Parry, Ellwood C., III. *The Art of Thomas Cole: Ambition and Imagination.* Newark, Delaware: 1988.

The Voyage of Life by Thomas Cole, Paintings, Drawings, and Prints. Exhibition catalogue. Exhibition organized by Paul D. Schweizer, Museum of Art, Munson-Williams-Proctor Institute. New York: 1985.

Wolf, Bryan J. *Romantic Re-Vision.* Chicago: 1982

Index

Photograph Credits

E. Irving Blomstrann: pp. 24–25; Will Brown: p. 37 top; Deloye R. Burrell: p. 15; New York Public Library: p. 43 Anthony Potter: p. 94; Sotheby's New York: p. 103.